What's a Homeowner to Do?

Also in This Series

What's a Homeowner to Do?

Stephen Fanuka and Edward Lewine

ARTISAN

Copyright © 2011 by Stephen Fanuka and Edward Lewine
Photographs copyright © 2011 by Marc McAndrews
Illustrations copyright © 2011 by Ralph Voltz

Published by Artisan
A division of Workman Publishing Company, Inc.
225 Varick Street
New York, NY 10014-4381
www.artisanbooks.com

Published simultaneously in Canada by Thomas Allen & Son,
Limited

Library of Congress Cataloging-in-Publication Data

Fanuka, Stephen.
  What's a homeowner to do? / Stephen Fanuka and Edward Lewine.
    p. cm.
  Includes index.
  ISBN 978-1-57965-433-7
1. Dwellings—Maintenance and repair—Amateurs' manuals. I. Lewine, Edward. II. Title.
  TH4817.3.F36 2011
  643'.7—dc22   2011005684

Printed in Singapore
First printing, November 2011

10 9 8 7 6 5 4 3 2 1

Disclaimer: The publisher and the authors disclaim responsibility for
any loss, injury, or damages caused as a result of any of the instructions
described in this book. The advice and instructions contained herein may
not be suitable for every situation. If professional assistance is required,
the services of a competent professional person should be sought.

Contents

Preface: Green Manifesto

Before we get started, let's take a moment to think about how what we do in our homes affects the environment. This is so important that we would like to urge you to keep the environment in mind no matter what you are doing around the house. Here are a few ideas to consider while you work.

How Can I Save Energy?

- Insulate windows, doors, attics, and basements.
- Buy well-made doors and windows.
- Use curtains and other window treatments to keep out the sun during the summer and keep in the heat during the winter.
- Switch from incandescent bulbs to compact fluorescent ones.
- Buy energy-saving appliances.
- Add trees and bushes to your landscaping that provide strategic shade during the summer but lose their leaves to admit sun during the winter.
- Install a thermostat that has variable settings, so you can adjust heating and cooling when people are asleep or away.

How Can I Save Water?

- Buy water-saving plumbing, such as faucets, showerheads, and toilets.
- Have older, nonefficient toilets and showers, etc. retrofitted with water-saving gaskets.
- Use so-called gray water from washing machines and baths to water your lawn.
- Instead of planting a water-sucking lawn, create a landscape with water-retaining plants.
- Fix leaky pipes, faucets, and toilets, which can drip away countless gallons of water a year.

How Do I Reduce Toxicity?

- Whenever you can, use natural cleaners instead of chemical ones. For example, white vinegar works well and can replace most cleaning agents. Another alternative is a mixture of hydrogen peroxide and water.
- Use water-based or latex paints, stains, and sealers rather than oil-based versions of those products.

How Do I Reduce My Carbon Usage?

- Take good care of the wood in your house so you don't have to replace it.
- If you are doing a renovation, try to reuse as much of the wood as you can.
- Buy recycled products whenever possible.
- Buy products that have been sustainably produced.
- Buy products that are produced locally and don't have to be shipped around the world.

How Can I Think Big about This?

- Install wind or solar power in your house.
- Install geothermal heating.
- Put in a so-called green roof that helps insulate your house.
- Install a system to capture rainwater for use in watering the landscaping.

Introduction

The universe is slowly falling to pieces. The Second Law of Thermodynamics tells us this, and so do our homes. The minute a home is built, it starts decaying. Some of us resign ourselves to this gentle destruction; others fight it. Either way, the decay of our homes makes most of us a little bit batty and drives some of us to depression. In an interview a few years back, the writer Alain de Botton said the saddest part of his London home was the limestone floor in his kitchen, which had suffered its share of knocks, scratches, and cracks. "It's the beginning of the ruination of the house," de Botton observed, "a reminder of death and collapse."

We wrote this book to help the average homeowner take control of his or her home and keep it from ruination. We don't recommend battling against the inevitable: to retain mental health, a homeowner has to accept some wear and tear. At the same time, there's no reason to just let your house slide downhill. The average person can learn how to care for a home and handle its everyday problems. That's what this book is about. In *What's a Homeowner to Do?,* we explain how to maintain your home, when to ignore the small stuff, how to fix the medium stuff, and how to call in the pros when the big stuff hits. (We also tell you how to get amazing water pressure in your shower, how to unscrew a broken lightbulb using a raw potato, and why a monkey wrench is called a monkey wrench. You need this book.)

We're not here to offer design ideas and decorating tips or to show you how to organize your closets or undertake large building projects, like adding on a new room. We start by showing you the tools you'll need around your house and how to use them. Then we head to the outer shell of the house and take you on a tour, from the roof to the windows, plumbing, doors and walls, basement, yard, garage, and safety and security. Along the way, we'll explain how things work, how to keep them from breaking, how they break, and how to fix them. We'll also discuss what you need to know in order to hire someone else to fix them for you. Even if you never intend to work on your house yourself, you should have this book. It will make you a much better employer of handymen, painters, plumbers, electricians, and contractors.

That's a lot of material, and we're proud of how much information we've packed between the covers. At the same time, we can't pretend we've said the last word on any of these topics. What you'll read here may prompt deeper questions, and you may find yourself wanting more information on a given topic. We're fine with that. We know people have written entire books on subjects we deal with in a single paragraph. But hey, we figure most homeowners don't want to read four hundred pages about electrical wiring. They just want to know how to replace a faulty light switch. If that sounds like a good description of you, then this is your book.

We've made some other assumptions about you. We assume you are intelligent and have a basic grasp of how to work with potentially dangerous tools and substances without maiming yourself. We assume you've lived long enough on planet Earth to have some basic awareness of tools, materials, and the contents of a house. If you really aren't sure how to hold a hammer, it's too soon for you to attempt a project out of our book without some adult supervision. On the other hand, we also assume you aren't some kind of fanatical do-it-yourselfer. If you've already replaced all the plumbing in your basement or built a bookshelf, you probably don't need our book. (Although we do recommend you buy it for kicks, or maybe as a gift for someone, or to find out why a monkey wrench is called a monkey wrench.)

There are few absolutes in the home-repair biz. Never stick a wet finger into a light socket comes to mind. But most household repairs are like recipes: there are various ways to get from A to B. Often the choice is between doing a job the detailed professional way, the solid amateur way, or the quick-fix Band-Aid way. Our preference is always to show you fixes that are safe, effective, lasting, and within the skill level of what we assume to be an average person. If you think you've got a faster, smarter, better way of doing a given project, that's marvelous. Just don't get mad at us. As we said before, we've never claimed to offer the only solutions to problems, just the ones we prefer.

So, in case you haven't noticed, we hope you buy our book. But we also hope you use it as more than bathroom reading or a way to hold up a broken window. (By the way, in the book we show you how to fix broken toilets and windows.) The biggest thing stopping most people from making simple home repairs is the same thing that stops people from speaking foreign languages or asking their crushes out on dates: fear. If we can leave you with one thought, it's be brave! If you try some of this stuff at home, you may make a few mistakes along the way. But you will also learn, and as time goes by you'll find that what was once mysterious and frightening has been made plain.

Cheers,
Stephen Fanuka and Edward Lewine

What's a Homeowner to Do?

Tools and Techniques

Before you can maintain your home properly, you have to learn about the tools you'll need and how to use them. Of course, there are thousands of different tools out there and ten thousand ways to use all of this wonderful and cool specialty gear. That said, you would be surprised at how much you can accomplish with a basic kit that's easy to put together. This chapter outlines the basics you will need to keep a good-size home in good working order. And just as important, it explains how to use those tools safely.

1 How to assemble a basic toolbox

Whether you own a five-bedroom Colonial in the suburbs or a studio apartment downtown, you should have a well-equipped tool collection at the ready.

To begin with, you'll need a good hammer (see entry 4), an adjustable wrench (entry 32), and two kinds of pliers (entry 29), needle-nose and standard (also known as lineman's pliers). Add to those the items illustrated opposite and a bottle of white glue, a tube of silicone, and a tube of white caulk, and you're all set!

2 What kind of toolbox do I need?

The most basic solution is simply to use a milk crate or any other container that will support the weight of all those tools. That would work just fine for someone who isn't going to be using his tools all that much. If you are planning to keep the box stationary and carry individual tools to where you are working, you can buy a larger, more involved version. But if you really want to keep your entire tool collection mobile, then you'll want something smaller. You may also choose to purchase a larger, stationary kit for storing all your tools as well as a smaller kit for carrying selected tools around the house. A really handy stationary box for the person who's going to use it a lot is a multidrawer kit. If you have children, you'll want something that has a good lock. If the box is going to be indoors all the time, you can select a metal model. But if you are exposing it to the elements, find one made of a rust-free material, such as plastic or stainless steel.

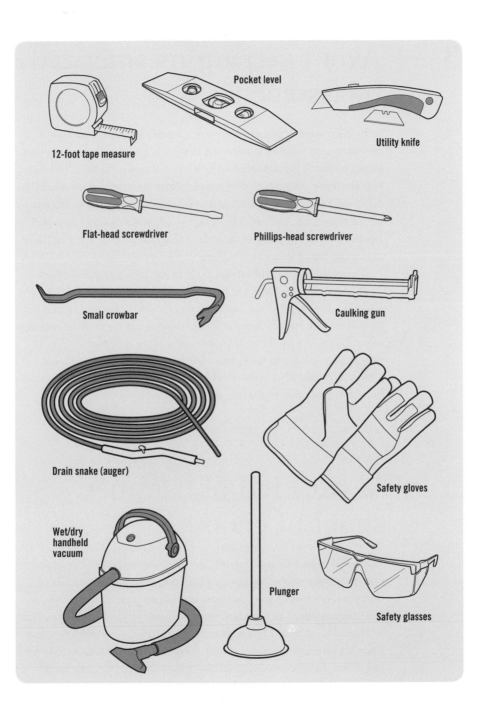

Pocket level

Utility knife

12-foot tape measure

Flat-head screwdriver

Phillips-head screwdriver

Small crowbar

Caulking gun

Drain snake (auger)

Safety gloves

Wet/dry handheld vacuum

Plunger

Safety glasses

3 Avoid getting mesmerized by fasteners

In builder-speak a fastener is a nail, a screw, a bolt, or any item that gets driven or screwed into two pieces of material to hold those two together. We'll get into this a little further down the line, but let's just say there are enough different kinds of fasteners in the world to fill many volumes of a book, and all those shiny little bits and pieces are pretty neat to look at. The temptation, when you get into the hardware store, is going to be to buy box after box of every fastener under the sun. Please don't.

The plain truth is that most of them are going to collect dust in your tool kit, and when it comes time to do a specific job you'll find that despite all these fasteners you may have bought, you don't have the right ones on hand anyway. But you do want some fasteners around, just in case. Your local hardware store will likely have for sale some small boxes with miscellaneous selections of nails and screws in them. If you buy a few of those, you'll have something on hand for small jobs and will have saved yourself a lot of money.

4 What kind of hammer should I choose?

Stay away from a hammer that's too small or too large. The little ones make you work too hard, and the big ones are impossible to deal with. Pick up a few hammers and choose one that makes you feel comfortable. The standard hammer head is 4½ inches from front to claw. The standard hammer length, including the head, is 1 foot. Handles come in wood and metal. Choose whatever feels best to you, but make sure the handle is solid. Hollow handles tend to break.

Also make sure the hammer head is attached tightly to the handle. A flying hammer head is a dangerous thing. There are various kinds of hammers for different jobs. For your tool kit you'll want a curved-claw hammer, meaning the two prongs in the back of the hammer's head are curved for removing nails. The following are some of the most common hammers.

Curved-claw: the basic tool for knocking in nails.

Straight-claw: for installing Sheetrock.

Tack: for the tiny nails that are used in making upholstery or picture frames. (If you have space for one of these in your tool kit, pick one up—it will come in handy.)

Ball-peen: used for metalwork.

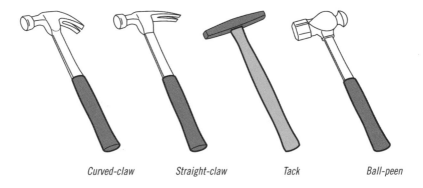

| Curved-claw | Straight-claw | Tack | Ball-peen |

5   How to hammer a nail

Use a pencil to lightly mark the spot where you want the nail to go. Before anything else, do your best to make sure you are driving the nail into a material that will accommodate a nail of its type or any nail at all. This is particularly important when you are hammering something into a wall. There may be a thin layer of Sheetrock that the nail won't hold in, or a brick wall behind the plaster that the nail will bounce out of. A nail should be held between the thumb and the index finger at a 90-degree angle to the surface you are working with. If you're right-handed, hammer with the right. Left-handed, go with that. If you swing both ways, as they say, choose the hand that is most comfortable for the job. Keep your wrist firm, and drive the hammer with your forearm. Hold the nail against the desired spot and tap the nail head lightly with the hammer, making sure you drive the nail perpendicular to the material you are nailing it into. When you feel comfortable that the nail has gone in straight and true, tap more firmly until you've driven the nail in. Don't swing the hammer with too much force. Instead, concentrate on hitting the nail firmly and driving it straight down into whatever you are nailing. Be especially careful to have a light hand when you get to the end of the job, just before the nail disappears into the wood. If you bang too heavily at this stage, then you will damage the surface you are working with.

TRICK OF THE TRADE: *There are two techniques you might consider when hammering in a nail. First, hold the nail with a pair of pliers instead of with your hand for greater control and confidence. Second, lay an index card down on the surface and push the nail through that first, as a way of stabilizing the nail and preventing surface damage.*

6 What do I do about a nail that's gone off-kilter?

Okay, here's the scoop: even the most skilled woodworker is going to end up with some crooked nails. The best way to prevent this is to concentrate on hammering the nail in perpendicular to the wood. One way you can do that is by making sure you've used the proper grip on the hammer, as described in entry 5, and if you are hammering a nail downward, that you are keeping the handle of the hammer pointed at your hips as you work. But you'll make mistakes. It happens, and when it does, start over. The worst thing you can do is try to toggle the nail around in the hole, hoping that this will straighten it out. It won't. Remember, when you hammered in that nail, you created a channel in the wood, and if that channel is on an angle, there is nothing you can do to make it right. All you will get for your efforts is a big, misshapen nail hole in the wood. Yank that nail out with the claw of your hammer and start over.

7 How to remove a partly driven-in nail

Let's assume, for the sake of argument, that the nail you are dealing with is still sticking out of the wood a little bit. If so, your task is an easy one. The only real issue here is getting that nail out while doing a minimum of damage to the wood or other surface you are working with. Before you start, do you have the right hammer? For this job you need the aforementioned curved-claw version. Turn the hammer around and wedge the nail head as deeply into the claw as you can get it, and roll the hammer toward you steadily and easily, using the surface of the material you've nailed the nail into as a fulcrum for leverage. Chances are this is going to do some harm to the surface of the material you are working with.

TRICK OF THE TRADE: *If you don't want to hurt the surface of the material you are pulling the nail from, consider placing a rag or an index card or other buffer beneath your hammer to blunt any damage.*

8 Removing a nail that's all the way in the wood

Using a cat's paw

If all you have is a hammer, then you are going to have to use the end of the claw to kind of chip your way underneath the nail head. If you have two hammers, you can try to wedge the claw of one hammer underneath the nail head and use the other hammer to tap the first hammer into position. This will likely work, but not only is it ineffective, it can also cause all sorts of damage. A better idea is to buy something called a cat's paw, which is a small crowbarlike device used specifically for this situation. It will have a claw at one end that you can tap underneath the nail head with your hammer. You are still going to do some damage but not half as much as if you'd tried to use the hammer claw alone. Once you have the cat's paw underneath the nail head, you can pull the tool back gently, lifting up the nail.

9   Hammers: **THE DARK SIDE**

We use hammers every day, but there's no end to the mischief a hammer can cause if you let it. Here are some tips:

- Make sure the head of the hammer is tightly attached to the handle and that the handle is sound; never use a chipped hammer.

- Never use an everyday curved-claw hammer against a metal surface.

- Check the handle for cracking.

- Always be in the present with a hammer or any other tool. If you let your attention flag for even a second, you can easily slam your fingers with a hammer, producing the inevitable black-and-blue bruise. Professionals do this all the time, so beware.

- If you fail to keep a firm grip on the nail, it can flip back and hit you in the face, doing some serious damage.

- If you forget to line up the nail properly, you'll find you've driven it through whatever you are nailing, causing damage to whatever you are working with and maybe to yourself.

- Wear a pair of safety glasses when hammering because you never know what is going to come flying back at you, but you can be sure that whatever it is, it will be sharp and moving at a good speed.

10   Choosing the right nail for the job

As we mentioned before, there are hundreds of different kinds of nails out there, and you could stand in the aisle at the hardware store until they throw you out before figuring out which one you need. But let's begin at the beginning. A nail is typically a cylinder of metal with a flat or rounded head at one end and a sharp tip at the other. Nails are meant to be driven into two pieces of wood or other materials to hold those two pieces together. Nails tend to be made of steel, but you can find them in brass, copper, or aluminum. Among the more useful kinds of nails you'll find out there are the following.

Flat-head: for general wood work.

Box: like flat-head nails but lighter, to prevent splitting or cracking in more delicate or weaker pieces of wood.

Finishing: these have small heads that barely leave a trace once they're hammered in.

Brad: finishing nail with a more rounded head.

Roofing: used for nailing down shingles and are water resistant.

Threaded: look sort of like screws but are driven into the wood with a hammer.

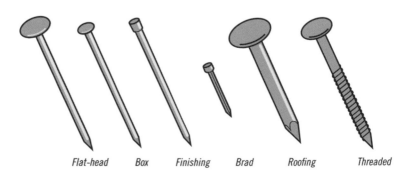

Flat-head   Box   Finishing   Brad   Roofing   Threaded

11 Choosing the right size nail

You'll need a nail of narrow enough width that it will not crack or break the materials you are working with. If the nail is too short, it won't secure the two pieces of material. Too long and it will go straight through whatever you are nailing. If you are asking the nail to support a lot of weight, it needs to be strong enough for the job. Most of these questions are best posed at your local hardware store when you have a specific project in mind. Length is something you can figure out for yourself. In general, put the two pieces of wood or other material that you are joining together and measure them horizontally. To do the job properly, the nails you use should go all the way through the first object and about halfway through the second. Remember, if you are working on a project that will be outdoors, you will want to buy nails that are rust resistant. Galvanized steel nails will do for most situations. If you must, you can buy stainless steel nails. They won't rust, but they are expensive.

12 How nails are measured

The most commonly used sizes of nails are measured in pennies. The term *penny* originally referred to the cost of a hundred nails in England during the fifteenth century. Larger nails cost more per hundred. The penny is a measurement of height. The abbreviation for penny is "d," which is confusing, but it comes from the word *denarius,* which was a Roman coin that was worth around a penny. These nails range from two pennies, which is 1 inch long, to ten pennies. The standard nail is a fourpenny, which is 1½ inches in length. Nails smaller than one penny are known as "wire nails." Wire nails are the thickness of a paper clip and come in a variety of lengths. Nails that are larger than ten pennies are called "framing nails," and are used by professionals for major construction. Once

tools and techniques

13

you know generally what size nail you need, you can go to the people at the hardware store and describe your project, and they can point you in the right direction.

13 The hammer's best friend

What we are about to tell you is not a cheat. It is something the professionals do. The best thing you can do for your hammer, beyond using the correct nail, is to apply a bit of glue to whatever you are hammering. Think of the glue as insurance in case you use a nail that is too short or drive it in the wrong way. Take the bottom piece of the two pieces you are nailing together and put a ½-inch dot of glue about a quarter of the way down the length of the wood. Place the top piece on the bottom one and align them. No need to let the glue dry. Just hammer away. Glue comes in regular (white glue) and quick drying (yellow). In general, the basic, white glue, of the type kids often use, is perfect for this kind of job. But the quick-drying glue is still something to consider having in your tool kit. You'll use it in other contexts, just not for this kind of job. The quick-drying stuff doesn't give you enough time to line up your project, which adds a layer of unneeded tension to what you are doing.

14 How to choose a screwdriver

A basic screwdriver is a tool with a plastic, metal, or wooden handle at one end and a narrow steel blade at the other. The blade is designed to fit into the head of a screw. There are many kinds of screws out there, but the two most common are the slotted screw, which has a single indentation along its center, and the cross-head screw, more commonly known as the Phillips-head. You'll need at least one Phillips-head and one slot-head screwdriver, but there is a problem. To work well, a screwdriver needs to fit snugly into the head of the screw. Too tight, and the screwdriver will slip out of the screw; too loose, and it will rattle around in the slot—either way you'll damage the screw. You might consider buying at least four slotted screwdrivers of different sizes, starting with a small one, at 2½ millimeters, and going up to a 9½-millimeter model. That would cover most situations. Phillips-head screws also come in varying sizes, which are measured in gauges, and you can think about purchasing a similar spread in those. As with hammers or any other tool you are buying, you don't need the Rolls-Royce model, but buy good, well-made screwdrivers. You are going to use these all the time.

TRICK OF THE TRADE: *The larger the handle, the better control and the more torque you'll have in using the tool. So think big handles.*

15   You can't generalize about screws

On the most basic level, a screw is a fastener, like a nail, except its shaft is threaded with a spiral groove and its head has a slot or other indentation meant for use with a screwdriver that will twist the screw into whatever material you are working with. Beyond that all bets are off. There's an endless variety of screws outfitted with about a dozen different kinds of heads. If we tried to make any generalized statements about screws, someone would write us and tell us about an exception. But let's generalize about screws anyway.

BASIC SCREW TYPES

Wood screws: these have a point at the end of the shaft and are meant for use with, well, wood.

Machine screws: blunt at the end and designed to be used with metal.

BASIC SCREW-HEAD TYPES

Slot-head: used with a flat-head screwdriver; excellent for basic jobs involving wood or metal.

Phillips-head: used with that type of screwdriver; typically found on complex machinery or in other involved jobs.

 Slot-head Phillips-head

Flat-head: a slot-head or Phillips-head screw designed to sit flush with the surface you are driving the screw into; the basic screw for any project that doesn't involve metal.

Pan-head: a slot-head or Phillips-head screw that's designed to sit atop the surface you are driving the screw into, most often used in projects involving metal.

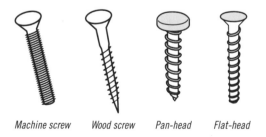

Machine screw   Wood screw   Pan-head   Flat-head

TRICK OF THE TRADE: *One way you can get a screw to slip more easily into wood, for example, is to wet a bar of soap and coat the threads before using the screw. This will lubricate the whole deal and allow you to twist that screw home with a lot less elbow grease.*

what's a homeowner to do?

16 Choosing the right size screw

Screws come in different lengths and widths. As with a nail, you need a screw of narrow enough width that it will not crack or break the materials you are working with and long enough that it will go all the way through the first layer you are fastening and about halfway into the second layer. As with nails, you'll want to bring your project to the hardware store and get some advice if you aren't sure about what you are doing. Screws are measured with three metrics, and these will be marked in the hardware store. You'll see a series of numbers that look something like this: "4-40 x .5." The first number tells you the width of the screw. These numbers go up from 0 to 14, but when the numbers go above 10 they'll typically be written as fractions, such as ¼, which would mean a ¼-inch diameter. (That, by the way, is a pretty big screw.) The second number, after the dash, is the number of threads. The third number, after the x, is the length. Be aware that some screws are measured in inches and some in metric measurements. To calculate the correct length of the screw you need, you should do exactly what you did when choosing a nail. Put the two pieces of wood or other material that you are joining together and measure them horizontally. To do the job properly, the screws you use should go all the way through the first object and about halfway through the second.

17 How to screw in a screw

It goes without saying that you are going to choose the right screw for the job and the right screwdriver for that screw. If you are working with wood, you can use a hammer and ever so lightly tap the screw gently into the wood until it penetrates the surface; often you can achieve this effect just by pressing down on the screw with your hand. If you are concerned about splitting the wood or about being strong enough to drive in the screw, you can also consider using a drill to create a hole that is smaller in diameter than the diameter of the shaft of the screw. This will make the job go a lot more easily.

If you want to twist away with the screwdriver, hold the screw steady between your index finger and thumb and turn the screwdriver until the screw is sunk all the way in. When you are using a screw with metal, you will usually have a premade hole to work with. So twist the screw in with your hand until you meet some resistance, then finish the job with the screwdriver. Remember to stand over the screw if at all possible and exert a steady downward pressure so that you drive the screw into the wood at a 90-degree angle to the wood surface.

TRICK OF THE TRADE: *When you are twisting a screw into wood, you'll feel it getting tighter and tighter as it goes in. Then there will come a point when the screw stops tightening and it will loosen, and the screw will turn and turn. If you get this far, you have overscrewed. You'll need to pull that screw out, and if you want to use that same hole, you'll need to start over with a wider screw that will catch into the wood.*

18 How do I screw out a screw?

Part of the magic of screws is that they are designed to come out of the material you are working with as easily as they go into it. This means that in most cases you can remove a screw in no time at all. Choose the right screwdriver for the screw you are loosening. Stand over the screw. Insert the screwdriver into the screw and press down firmly into the screw. Yes, press down. Then turn gently but firmly to the left. Counterintuitively, the threading on the screw will push the screw out of the wood or metal, even as you press down on the screw. Don't overpress but exert just enough pressure to move the screw out.

TRICK OF THE TRADE: *We want to introduce you to one of the most common and useful little phrases you can ever employ around the house. You may have heard it: "Righty tighty. Lefty loosey." It means what it says. With everything from screws to lightbulbs and faucets, you tighten by turning to the right and you loosen by turning to the left. Voilà!*

19 Stripping screws

This topic may sound kind of fun in a naughty way, but in reality it is a big and boring problem. The screw has a head on it, usually with a slotted or cross-shaped indention in it. You are supposed to put the screwdriver into those slots and use the screw, but often—very often, all too often—the slots will become broken, weakened, or worn out. This can happen for a variety of reasons. The most common reason, really, is poorly made screws. There are a lot of cheap ones out there, and they don't wear well. Another reason is rust and age. Over time, even the best-made screw will begin to degrade a bit, and if that screw is subjected to moisture, it can really rust out. Finally, any screw can become stripped by being used improperly. Most screws are stripped after contact with screwdrivers that are either too large or too small for them. If you exert force on a screwdriver that doesn't fit the slot properly, it will rattle around inside the slots or press up against them and wear them down.

20 What do I do about a stripped screw?

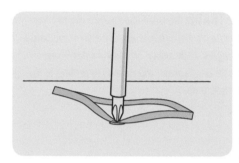

Like the doctors say, your first commandment in this case is: do no harm. If the screw is stripped, be extra careful when choosing the right screwdriver to use with it. Don't be tempted to use a power tool. You are better off getting over the screw with a manual screwdriver and exerting a steady, strong, and slow pressure. Try experimenting with different kinds of screwdrivers to see which one will work. To give yourself added traction, take a rubber band and place it in the head of the screw, then apply the screwdriver. With a Phillips-head that has stripped in a project involving metal, you can take a power tool and literally drive another screw through it. Alternatively, you can leave the stripped screw alone and drill a new hole near it and put in a new screw. For a flat-head screw, you may be able to deepen the stripped slot by banging a screwdriver into the slot with a hammer. If you are encountering a rusted screw, spray a lubricant onto the screw. Let it sit for a few minutes. Then try unscrewing it again.

TRICK OF THE TRADE: *There's a neat little tool for dealing with a stripped screw called a screw extractor. It's a screwdriver or screwdriver bit that has rough threads designed to bite into the head of the stripped screw and give you the traction to really screw the thing in or out. You use the extractor as you would any screwdriver in this situation. Stand over the screw, exert slow and steady pressure, and turn.*

21   Don't screw in at an angle

Chances are, now and then (but likely less often than you will with a nail) you're going to somehow twist a screw in at a bad angle. Remember, just as with a nail, the way you start is the way you'll finish. Start crooked and you'll end crooked. So before you drive the screw in all the way, make sure it is standing straight and perpendicular to the surface you are working with. If you end up driving the screw in at an angle, you may have to accept defeat. Trying to toggle the screw around in the hole is just going to create a bigger and more unsightly hole. Pull the screw out of the hole and start the entire process over in a slightly different spot. Alternatively, you could drill a straight hole down through the angled one.

22   Fixing a bad screw hole

You've put a screw in at a bad angle and decided to start over. Great, except now you are stuck with an unsightly hole in your wood. No fear, because there's a product called wood putty or wood filler. It comes in two main styles, water based and solvent based. The solvent-based variety has been the industry standard for years. It works great. The water-based variety is supposed to be more eco-friendly, and in recent years the quality and effectiveness of this kind of filler have improved greatly. Water-based fillers are much easier when it comes time to clean up your project, and they last longer in the can. The choice is yours. Wood filler comes in different shades to match different types of wood. If the piece of wood you are working with is unfinished, you fill the hole with the putty, to just above the surface. Let it dry for an hour, and then sand it down. If the wood you are working with is finished and you don't want to abrade it, right after you fill it with the putty, use a wet rag and wipe the excess putty away. We will discuss this topic in greater detail in chapter 7.

23   Screwdrivers: **THE DARK SIDE**

It's always our closest loved ones who hurt us the most. The screwdriver is an innocent-looking thing, and because it's an everyday tool, we tend to treat it lightly, and that leads to injuries.

Take a moment to consider whether you have the right tool for the job, and if you don't, go out and get what you need. The most common problems with screwdrivers come when the tool slips out of the slots in the screw and flies around, or drives into the leg of the person using the screwdriver, or slips and drives into the hand of the person using the tool. These and other nasty little incidents happen when you aren't using the proper equipment for the job. Here are some pointers:

- Confine your screwdriver use to screwing and unscrewing. The screwdriver is not the tool for prying open cans, punching holes in metal, or prying apart bits of machinery.

- Do not try to drive your screwdriver into anything using a hammer.

- Obviously, don't go sticking your screwdriver into anything that is electrified.

- Don't expose the screwdriver to excessive cold or heat.

- Don't use a damaged screwdriver, whether it has a blunted head or a broken handle.

- Wear your safety glasses.

24 Using screws in walls

We'll go into this in more depth later, but for a short overview, the walls in most new construction buildings will be made of drywall, also known as Sheetrock. Most buildings constructed before World War II will have plaster walls. Each of these kinds of walls poses a different problem when you want to place a screw in them, but there are small devices available that can help you do this.

TOGGLE BOLTS

Sheetrock walls tend to be less than 1 inch thick, so there isn't much material to hold your screw in place. The solution here is a toggle bolt (commonly known as a butterfly in the business). This is a small wing-shaped device that closes over the screw before you twist it into the wall. Once the toggle bolt has been screwed inside the drywall, it will open up on the other side (once pressure is applied between the back of the Sheetrock and the wing by a spring) and stabilize the screw against the inside of the drywall.

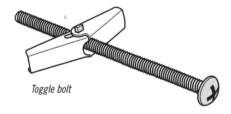

Toggle bolt

ANCHORS

Plaster and brick walls are brittle and will likely crumble around the screw. Use an anchor, which is a plastic sheath that goes around the screw. When the screw is screwed into the anchor, the anchor expands, and this helps secure the screw and anchor in the plaster. Choose an anchor that is just slightly narrower in diameter than the screw you are going to use. This will allow it to work properly, expanding inside the hole as the screw is being twisted into it.

25   Nuts and bolts

If you look around, chances are you'll see that your world is filled with items that have been put together using nuts and bolts. To state it simply, a bolt is like a machine screw, a threaded screw with a head and a blunt end. A nut is a doughnut-shaped object with threads on the inside of the hole that is meant to have the bolt screwed into it. Nuts and bolts are almost always used together. The bolt is screwed into two objects that are meant to be fastened. The nut is put on the other side of the two items, and the bolt is also screwed through it. End of story.

We've already dealt with the kind of bolts you are going to encounter. They are the same as machine screws. Nuts come in many shapes and sizes. Remember, the outside of the nut may be fashioned in various ways.

Wing nuts: are made for use by hand and have two little projections, or wings, that are turned, using the index finger and thumb.

Hex nuts: are six sided and made for use with the most common spanner wrenches (see entry 32) or socket wrenches.

Coupler nuts: are like hexes, except they're wider and are actually used to connect two different bolts.

Lock nuts: have built-in imperfections in their threads that make them very hard to take off.

Cap nuts: are like hexes, but with a top that covers the threading at one end of the nut. They are used for jobs where the end of the nut will be exposed and on view.

26   How to use nuts and bolts

Nuts and bolts are most often found in store-bought metal furniture and toys that require assembly. There's nothing all that fancy about using them. You need two hands or, failing that, a screwdriver and a pair of pliers, or a ratchet wrench. To go tool-less, use one hand to hold the bolt on one side of whatever you are fastening, while the other hand holds the nut on the other side. Begin screwing the bolt in with your fingers, screwing it through whatever you are fastening and into the nut on the other side. Whenever you begin to meet resistance, use a screwdriver, and if you need to you can hold the nut with a pair of pliers. That should do the trick.

Loosening a nut and bolt can be a bit more difficult, especially if the nut and bolt have been screwed into each other for a long time. You start by loosening the nut. The primary problem is if the bolt turns with the nut and you can't get any traction. The simplest solution here is to have two pliers or wrenches, one to turn the bolt, the other to turn the nut.

TRICK OF THE TRADE: *If you don't have two pliers, you may be able to secure the bolt with a screwdriver and turn the nut with a set of pliers.*

27   When to use a washer

Washers are flat, O-shaped metal discs that are positioned between a screw head and the surface of the material the screw has been driven into. The washer does two things: it strengthens the fastening action of the screw, and it protects the surface from damage by distributing the pressure that the screwed-in screw exerts on the surface. A washer allows the nut and bolt to be turned without affecting the finish of the part and creates a smooth-bearing surface.

Some washers have a series of small teeth around the edges, or are split to prevent the bolt from loosening. These are called lock washers. They are used in areas that might also use a lock nut.

TRICK OF THE TRADE: *Now and then you are going to be faced with a bolt, screw, or other fastener that doesn't have any indentations in it. When that happens it's time to pull out the pliers. Take the pliers in one hand, open them wide, close the ends over the top of the bolt or screw, and turn left to loosen. Be sure to hold your pliers carefully on the screw to avoid scratching it up against the surface of the object.*

28   What is an Allen wrench?

Many bolts and screws, particularly those used in furniture and fixtures like doorknobs, are designed for use with a tool called an Allen wrench, which is an L-shaped, hexagonal device. Allen wrenches, which are sometimes called hex keys or zeta wrenches, typically come in sets of different sizes and are great little things to have. They are small, light, and easy to understand and use. They work really well everywhere, including in tight spaces. They don't cost much. Insert one tip into the top of the bolt and twist. If you can insert the short end of the wrench, do that first, because you'll get more torque using the long end. If you don't have enough space to turn the long end around and around, by all means insert that into the bolt and use the short end as your handle. If you meet resistance from the bolt and your hand begins to hurt, a handkerchief or other rag will ease your pain and give you added leverage. You can also consider using pliers on an Allen wrench.

29 Choosing the right type of pliers

A pair of pliers is a tool that looks rather like a pair of scissors, except the business end of the pliers will have two pincers rather than a pair of blades, and a small cutting surface right at the fulcrum, where the two pincers meet the handle. Pliers are used for holding objects, for cutting, and also for bending or crimping materials like metal wire. The following are the basic pliers types.

Lineman's or standard pliers: the basic pliers, which have stubby little arms. Used for gripping and cutting and are best for small, hard-to-grasp objects.

Needle-nose or long-nose pliers: these do the same kinds of jobs as regular pliers, but with their long, graceful pincers, they are great for working in tight little spaces.

Slip-joint pliers: they have two settings, larger and smaller.

Locking pliers: they lock onto objects.

Parallel pliers: they are designed so that the two pincers are exactly parallel to each other so that they meet over a greater surface area.

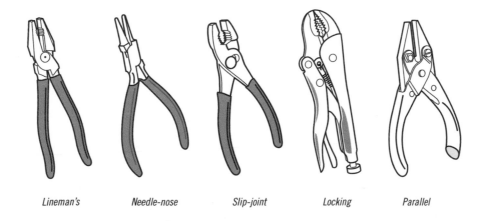

| Lineman's | Needle-nose | Slip-joint | Locking | Parallel |

tools and techniques

30 Pliers: THE DARK SIDE

The best advice we ever saw on what not to do with pliers came from a do-it-yourself Web site that advised its readers not to use pliers to grab their brothers' noses like the Three Stooges used to do. Excellent point. Also, make sure to use a rag or some other buffer if you are using a pair of pliers on a finished fixture like a faucet or on a polished pipe in a bathroom—otherwise, you'll ruin the finish. You can break a pair of pliers, especially needle-nose, if you bend or twist it too much.

Do not try to get greater leverage on a pair of pliers by putting pipes or other extenders on the handles. (Yes, people do that.) You are going to cause an accident. If you need more grip, get a bigger pair of pliers.

Above all, make sure to keep all parts of your body—especially your fingers and the meaty part of your palms—away from between the two handles of the pliers. Man, does it smart when you pinch skin in there, and it happens all the time. You get a nice, bloody little bruise.

31 How to use a pair of pliers

Locking pliers have a screw at the end of the handle that allows you to lock the pliers onto whatever you are looking to grip. This is a great way to secure something so that you can then use your free hands for loosening, cutting, or otherwise dealing with it. Lineman's pliers, with their serrated pincers, can get right in and grip onto bolts, nuts, nails, and other objects that need loosening or pulling out. Needle-nose pliers are the best. They grip like anything and fit into any little space. They are great for precision work, such as removing a tiny nail from a picture frame. Both needle-nose and lineman's pliers have small cutting surfaces near the fulcrum. These are great for cutting wire, for stripping the plastic insulation around small wires, and for other cutting jobs, mostly involving metal. To cut something, position it down at the point where the two jaws of the pliers meet and close the pliers for a clean snip.

32 The lowdown on wrenches

Our friends and allies over in England call them spanners, but here in the USA we apply the name "wrench" to a variety of different tools primarily designed to grip onto nuts, bolts, and other fasteners. There is also an entire category of wrenches designed for use with pipes, but we are not speaking about those right now. Wrenches differ from pliers in that a set of pliers works like scissors, gripping an object between two pincers, whereas a wrench has a circular or U-shaped end that in most cases is designed to fit exactly over the object that it is turning. For this reason you tend to need to buy rather large sets of wrenches. Here are various commonly used varieties.

Adjustable wrench: by far the most useful for the average homeowner, it has a jaw that moves up and down toward the other, stationary jaw, allowing you to accommodate your wrench to many objects of different sizes.

U-shaped or open-ended wrench: the most common.

Circular or ring wrench: fits around the nut or bolt.

Combination wrench: has a ring at one end and an open end at the other.

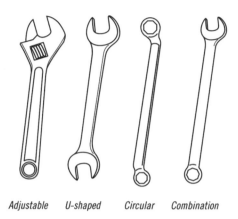

Adjustable   U-shaped   Circular   Combination

TRICK OF THE TRADE: *Well, this one is more like a nice bit of trivia to impress cocktail party guests with. The famous monkey wrench is an adjustable wrench that was popular in the nineteenth century but is rarely used today. It was named not after a primate but rather after its inventor, one Charles Moncky of Brooklyn, New York.*

33   How to use a wrench

Make sure you have the right tool for the job. Do not use a pipe wrench for work with nuts and bolts. Take care selecting the right size wrench so that you have no slipping or sliding around the object you are working with. Place the wrench over the object that you are loosening and make sure the fit is snug and secure. Pull. When you do exert pressure on the wrench, do so in a slow, steady, even way. No jerking or sudden motions. Never push on a wrench; always pull.

Pushing will cause you to lose balance. If you are using an adjustable wrench, get it tight and well adjusted before going to work. Don't try to make a wrench fit better by inserting some kind of shim.

TRICK OF THE TRADE: *Here's an important piece of advice: make sure you have a firm footing when you use a wrench (same goes for any tool) so that when you begin to exert pressure on the wrench you don't slip, fall, and bang your jaw onto whatever you are working on.*

34 Crowbars: they aren't just for demolition anymore

Crowbars, also known as jimmy bars, wrecking bars, and pry bars, are great for a variety of purposes, none of them felonious. A crowbar consists of a metal bar with a single curved end that flattens into a two-pronged claw that looks rather like what you'd see at the back of a hammer head. Many crowbars will also feature a second set of claws at the other end of the bar. Crowbars are ideal for removing nails, prying shingles off roofs, opening large wooden boxes, providing leverage for lifting heavy objects up onto wheelbarrows, and destroying stuff. It is generally accepted that the name dates back centuries to England and refers to the way a crowbar's claws look like a crow's foot.

If you are prying something apart, find a snug crack to insert the crowbar into and then put pressure on the bar slowly and evenly. If you are lifting something up, place a piece of wood next to the object you are going to lift, for use as a fulcrum. Place one of the claws of the crowbar underneath the object, the shaft of the crowbar resting on the piece of wood. Gently push down on the crowbar to lift the object you are working with.

35 Crowbars: **THE DARK SIDE**

When you use a crowbar, there is a lot of potential for accidents, so be very careful and watch the following:

- Things you are demolishing may fall on you. Always pry objects—like two beams that have been nailed together—away from you.

- Check to make sure there is a safe landing area for whatever you are demolishing.

- Before using the crowbar, make sure the object you are working with is in fact secured to something else; it might just be lying there, in which case you are going to send it into the air when you use the crowbar.

- Do a check to see whether there are any objects, like nails, splinters, or glass, that might go flying.

- If you use a crowbar, you might not only end up with debris all over the place but also twist or otherwise strain your back.

- If you are swinging the crowbar during a demo project, look around you—through your safety glasses—before having at it.

TRICK OF THE TRADE: *Whatever you do with a crowbar, never go in for a quick motion. Jerking the crowbar may send projectiles flying around.*

36 Using a tape measure

A tape measure is a device that will typically have a spooled metal tape marked with inches and millimeters and is rolled up inside a box. The tape is on a spring and will roll back into the box if you let go, although there is usually some mechanism for locking the tape into place. The tape will also have a metal hook at the end. To use the tape measure, you just pull out the tape. Either hook the hook at the edge of the object you want to measure, or if you don't have an edge to work with, line the tape measure up at the 1-inch mark. Lay the tape out between the A and B you are measuring and take the measurement. Remember, if you have measured the distance starting from the 1-inch mark, you are going to have to subtract an inch from your measurement to be accurate.

TRICK OF THE TRADE: *Be very respectful of measuring. It is really hard. You probably reckon you can measure something accurately. Well, think again. Thus the old woodworker's axiom, "Measure twice, cut once." What this means is, even an experienced craftsman has to double-check his measurements.*

37 Calibrating multiple tape measures

Beware of using multiple tape measures. Chances are each one is going to be slightly different from the others, by as much as ⅛ inch. And that is a lot! So, be consistent. Use one tape measure per project.

If you aren't sure whether you've been switching measures, you can calibrate them by taking a piece of wood, measuring a distance—say, 1 foot—on the wood, and marking it. Then take the same measurement with your other tape measures and see what the spread is. If you have a slight variation, you can adjust it by taking a pair of pliers and bending the little hook at the end of the tape measure out a little to make it take a longer reading, or in a little to take a shorter one.

.

38 Advanced measuring techniques

The simplest kind of measuring you do with a measuring tape is from one end of a piece of wood to the other. That is, you have something that you can hook the tape measure onto and unspool it from there, and the distance you are measuring is relatively short, say, less than 3 feet. But many situations are more complex than that.

The first one is measuring a large distance, say, longer than 5 feet. This is not so easy to do, especially if you are alone. What you'll find is that the tape will bend as you spool it out, and that will warp your result. Having a pal at the other end is the simplest solution, but you may need a new tool—a wider tape measure. For big measuring jobs, buy a tape measure that is the widest you can find. These will resist bending at longer distances.

What if you are trying to measure a distance in the middle of a space? As we said before, tape measures are meant to hook onto something. But when you want to measure between two points—say, from one part of a floor to another—and there's no possible object to hook onto, try this: pull out a section of tape and get your thumb at the 1-inch mark. Hold that down right at the first point you are measuring, then spool out to the second point, and do the math.

39 Tape Measures:
THE DARK SIDE

Here's the dirty little secret about tape measures. They are fine for most of the measuring you want to do, but know this: even though you can take readings to $\frac{1}{16}$ inch with a tape measure, it is almost impossible to be accurate to within $\frac{1}{8}$ inch with a regular tape measure. If you want greater accuracy than that—and when you are doing precision woodworking or cabinetry, you may well want that level of accuracy—you need a different tool, but before we go there (entry 40), here are some tape measure warnings:

• If your tape measure is cut, bent, or damaged in any way, throw it out. You can slice your hand open with it in a split second and you'll be ER-bound.

• It is really fun to do, but don't attempt any violent spooling of the tape. Letting it wham back into its box is impressive but will degrade the spring mechanism fast.

• Another easy way to break your spring mechanism is to pull the tape out as far as it will go. Bad idea. If you need to make a larger measurement, buy a longer tape measure. They come in sizes up to 100 feet.

• Tape measures come with locks that can secure the tape in place, but using this mechanism can damage your tape, bending it and giving you inaccurate readings.

• Be gentle when bending the tape. You will naturally bend the tape a bit to take accurate measurements, but bending it too far over or too roughly will damage the accuracy of the instrument.

40 How to obtain a really accurate measurement

There are some jobs that require more accuracy than others. Framing a wall with wood beams does not require accuracy down to $\frac{1}{16}$ inch. Making a chair might. So if you need to be superaccurate, buy an extension ruler. An extension ruler—or, more exactly, an extension rule—is just what it sounds like: a 6-, 8-, or 12-foot ruler, made out of wood and broken into segments that fold and unfold (see the photograph on page 3). This is an old-fashioned device, and there are plenty of people who will advise you that you just don't need one. But don't heed that advice. Sometimes the old ways are the best ways, and this is the perfect tool. It is great for measuring distances up to 6 feet, where you might find a tape measure cumbersome. It also affords you much greater accuracy in taking small measurements than a tape measure does, because you can always lay the extension rule flat.

TRICK OF THE TRADE: *The extension rule also makes a great back scratcher.*

41 How to use a utility knife

They go by so many names—box cutter, Stanley knife, razor blade knife—and you see them everywhere. The utility knife is essentially some form of handle that has within it a razor blade that can extend out of the handle. Some knives come with segmented blades that can be snapped off as the tip dulls, revealing a new, sharp blade. Other utility knives, meant for precision work, have fixed blades. These will come with some kind of cap or safety covering. Obviously you use these tools for cutting, and boy, are they handy. Before you start, make sure you have the right utility knife for the job at hand.

If you are opening boxes, then you'll want a larger, stronger knife. For doing intricate work in wood, take out one of the pen-size jobs. Extend the blade and make sure it is locked, in whatever way the blade locks for that kind of knife. Then stop. Now think hard about where you are placing the hand that isn't on the knife. Never place this second hand underneath the surface you are cutting or near the path the knife is going to take, or anywhere in the direction you are cutting. Utility knives slip, and when they slip they cut a path of destruction. If all this sounds a bit obvious, then just remember that professionals are always slicing off bits of themselves with utility knives.

42 Don't I need some kind of saw?

You might. So, go with a hacksaw. This is a cutting device with a fine-toothed blade that is held in a frame. Hacksaws are great for any small sawing chore, but they are mostly used for cutting metal. (They were also used by doctors in earlier eras for amputations, but please don't try that at home.) Most hacksaws will come with what's called a pistol grip, which looks exactly like what you'd expect—a grip that would seem appropriate on a handgun.

The blades are disposable and can be detached from the saw by loosening pins or screws at either end. Some hacksaws can accommodate blades of only one length, while others can be used with blades of varying lengths. Changing blades can come in handy, because not only do the blades wear down but you can also attach blades of varying styles and quantity of teeth for use in cutting materials of varying degrees of difficulty.

43 How do I use my new hacksaw?

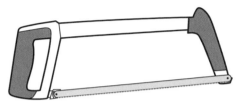

You can attach the blade with the teeth facing toward you or away from you, depending on the job and your preference for which stroke will do the cutting. Hold the object you are cutting with one hand, making sure to keep that hand away from the hacksaw. If you are cutting something intractable, like piping, you should put it in a vise. Cut slowly and carefully. Do not rush or use many strokes per second, as the friction of the saw on metal will heat things up pretty fast. Use the entire blade in each stroke. Think about using a drop of oil or other lubricant to reduce friction.

44 But what about power tools?

We have mixed feelings about power tools. Power tools are a beautiful thing. They get jobs done quickly and cleanly, and there are some jobs that are hard to finish without them. At the end of the day, however, if you aren't a professional, using power tools is a hazardous activity. To put it differently, you don't need an Italian sports car to commute to the train station. That said, there are a few power tools that you should think about having in your arsenal, or, perhaps, keeping in mind and buying if you find you really need them. In general, the rules for buying power tools are much the same as the rules for buying hand tools. There is no need to get the top-of-the-line, most expensive tools money can buy. But you want to be sure you are buying quality, because shoddy tools are simply unsafe.

The next few entries (45 to 48) outline a few basic power tools that ought to see you through most of the jobs you'll want them for. Now and then we may also mention a few others for specific tasks.

TRICK OF THE TRADE: *With power tools, please remember that in many instances you can borrow them from friends. You can also rent them from hardware stores, big-box stores, and companies that specialize in power tool rentals. Indeed, renting power tools is remarkably easy in most parts of the country. So look into that before plunking down your cash for something you may use only once.*

45 How to use a power drill

If you are planning to buy just one power tool, it should be a power drill. It's one of the most useful things a person can own. What does a homeowner do more of than anything else? Tighten screws—and if you attach a screwdriver bit to a power drill, you'll be tightening screws all over your house in seconds. With a power drill you can also choose to use screws rather than hammer-driven nails for projects, and as we've said before, the screw is a superior fastener to the nail.

A power drill is nothing more complicated than a motor that rotates a removable bit. There are endless power drills out there, but the most basic choice you are going to have to make is between a cordless, battery-operated drill and an electric drill with a cord. We advise getting an electric model. The cordless drills often don't have the power, and you can always buy an extension cord for jobs away from your power sources. You will also want, at bare minimum, a drill that can go in reverse and has variable speeds for different jobs.

As with all power tools, learn about your drill before you use it. Read the instructions. Try putting bits in and taking them out before you plug in the machine. To use a drill, first make sure the ON/OFF switch is off and the drill is unplugged. Then unscrew the open end of the drill and insert the bit you want. Make sure when you put the new bit in that you have properly tightened the drill. Set the torque adjuster to the right amount for the job at hand. (If you apply too much torque to a screw, you'll strip it.) Turn on the power, place the drill where needed, and pull the trigger to rotate the bit.

46   What if I want just one more power tool?

This is what we were afraid of. You are getting into the whole power tool thing. Okay, if you must have one more, you might want a power saw. In fact, in a perfect world you might actually want two power saws. But if you had to choose one, the first we'd recommend buying is a reciprocating saw. This is a gun-shaped saw with a motor that drives the blade back and forth as you might do with your arm. They are small, light, and handy for a wide variety of demolition projects. With a good reciprocal saw you can cut

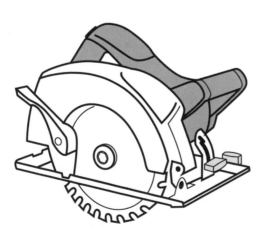

Reciprocating saw

Handheld circular saw

through just about anything, from wood beams and walls to pipes and other metal objects. All you need is the right collection of blades.

But reciprocating saws are not all that great at making long, straight cuts. If you have that kind of sawing in mind, then go for a handheld circular saw. These are portable, like reciprocal saws, but have a circular blade that rotates. They are marvelous for making those long, straight cuts that carpenters and general contractors need for various purposes. Circular saws come in a variety of styles and price ranges. For most homeowners a nice sidewinder, the style with the motor beside the blade, is a great acquisition.

47 Saw safety

Since we're the guys who told you manual screwdrivers were dangerous, imagine how we feel about saws. Handling a saw is like handling a gun. You are in possession of a deadly weapon and need to be awake, alert, sober, conscientious, and a full-fledged adult before even approaching such a tool. Saws account for thousands of injuries a year. Wear safety goggles. Avoid wearing loose-fitting clothes and jewelry. Think about getting some kind of dust mask. Use the correct blade for the job. There are blades for cutting against the grain of wood, for cutting with the grain of wood, for clean cutting wood, and for cutting concrete, metal, and tile. If you don't know which blade you need, go to the hardware store and ask. Keep your blades keen and sharp by sharpening them as you would a kitchen knife. Never use a dull blade, a broken blade, or a dirty blade. Know where your hands are and where the power cord is. Keep everything away from the saw. Make sure that whatever you are cutting is properly supported and that there is nothing underneath that you are going to slice into. Once you start cutting, if you feel the blade slowing, hear it screeching, or feel it shaking, then just stop. Don't lean into the saw and try to force things. Wait for the blade to stop completely before you set down the saw. Lock up saws and keep them away from children.

48 Using a Dremel

Okay, the proper description for this kind of tool is actually "rotary power tool." Dremel is a brand name, but many people use that term interchangeably with the generic name. Rotary power tools are used for an amazing variety of different tasks, including drilling, sharpening, grinding, engraving, and routing out spaces in wood. A rotary tool is a handheld device to which you can attach any number of different bits to turn it into a sander, a polisher, a carver, a grinder, and more. You might have seen a similar kind of tool, with much regret on your part, in the hands of your dentist as he or she was about to drill or polish your teeth.

Learn the proper method for installing and removing bits and turning the machine on and off. Then buy some scrap wood and spend a few hours practicing with this tool. Hold the device properly, as instructed by the manual. Turn it on and lay the tool on the wood, using the power of the engine, not your force, to do the work. Remember that the tool will heat up rather quickly with all the friction it is generating, so do your projects slowly, carefully, and in small segments to give the rotary tool plenty of time to cool off.

TWO TRICKS OF THE TRADE

1. *Whenever you start a project, make a note of exactly what you are doing, which materials you are using, and where you bought them. That way, when you have to make a repair or other fix on that job, you'll know exactly what materials to buy and where to buy them.*

2. *Use a digital camera to make a visual record of any project you are undertaking. This will help you recall exactly what you did and how you did it.*

The Outer Shell

When you're thinking about maintaining your house, it makes the most sense to focus your attention on the outside and work your way in. Why? Because if the outer shell of your house is damaged or compromised in some way, then it really doesn't matter what is going on inside the house. You are in big trouble. You cannot ignore a damaged wall or roof, because if you do, you'll have the outside coming inside. There are some aspects of fixing up the outer shell of your house that you're going to want to farm out to pros, but there's a lot you can do yourself.

49 How is a roof constructed?

We're not suggesting that you go out and build a roof, but it's very helpful for you to know how your roof is put together. There are essentially two kinds of roofs: pitched and flat. The underlying bones of a pitched roof will typically consist of some kind of triangular wooden trusses, which are triangular frames that give the roof its pitched shape, framed out in wooden beams. Plywood is laid on top of this base to form the roof. A flat roof has a flat wooden frame with plywood over it.

But that is just the first level of the roof. Atop the plywood are layers of insulating material. There are many ways to insulate a roof, but we'll describe the most basic methods. First you'll have a waterproofing layer of either tar paper or roofing felt. Tar paper is exactly what it sounds like—a heavy-duty paper impregnated with tar to form a waterproof sheet. The usual grade of tar paper is fifteen-pound, which means that it weighs fifteen pounds per 100 square feet. Roofing felt is a kind of fibrous material impregnated with tar. It is installed either by being nailed to the roof with roofing nails, melted on with heat, or attached with some form of cement. On top of this you'll find the outer layer of the roof, the part that everyone can see. This outer layer can be made from a variety of materials.

50 Asphalt shingles

When it comes to houses, "shingles" does not refer to the horrible illness that strikes people who've had the chicken pox, but to flat rectangles that are laid overlapping one another. Shingles can be made from asphalt, wood, or slate. You can also find shinglelike

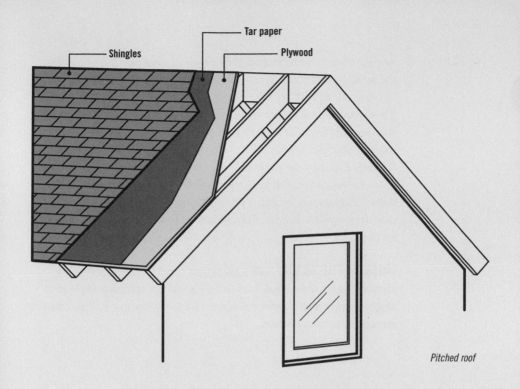

Shingles

Tar paper

Plywood

Pitched roof

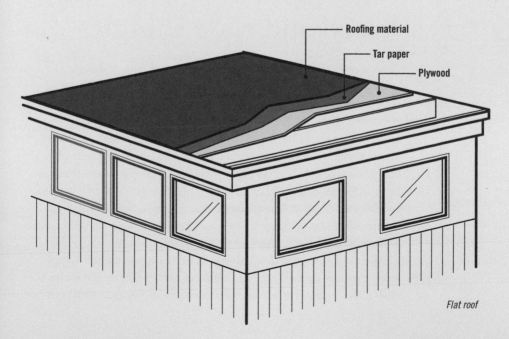

Roofing material

Tar paper

Plywood

Flat roof

roofing materials made from clay tiles and even metal roofing. But the most typical shingled roof is made of asphalt. Asphalt shingles aren't much to look at, but they're cheap and easy to deal with. They're made from paper or fiberglass, which is then impregnated with various forms of asphalt and other metals to make it waterproof. Asphalt shingles are installed with nails, struck straight through the shingles and into the plywood. A good asphalt shingled roof can last up to twenty years, which is a long time, but some other kinds of roofs will last even longer. The other issue with asphalt shingles is that they tend to come in dark colors, which absorb heat and warm up the house.

TRICK OF THE TRADE: *Heat is the biggest factor to consider when using asphalt shingles, which break down both under the rays of the sun and in warm weather. For this reason, asphalt shingles are a better choice for building structures in cooler, more cloudy climates.*

51   Wood and slate shingles

Wooden roofs actually come in shingles and shakes. A shingle is a rectangular, flat piece that is precision cut. A shake is more roughly split and is from the larger piece of wood, which creates a rougher, more old-fashioned, organic look. Wood shingles tend to be made from cedar. Cedar shingles are a popular look in beach communities such as those on Long Island and in New England (think Nantucket). You also find them in California, where there are beautiful trees to make them out of. A good cedar roof, well tended, can last two decades. But be aware that it will rapidly evolve from a warm red-brown to a gentle, weathered gray. Wooden shingles come with holes precut into them and are nailed to the roof.

The same is true of slate roofing. Slate is a naturally occurring stone that is mined all over the world as well as here in the United States. Slate comes in various colors and grades but is most typically a dark gray. Slate is expensive to both buy and install, but it lasts beautifully. A good slate roof can go more than fifty years. Slate is fireproof and waterproof and doesn't need much maintenance, beyond replacing a shingle here and there each year. Slate is also quite heavy, so you need to make sure you have a roof frame that can support it.

TRICK OF THE TRADE: *Can't afford slate shingles but like the look? Keep an eye out for synthetic ones that are dead ringers for slate and a lot cheaper than the real deal.*

52 Clay tiles and metal roofing

A clay tile roof is one of the oldest kinds of roofing out there. Think ancient Greece. Contemporary tiles can be made of clay (as they were in olden times) or of concrete. The tiles will come with holes punched in them and are nailed to the roof, although in some roofing systems not all of the tiles are nailed down. Tiles offer many advantages. They are durable, lasting more than fifty years if well maintained. They keep homes cool (which is why they are popular in places with warmer climates) and come in many styles, shapes, and colors. The upkeep is minimal. On the other hand, tile is a specific look that not everyone wants, and some tiles, particularly the curved ones, are also prone to being infested by animals.

High-end metal roofing, made from aluminum, steel, copper, and other compounds, is growing in popularity, and it is easy to see why. Metal roofing is lightweight and simple to maintain, reflects sunlight and heat away from the house, and comes in many different colors and styles. Unfortunately metal roofing is very expensive, more so even than slate in some instances. It can also be noisy. Imagine a night of listening to rain falling on a metal roof. These roofs do deteriorate over time, acquiring dents and ruts, and the paint can become chipped and peel. These problems are hard to fix without the help of a professional.

53 Roofs: THE DARK SIDE

Every once in a while, perhaps twice a year, you should take a few minutes to eyeball your roof from the street. Use a pair of binoculars. If you see a shingle or two loose or missing, you'll need to make repairs. However, the most common way people realize there's something funky happening on their roof is the appearance of water. You'll see water in the attic, or water stains on your walls or on the ceiling. Chances are this water has come from somewhere on your roof, although there could be other culprits, like window frames.

If you do find water or the evidence of it, don't assume the problem stems from directly above the spot. When water leaks in, it will flow with gravity down the path of least resistance. That means a leak can occur on your roof in the back of your house and the water may actually appear somewhere on the lower floor in the front of your house.

So, to avoid that diagnosis problem, here's a bit of advice. Every few months, on a day when you have a good, strong downpour, take a trip up to the attic and just scan it for water staining or dripping. You may end up finding a small problem, but if you don't nip it in the bud, it can turn into a big problem fast. Either way, if you see some loose or missing shingles, or some water in the attic, you'll have to make a roof repair.

54   Why do I need proper roof ventilation?

Trust us: roof ventilation is a huge issue and one that is often overlooked by homeowners. One of the biggest factors in the health and longevity of your roof is whether it is properly ventilated. Proper ventilation will reduce temperature extremes and moisture in your attic, and this in turn will prevent a variety of ills, including condensation in the attic that will rust nails, screws, and metal roofing; frost forming inside the attic and causing wood to rot; and ice forming on the outside of the roof and driving up under the shingles, where it melts and causes leaks, mold, and mildew. Just as important, a properly ventilated roof can cool your house by many degrees all summer long and reduce your energy bills.

There are all sorts of roof vents, but a good system will have:

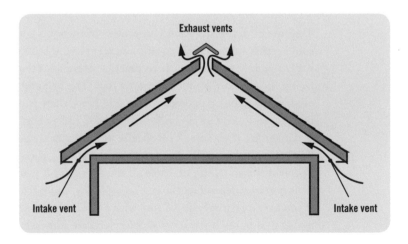

- Intake vents, which are situated at the bottom of the roof, often under the eaves, and which allow air to flow into the attic;
- Exhaust vents, which sit at the top of the roof and allow air to flow out.

If you're not sure how well your roof is ventilated, ask a roofing contractor to come in and do an inspection. If he thinks you need more ventilation, consider hiring someone to do this. It is theoretically possible for a homeowner to install roof venting, but the job is complex, because it requires knowledge of just how much venting you need.

TRICK OF THE TRADE: *Remember that you can actually have too much venting. An overvented roof will function just as poorly as an undervented one. Having too much ventilation can reduce the proper exchange of air that venting relies on and can bring too much weather inside your roof.*

55 Can I repair my own roof?

The answer to this question is complex. In theory, a homeowner could repair almost any kind of roof except metal roofing, which really requires a professional. In practice, there are a few big issues facing the amateur trying to repair a roof. The first and foremost is: should you be up on your roof at all? Now, there is no reason a healthy adult can't go up on his or her roof, except that it is kind of dangerous. If you aren't physically fit, or if you are panicked by heights, or if the whole idea gives you the willies, then don't bother. People die from falling off roofs all the time, and it just isn't worth it.

It also may depend on the size, complexity, and pitch of your roof. If you have a relatively small roof with a relatively flat pitch, it may be no big deal to reach whatever problem you are addressing. If you live in a vast mansion, with all sorts of little peaks and valleys in the roof, you might think twice before going up there. Finally, assess the size of the job. If you are talking about replacing one shingle, you might give it a shot. If you are talking about a major portion of the roof, we strongly recommend bringing in a pro. If you are going to try it, you'll have to purchase and learn how to use a ladder. See the next entry.

56 Buying the right ladder for roof work

If you're going to maintain your own roof, you'll need a good, solid ladder. Chances are you already have the kind of A-shaped, folding ladder that most people keep around for replacing lightbulbs and doing other work inside their homes, but this is not the right tool for the job. For roof work you'll want to buy what is known as an extension ladder. An extension ladder is not shaped like an A. It comes in a single length, normally divided into two or more sections that can be slid up or down to make it longer or shorter, and then locked into place at whatever length you desire. This forms a single, long ladder that is meant to be leaned up against the house. Before you even think about leaning the ladder against your house, take a moment to get the ladder in order. It could be all that comes between you and a rather nasty encounter with Mother Earth.

57 How to use an extension ladder

Remember, it's not safe to extend the ladder all the way. Make sure you leave at least three steps overlapping to ensure that the ladder is rigid; four would be better. Make sure the two sides of the ladder are clipped together firmly with whatever locking system your ladder uses. Some ladders even come with a rope that you loop around the steps of the two sides. Use it. Make sure the surface you are standing the ladder on is level, dry, stable, and not slippery. Sweep the ground to get rid of small rocks or detritus the ladder might slip on.

The ladder should extend three steps above the gutter. There is a three-to-one ratio for how high the ladder goes in relation to how

far away from the house it should stand. Lean the ladder against the house at an angle so that if it were 30 feet high you'd have it 10 feet from the house. Shake the ladder a bit to make sure it's sitting against the house in a stable way. Have someone strong and trustworthy around to hold the ladder while you climb.

TRICK OF THE TRADE: *The right footwear for use with ladders is rubber-soled shoes. Those new, leather-soled penny loafers are a bad fit for this job.*

58 How to be safe on a roof

Before you go up on your roof, take a moment to go over a few things in your mind. Choose a day that is clear and sunny with no precipitation. Do not go up on a roof that is wet, snowy, or icy. Wear the right shoes. Always inform someone that you are going up on the roof and ask him to either watch you or, at the bare minimum, check in on you now and then. When you are on the roof, always keep in mind where the roof ends, especially if you are concentrating on a task that entails moving slowly backward down the roof. Take a cell phone in case of emergencies.

Check your ladder to make sure it is sound. Experiment with it and get it set to the right height and locked. Find the right place for it, and make sure it is solidly up against the wall of the house and at the proper angle. When you are up on the roof, make sure you have solid footing and that you are avoiding any dangerous power lines.

TRICK OF THE TRADE: *Consider using a roof harness or other safety system that can help break your fall in case you do slip. There are various kinds of harnesses out there, but they mostly work with a harness that is worn on the body and a lanyard that is attached to the house. The two work together to cushion the fall of the wearer.*

59 Replacing a damaged asphalt shingle

In this section we are dealing with replacing a single shingle, which you can do yourself, if you are fit and willing to go up on the roof. For this job you'll need a crowbar, a hammer, galvanized roofing nails, roofing cement, a caulking gun, a putty knife, and some rags (before you climb up the ladder, put them all in a bucket; don't cradle them in your arms or jam them in your pockets). First, you'll need to loosen the good shingles above the damaged one by taking your crowbar and gently shimmying it between the damaged shingle and the ones above it to pry them loosely apart (fig. 1). You should now be able to take the damaged shingle in your hand and rock it gently until it comes out. Then, lift the shingle above the empty space and use your crowbar to pry away as many of the old nails as you can (fig. 2). Any nails that cannot be pried away should be hammered flush with the roof (fig. 3). If you see rips or tears in the underlying tar paper or roofing felt, squeeze roofing cement into the damaged area and smooth it out with your putty knife, wiping away the excess with your rag. Gently lift up the good shingles above the open space and place your new shingle in the same spot where the recently removed, damaged shingle was (fig. 4). Hammer four nails across the new shingle at about the level that would leave them ¾ inch under the shingle above. Lastly, lift up the shingle on top of your new one and apply a dab of roofing cement onto the new shingle at a point that will be underneath the one above it. Let the shingle on top fall down onto your new shingle.

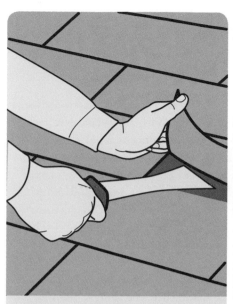

1. Lift up the old shingle with a crowbar.

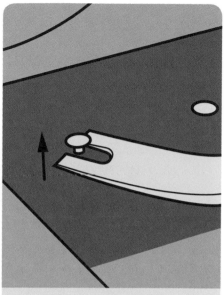

2. Pry up any nails or . . .

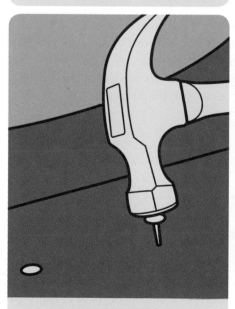

3. . . . hammer them flush with roof.

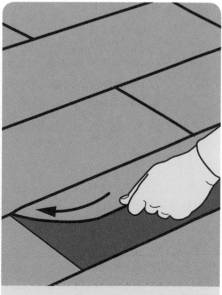

4. Place the new shingle.

60   Replacing a damaged wood or slate shingle

The process with either of these materials is almost exactly the same as with asphalt shingles (see entry 59). With a wood shingle your main concern is the fit. Wood shingles are not as regular as asphalt shingles, so you may have to experiment a bit with getting exactly the right size of shingle. Remember that with wood shingles, you need to leave just a touch of space between the shingles to allow for the expanding and contracting that all wood does with changes in temperature and humidity. You don't want too snug a fit.

The special issue with slate is the color. Slate, obviously, is a natural stone, and there are many variations in hue. For this reason, you'll want to remove the slate shingle, install a garbage bag or other form of insulation in the space where the shingle was, and take that shingle down to the store to replace it with one of similar hue. Then, when you've matched it properly and fitted it into the space, you'll want to mark two spots for nails, take the slate down, and drill two nail holes (some slate shingles have predrilled holes). During installation of the new tile, make sure to place a piece of tar paper or roofing felt to cover the spots where the nail heads are, which will protect the shingles above the new one you have installed.

61   Replacing a damaged roof tile

This is an exponentially more difficult job than dealing with other forms of roofing, and you should consider hiring a professional. The issue is that in many roofs not all the tiles are nailed down, and what that means is you risk a small avalanche if you begin messing with the delicate balance of the roof. There are also many other little bits and pieces involved in the installation of roof tiles.

But if you must, here is a general outline of how you'd replace a broken tile. (Please be aware that there are various kinds of tiles, which work in various ways, so this is just a general outline, and you'll need to do a bit more research before attempting it.) Using a bricklayer's trowel, you will need to lift up the unharmed tiles above the damaged one and wedge them up, using small pieces of wood. If the tile isn't nailed, you might be able to jiggle it out by hand. If it is nailed, you may need a tool called a slate ripper, which is designed to go up under the tiles and rip out the nails. This can be damaging to the roof, and you might stop here and consider hiring a professional. You may also, in some circumstances, actually have to remove the tiles from the row above and below the tile you are repairing. As we said, this is quite an operation.

62   What's on a flat roof?

Like pitched roofs, flat roofs begin with a wood framing system over which is laid a plywood base. In a flat roof, this base is covered with asphalt-saturated paper or roofing felt for insulation, on top of which you'll find an asphalt-based flat roofing material, or a rubber material and perhaps some gravel. These substances usually come in sheets that are rolled onto the roof and more often than not attached by heating them until they are tacky and then sticking them to the roof, or by using an asphalt-based adhesive. As with roofing shingles, the advantage of the conventional, black, tar-based flat roofing is that it is cheap and easy to install and work with. The downside is that the material will attract a lot of heat to your home. The rubber material is a bit more expensive but tends to be a kind of silvery color that reflects sunlight away from the home.

To cover an entire roof will require using multiple sheets of roofing material. The sheets are laid down so that they overlap one another generously (typically it's a 4-inch overlap), and the places where the sheets overlap are sealed with the same asphalt-based adhesives that attach the roofing to the felt paper. The place where you'll have problems with a flat roof is in the seams, where the pieces of roofing material meet one another and where the roof meets the sides of the house. For more on this, see entry 63.

63   What is flashing?

In a roof context, the word *flashing* has nothing to do with creepy guys in raincoats. Flashing is used to seal up the areas where the roofing material meets the sides of the building: chimneys, skylights, or anywhere there's a seam between the roof and the house. You will find it on pitched roofs around chimneys, but it is used more extensively on flat roofs. Typically flashing is made out of some form of metal, from lead to steel and aluminum. The metal is laid down over the roofing material and then bent up the side of the roof over the transition between the roof and whatever the roof is meeting, say, a chimney. Then liberal amounts of roofing cement are applied to attach the flashing. Roofing cement is usually a tar- or plastic-based liquid that is used as a fixative and sealant on roofs. It comes in a can ready to use, and you apply it with a trowel. After the roofing material is laid down, the flashing is installed at every seam. The roofing material is laid out 3 inches above the seam. Then the flashing is applied 6 inches on the wall and 6 inches onto the roofing, and then another layer of roofing is applied. Take a look at your roof. You'll see the flashing all around the margins.

Flashing

The flashing extends under the adjacent shingles as far as the dotted line.

TRICK OF THE TRADE: *Flashing is perhaps the most important feature for maintaining your home. Without flashing, you are guaranteed water damage every time it rains. With flashing, there's less chance of it, but over time flashing loosens, weakens, and goes bad. As we said earlier, check your roof at least once a year.*

64 How do I fix a bubble in a flat roof?

Make sure you are doing this on a day when there is no precipitation predicted for at least twenty-four hours. The process here is like patching a pair of jeans. You cut a square around the bubble and lay a patch over the section you've cut away. Go to the hardware store and buy a roll of similar roof material and roofing cement; you'll also need a utility knife, a trowel, roofing nails, and a hammer. Use the utility knife to cut a nice X in the bubble (fig. 1). Then expel the water or air and dry the inside of the bubble as best you can. Nail the

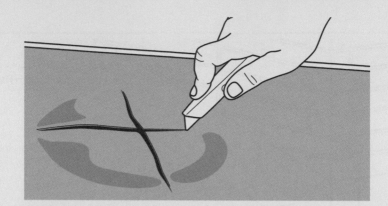

1. Cut an X in the bubble.

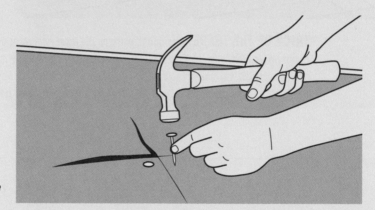

2. Nail down the loose flaps.

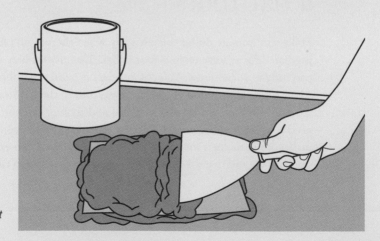

3. Apply cement liberally.

loose pieces of the X to the roof (fig. 2). Cut a section of roofing material that covers the space and extends at least 8 inches past the perimeter of the X on all sides. Put roofing cement over the X and lay the roofing material down and then cover the margins of the roofing material with another layer of cement (fig. 3). Use your trowel and lay the cement on thick. You don't want to see the perimeter of the roofing material when you are done. The following day, go up and make sure it looks good. If you think you missed an area, put on more cement. It isn't expensive.

65　How to fix a small puddle in your roof

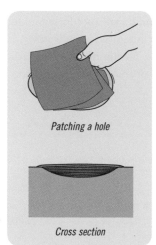

Patching a hole

Cross section

Sometimes you'll encounter an indentation, which is the reverse of a bubble and usually fills with water to form a puddle. Like bubbles, puddles can be the first step to a leak, as the standing water leaches into the roof. Standing water is caused by two things: either the roof itself is pitched improperly, allowing standing water to form, or you have certain spots in the roof that are sagging. Fixing the pitch of the entire roof is not a job for the typical homeowner. If you become convinced this is your problem, you are going to have to find a contractor to take some readings, pull your roof off and put a new roof on.

However, if you want a quick fix, you can actually dry the puddle out as best you can. Place patches of roofing material over the place where the puddle was, building them up with roofing cement until you have brought the small indentation up to the roof level or even a touch higher than the roof around it. That should take good care of that pesky puddle.

66   Flat Roofs: THE DARK SIDE

It doesn't take much for a flat roof to go bad, and when it does, it will usually bubble up. This tends to happen because of wear and tear from the weather. Variations in temperature can do the job—extremes of heat and cold, ice or snow on the roof, heavy rains, you name it.

A seam in the flashing may loosen or crack, and it only takes a pinhole for air or water to get underneath the roof. Once that happens, either you have a leak, or you are on the road to one. One way you can tell you have a problem with a seam is that bubbles will form in the roofing material. If you see those, you may not have a leak yet, but you are going to. The leak could occur away from the damage and bubbles, but most likely you'll see a leak within 4 to 8 feet of the bubbles.

This would also be a good time to check the contract you had with your roofer. Most flat roofs come guaranteed for at least ten years. If you have a good contract with a solid roofing company, it may be their responsibility to come over and fix the roof for you. On the other hand, you may have purchased or inherited a home and have no idea what the story with the roof is. So you may be left with the choice of either fixing the roof yourself or making an expensive phone call to a roofing contractor.

67 When you have a leak but don't see any bubbles

Okay, you've probably got one of two problems. Someone—maybe the telephone or cable guy, or you putting up your Christmas lights—walked on your roof with a pebble in the sole of his shoe or a nail sticking out, or dropped something, and you have a puncture somewhere. This can easily happen on the best of roofs. Walk the roof. You might be able to spot the hole. If you don't have a visible puncture, you likely have a problem with the seam where the flashing meets the structure of your house. Again, take a close look; you might just be able to spot the problematic seam.

TRICK OF THE TRADE: *For the technically inclined, it's worth noting that roofing contractors these days have thermal imaging machines that can scan your roof and take a heat picture of it. The variations in heat can tell the device exactly where the punctures have occurred. If you hire a pro to do the job for you, make sure to hire one who has thermal imaging technology in his arsenal.*

68 Fixing a roof puncture or a flashing issue

Taking care of a puncture is just like patching a roof bubble, and you don't even have to cut into your roof. Wait for a day when there is no precipitation. Cut a piece of roofing material that covers the problem with an 8-inch margin. Lay the new piece over the puncture and cover it liberally in cement.

If you can see a problem with a flashing seam, you don't even need to make a patch. Just cover the area in cement, and while you're at it, if your roof isn't too big, you could just tar the entire perimeter, and then you don't even have to sweat trying to find the fault in the seam. That might be a lot easier than going through the trouble of finding the exact problem.

69 Locating a roof problem that persists

If you've tried some fixes but still have a problem with your roof, keep in mind that finding a trouble spot on your own is going to be an involved process. At this stage many people will call a roofer, and there's no harm in that.

If you do want to keep trying to find the problem yourself, you are going to need a working hose on your roof, a hole in the ceiling, and two people. Basically, what you're going to do is inundate your roof with water and then look up through a hole in the ceiling to see where the water is coming in. If you have a crawl space in your roof, you can get in there and have a look. Before you knock a hole into the ceiling, ask yourself if there is any light, fan, or appliance installed that you can pull out easily. If not, you are going to have to go in yourself.

70 How to get into your ceiling

We realize it's a big deal to ask you to damage your own ceiling, but consider the following: if you don't put a hole in the ceiling, you aren't going to find the leak. Also, once you have water damage you're going to have to cut the damaged portion out and replace it anyway in order to avoid mold growth. So go to the spot where you have water damage and open up the ceiling. Most houses will have Sheetrock ceilings. If the ceiling is plaster, and this will be the case in older homes, you just take a hammer and bust through. Make a hole that is around 18 inches square. Get a friend up by the hole with a flashlight—meanwhile, you are on the roof. Isolate the distinct areas of the roof that you think might be problematic, and inundate them with water, one at a time. After each dousing with water, check with your friend to see if there's anything dripping through.

71   Maintaining a roof

There really is no maintenance for pitched roofs. Basically, they have a life span, typically decades, and when they wear out you replace them. For how to deal with various forms of shingles, see entries 59 and 60, and for gutters, see entries 72 to 79. However, there are some things you can do to maintain flat roofs. You should inspect them twice a year and patch any bubbles you see. You should also apply a coating to the roof once every five years. There are different coatings for asphalt or rubber roofs, which are the most common flat-roof surfaces. For asphalt roofs the idea is to install an asphalt-based coating, which resaturates the asphalt roofing product to keep it from drying out. With the rubber roof, the coating is aluminum, which helps to protect your house from the sun and prevents the rubber roof from degrading under the ultraviolet rays of the sun.

RAIN GUTTERS

72   What's so important about rain gutters?

We'll tell you: rain gutters are key. They save your house from untold damage and wear and tear. They are also quite fragile and need a lot of maintenance. Rain gutters are known as eaves, troughs, or simply gutters. They are channels located at the foot of the roof to collect rainwater and divert it away from the house and into some kind of drainage system. The gutter may be attached to the house or to the underside of the roof, or it may be built into the house or the roof. Gutters are made from various materials, including concrete, metals, plastics, and even wood. Gutters can be installed in parts, with seams in between the pieces, or they can be formed to fit the house exactly, in a single, seamless piece. The gutters will lead to downspouts, which are pipes that run down the side of your house and carry the water to a drain, or out onto your lawn. Gutters are an immensely important part of the weather protection of your house and should be scrupulously maintained and watched carefully for damage. Gutters are not only very important but also rather high maintenance, and many things can go wrong with them.

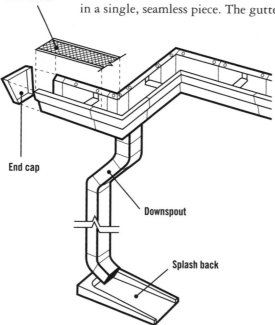

Leaf screen

End cap

Downspout

Splash back

73 Rain Gutters:
THE DARK SIDE

The most common gutter issue is water damming up because of leaves and other bits of debris that fall into the gutter over time. If your roof isn't properly ventilated (see entry 54) and you live in a place that gets cold, you may find yourself with an ice dam in the gutter. This doesn't sound that bad, right? I mean, the ice will melt eventually and drain away. Except that isn't always what happens. The problem is that ice and snow don't melt at the same rate all over your house. If you have a nice ice dam and the snow above it melts before the ice does, the water from that melted snow will run down the roof and collect at the ice dam, where it will begin to seep into the insulation of your house. Not good.

Then there are creatures, often birds, that will decide to take up residence in your gutter, filling it with whatever detritus or nesting material they decide to store there. You may also be bothered by noise from a downspout, the part of the gutter that allows the water to flow down to the ground. Finally, your gutters may pull away from the wall. That's a lot of stuff, but there are simple fixes for most of these problems.

74 How and when should I clean my gutters?

Obviously, you should clean your gutters. This ought to be done twice a year, in spring and in autumn. The right ladder for this job, if you have one high enough, is a good A-frame, because a leaning ladder might do some damage to certain kinds of gutters. Wear safety gloves, as there may be all sorts of sharp bits and pieces in the gutters. Working your way around the gutter, use a trowel or other tool to scoop out the gutter, and carry a solid garbage bag to deposit what you find. Then bring a garden hose up and inundate the gutters with water. At the bottom of the gutter system, around the foundation of your house, you'll find a few drainpipes, which drain the gutter water out into your garden and away from your house. These also need to be cleaned out now and then, and the best tool for this is a plumber's auger, or snake, which is a long, tightly wound metal cable with a crank at the end. Essentially, you crank it up into the drain and then pull it out, pulling whatever was up there with it. For more on augers, see chapter 4.

TRICK OF THE TRADE: *Cleaning gutters is a surprisingly messy job, so wear old clothes and be prepared for some ugly streaky dirt stains on your exterior walls until the next rain.*

75 Keeping your gutters clean without doing it yourself

You can pay a company to clean them for you. That really isn't a bad idea, especially since gutter cleaning involves ladders, and we've already been through how dangerous they can be. Consider entering into a cleaning and maintenance contract with the company that installed your gutters, which can be a big help if the gutters begin to break over time.

The other thing to do is have a contractor install a gutter cover. These come in a variety of styles, but essentially it's a grated lid that goes over the gutters, allowing water to flow easily into the gutter but preventing leaves, animals, branches, and other bits and pieces from falling in there as well. Gutter covers are a great thing—a must, really, if you live on a property that is full of trees—but they are not a cure-all. Even a properly covered gutter will still need to be cleaned every year. The cleaning, however, should be much easier than if you had not installed the covers at all.

76 Preventing ice dams in your gutter

We've said it before, but it bears repeating: please make sure your roof is properly ventilated and insulated. This is the best thing you can do to prevent ice dams. But even a perfect roof may form ice dams, especially in places that get really cold during the winter and where debris falls into the gutters. Another layer of defense against this problem is something called heating tape. Heating tape is an insulated wire that runs along your gutters, and when plugged in, it will heat up and prevent too much ice and snow from forming.

Heating tape is made by various manufacturers, but generally it is designed to turn on when the temperature falls below a certain point. The tape is installed in loops that run the entire length of your gutter and up along the overhang of your roof. Installation instructions are different for each brand, so follow them, but essentially you'll be stapling the tape along the roof and running the cord down to an electrical outlet. Heating tape usually works best when it is replaced every season.

77 Fixing a noisy downspout

As you recall, the downspout is the pipe that runs away from the gutter and down the side of your house and is designed to carry the water from the gutters to a drain or out onto your lawn. Typically, the bottom of the downspout will be L-shaped, with the small part of the L leading down to where the water is supposed to go. Obviously, as the water falls it hits the curve of the L, and that's where things can get noisy. How noisy? Well, we've heard downspout noise described as sounding like small explosions, artillery fire, the work of a Brazilian drum corps, or hurricane winds. Fortunately there is a simple and easy fix for this: installing noise-baffling material in the crook of the L. It usually comes in the form of a strip of matted material with an adhesive on one side. You just place it in the elbow of the downspout, and it should instantly solve the problem.

78 Repairing a gutter that has pulled away from the wall

You'll probably notice that your gutter is coming loose when you see water running behind it along the wall of your house. Bad sign. There are many reasons that gutters come loose, but typically it has to do with changes in temperature. As the gutter expands and contracts—and unfortunately all varieties of gutters in all materials will do this—the nails that hold the gutter to the roof begin to work their way out. This can be exacerbated by the weight of water and ice, if you have dams in the gutter caused by leaves or ice.

Follow the falling water to where the problem is. Now take a look at your particular gutter. There are variations, but most often the gutter is attached to your house by a series of metal strips that have been nailed or screwed into the wall. If you have a loose nail or screw, try injecting some roofing cement or other outdoor-grade liquid adhesive into the hole, and hammer the nail back in. It is a simple and easy way to take care of a nagging problem and avoid an expensive repair.

79 Repairing a gutter that is coming apart at the seams

If you are seeing water running down the side of the house, the other thing that could be happening—and again the villain is expansion and contraction caused by changes in temperature—is that sections of the gutter are coming loose from one another. Many gutters these days are seamless, and you won't have this problem with a system of that type. But if you do have a gutter that was put together in sections (and there's nothing wrong with this kind of system), you should follow the water to the place where the gutter is breaking down. If you see two sections of the gutter pulling away from each other, you can reattach them. Sorry for being vague, but each system is different. Essentially, however, the fix is a simple one. Take some caulking, tar, or other roofing cement and slather it 2 or 3 inches on either side of the loose seam. That ought to take care of the problem.

FAÇADES

80 What's on the outside of a house?

Almost all houses are built on wood frames. Over the frame goes plywood and sheets of insulation, and then you have the façade. The most common façades on American homes, in no particular order, are brick, stucco, aluminum siding, and wood shingle. The sturdiest and best insulating façade is brick, which is something to think about if you are looking to buy a house. In many cases a brick house should be worth a little more than the houses around it in the same neighborhood. If you already are in a brick house, be happy but realize there is some maintenance you'll have to do. Stucco is not only popular but also versatile and easy to fix. It is also prone to breaking down. The big attraction of aluminum siding is that it's cheap; it looks nice, and it can be installed on top of an existing façade if that façade is beginning to go bad. Wood shingles are also quite reasonable, and they age gracefully. Stone façades are a great look too.

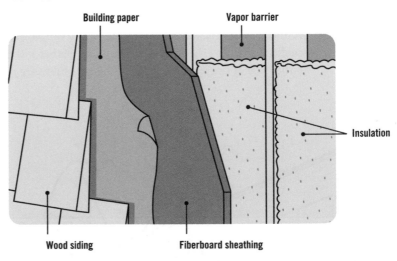

Building paper · Vapor barrier · Insulation · Wood siding · Fiberboard sheathing

81 How a brick façade works

There are many different kinds of bricks, but they are mostly rectangles made of clay or cement and heated at high temperatures. Bricks come in a variety of colors and sizes, but the most familiar bricks in the United States are of that wonderful red-brown hue. A brick façade is typically made of a single layer of bricks. The bricks are laid, one atop the other, in a pattern such that no seam between two bricks is over another seam, and they are attached to one another and to the main body of the house with mortar. Mortar is a binding agent made out of sand, cement, and water. There are different recipes for mortar, which comes in different shades of gray and black. There are two basic things you can do to maintain your brick home. Keep the bricks clean, which is optional and mostly aesthetic, and tend the mortar, which is not optional.

TRICK OF THE TRADE: *The craft of laying mortar between bricks is known in the business as pointing, and repairing or refurbishing that mortar is known as repointing.*

82 Repointing a brick façade

This is not something you are going to do yourself. Repointing is a real craft. The old mortar needs to be removed, usually with some kind of power tool. Then the new mortar has to be mixed correctly, which is an art in itself. Then the new mortar has to be applied to the bricks, and it takes real skill to do that. But there are things a homeowner needs to know about repointing in order to hire the right professional and get the best job out of him.

The first thing you need to know is that repointing isn't cheap. A good pointing job should last decades, but you have to pay for a job like that. Ask around, and find a contractor who specializes in exteriors and brick work and has good recommendations. Then you should demand that at least three-quarters of the depth of the old mortar be removed before repointing. If you don't remove the old mortar and just lay new mortar over it, you'll see cracking within a few years. You should also ask for a warranty on the job of three years. That way, you know you are getting someone who stands by his work.

TRICK OF THE TRADE: *In looking for a recommendation about repointing, ask a client who used the contractor at least five years earlier. The most accurate recommendation comes from someone whose façade has withstood the test of half a decade.*

83   Cleaning a brick façade

You can clean a brick house and make it look like new, and the process is not that expensive. In fact, if you have your house repointed, you should have it cleaned at the same time. You can even use cleaning as a bargaining chip in a price negotiation with your repointing pro. If you want to, you can also try this yourself. Rent a commercial power washer from the hardware store. Mix brick cleaner with water according to the instructions on the package, plug in the washer, and fire away. The only problem here might be if you need to get up to the top of a two- or three-story house. Make sure the power washer has a nice extension. Remember, if you are tempted to get onto a ladder, do not hold the washer too close to the house, or you may get blown back.

If you are thinking about painting your brick façade . . . stop. Once you paint brick, it is almost impossible to get the paint off 100 percent. It will never look like new brick again. If your façade is already painted brick, then you have the worst of both worlds. You'll need to repaint every decade, and you'll have the same repointing issues you'd have regardless, because the mortar will break down even if it is painted.

84 Brick Façades:
THE DARK SIDE

The weak link in a brick façade is the mortar. Over time, rain and wind will simply wear it away. You can see this on the outside of a house by looking for places where the mortar has receded and the bricks are standing there with spaces between them. Alternatively, you will discover that the mortar has worn away when you see water inside your house. Mortar doesn't wear away all at once. It's a process. Some parts of the house might show more wear than others, because of their exposure to the elements. Some batches of mortar may have been mixed more solidly or carefully than others, even on the same house. So the bottom line is that you just have to be alert.

Some wear in the mortar, otherwise known as the pointing, is just fine. But if you can stick a dime inside the crack left by the receding mortar, then you should think about making repairs. If you have this problem in one small spot, you can let it go for a time. But if you see it all around the house, you need to fix, or repoint, the façade.

85 Choosing the right color mortar

Mortar comes in a dizzying array of colors. You can find mortar tinted in hues ranging from white to black, with stops at yellow, brown, and gray along the way. This is no small matter, because in most brick façades the mortar joints—that is, the spaces between the bricks—make up at least 15 percent, and often more like 20 percent, of the total area of the façade. When choosing a color of mortar for a stone or brick house, think a little about how it will age and weather. If you live in a city, remember that air pollution is also a big factor in how a façade ages and that in your part of the world, lighter-colored mortar is going to darken over time. Also be aware that mortar color will change somewhat when the mortar is actually mixed, since no mortar mix is exactly alike and the pigment might come out looking slightly different, depending on the actual ingredients used.

86 How a stone façade works

A stone façade works on the same principle as a brick façade—it's held together with mortar—except in place of bricks you have stones. Because the façade is made of different stones, there's no uniformity in the design of the façade. The mortar joints—the spaces between the stones—will be wider in some places, to accommodate irregularities in the stones, and then narrow in other places. You have the same issues with pointing a stone façade as you do with a brick one. But there is another dilemma with stone: it sometimes will bleed mineral deposits. These will form whitish streaks on your home that are very hard to get off. If you like the weathered look, you can leave them on. Some people do try to clean these streaks off, but to no avail. The good news about stone façades is that they hide

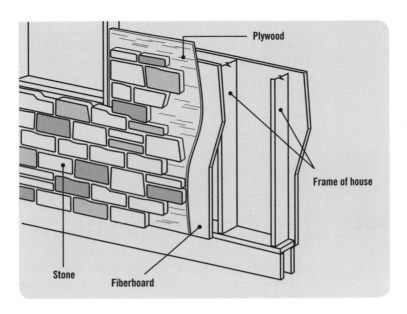

Plywood

Frame of house

Stone

Fiberboard

dirt very well, and depending on the kind of stone, dirt will wash off well in the rain.

87   What is stucco, and how does it work?

Stucco is made of a mortarlike substance that is troweled onto a metal mesh base. It is usually applied to a ¾-inch thickness, and in the hands of a skilled craftsman can be made to look smooth, rough, textured, rippled, you name it. Plus it can be tinted to any color in the rainbow. The other great thing about stucco is that it is relatively cheap, when compared with brick. In fact, we've seen a few cases where people have actually applied stucco directly over brick façades that were going bad, to achieve a fine look at much less expense than repointing. Stucco can last for decades, and it does a great job of insulating a house. Also, it's fireproof. Okay, that's the good news. The bad news is that stucco can be prone to cracking, chipping, flaking, and falling off. All it takes is for a small break to appear in the façade and then all of it can go bad really fast. There really isn't much you can do to maintain a stucco façade; you just have to wait for it to go bad and then fix it.

88 Maintaining a stucco façade

You can achieve a long life for your stucco façade with a minimum of maintenance. At least two or three times a year, hose down your façade. If you feel you must, you can even try a light pressure wash or chemical treatment, but seek advice from an expert before using any chemical wash. Once a year you will also need to repatch and repaint. If you see tiny cracks, you can simply paint those in. If the crack is a bit wider—say, the width of a dime—you will need to use a sealant. There are also preprepared stucco patch products out there that can do the job. The big issue with patch jobs is that they will look slightly different from the rest of the wall. So they must be left to cure properly. Keep the patched area dry and shaded for at least two days. If you have any cracks that are wider than, say, ⅛ inch, or severe flaking, you'll need to undertake a major fix.

89   Fixing a stucco façade

Here's the deal with stucco fixes: no matter how skilled you are, the area where the new stucco is applied will never, ever match the rest of the house. If you have a small area of flaking or chipping or cracking, you can fix it yourself. If you have problems on 40 percent of your home, hire a pro. To fix a small area, you first need to remove the existing stucco. You take a large Spackle knife and gently chip away at the area that is bad. If you need to, you should replace the steel mesh onto which the stucco is applied (fig. 1). Please be gentle, because you can easily take out a big section. Mixing and tinting actual stucco is not a job for an amateur, but if you have a small area to deal with, you can buy some cement from the hardware store, mix it at home, apply it with a trowel (fig. 2), and paint it to resemble the rest of the house with an oil-based exterior paint (fig. 3).

To fix a large area, hire someone who works with stucco. Make sure he is putting on at least a ¾-inch thickness of stucco and that he can work with the stucco so that the new area has the same texture as the old one. You should also get your contractor to promise in writing to return and make fixes where necessary.

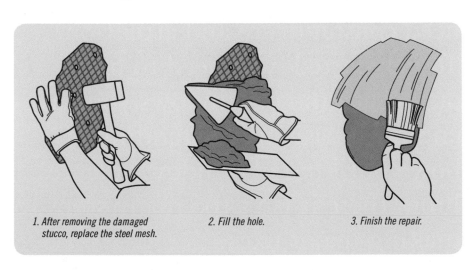

1. After removing the damaged stucco, replace the steel mesh.

2. Fill the hole.

3. Finish the repair.

Windows

A solid, see-through window that can be opened and shut is an enormous convenience, allowing you access to the world while providing almost perfect protection from it. But like most modern conveniences, windows can be a source of worry and bother. They break, they wear down, and they need constant care and attention. To get started, you need to figure out what kind of windows you have and get a basic understanding of how your kind of window operates. From there it isn't too many steps to making major fixes.

90   How to speak window

Windows have their own involved terminology, which you have to understand before we can go any further. The frame of the window is the window's perimeter, and it holds the window together. The sash is the smaller piece that holds the glass inside it and sits inside the window frame itself. Most windows have two sashes. Some windows have one sash, and a very few windows may have more than two sashes. The pane is the piece of glass inside the sash. Most sashes today are double-paned, meaning the frame of the sash supports two panes that are attached to each other for greater insulation. Until recently the most common window in the United States was a wood-framed, single-paned, double-hung window that operated on a simple weighted system. That means the windows had two sashes in them, one above the other, operating on a simple weighted pulley, and each sash contained a single layer of glass.

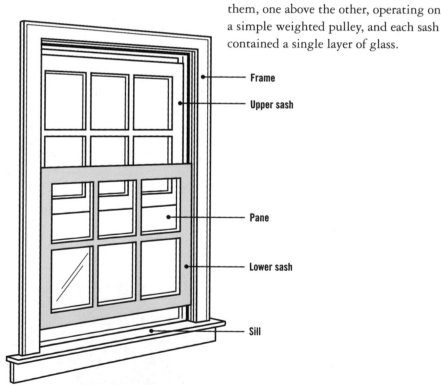

Frame

Upper sash

Pane

Lower sash

Sill

91 Telling one kind of window from another

Double-hung windows have two sashes, one above the other. The sashes are installed so that they work on two sets of parallel tracks, one set of tracks in front of the other. Each sash moves up and down on its track so that when one sash is all the way up and the other all the way down, the top of the lower sash and the bottom of the upper sash meet and lock and seal, and the window is fully closed. Double-hung windows are typically the least expensive variety of window, even when they are beautiful and well made. If your windows aren't double-hung, they are most likely casement windows. A casement window usually has a single sash that opens outward, like the cover of a book, with a crank controlling the pane. You will occasionally run into variants of the casement window where the pane tilts forward or pivots on a central axis, and some casement windows will have multiple panes.

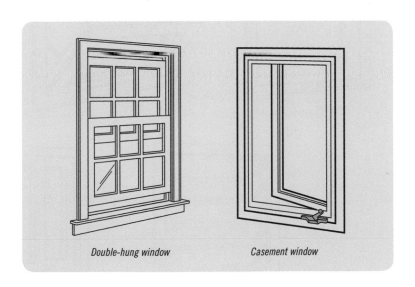

Double-hung window　　　　*Casement window*

92 What other kinds of windows are there?

Some less typical window types include:

Awning windows: a variant of casement windows with a sash that is hinged at the top and swings outward.

Hopper windows: are hinged at the bottom and swing inward.

Jalousie windows: very useful in hot, rainy places. They have multiple rows of narrow, horizontal glass panes that open and close like a Venetian blind on a crank.

Sliding windows: like double-hung windows, except the two panes slide horizontally across each other, rather than up and down.

Awning window

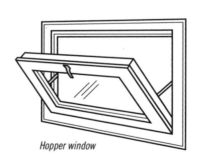

Hopper window

Jalousie window

Sliding window

93 What are windows made of?

The standard-issue window today is made of hollow aluminum. It's durable. It's easy to insulate. It looks good and is without doubt one of the least expensive material out there. Even cheaper than aluminum is vinyl, which does the job beautifully as well but may not be the look every homeowner wants. Homeowners who want a more upscale or traditional look, or have an older house that calls for a traditional look or a landmarked house that requires it, will use wooden windows. Wooden windows are more expensive, heavier, harder to maintain, and typically custom made, but they look great, and some homeowners just have to have them. The decision is up to you, but be honest with yourself. Even if you can afford them and can pay other people to keep them in working order, are you really interested in having to think about your wooden windows each year? If not, go with aluminum.

94 Can I change the colors of my aluminum windows?

Generally speaking, aluminum windows come in three not-that-exciting standard colors: black, brown, and white. If you want to change the color, you can try painting the windows, but beware: if you use a standard paint, it will peel and flake off. There is a simple fix, however, and it's called electrostatic painting. It's a service offered by a few companies; they will come to your house and spray on a special kind of paint that will adhere to the windows much better than any hand-applied paint. This method also produces an even, smooth finish that almost looks as if it came from the factory.

The process is relatively affordable, and you can give your house an entirely new look. If you are ordering new windows, you can have a custom color put on for an additional charge.

95 Are casement or double-hung windows better?

Perhaps this will get your attention: casement windows, on average, cost twice as much as double-hung. If you're redoing a house, you'll likely need around twenty windows, and that can add up fast. Because of the way they operate, casement windows do not work with window-mounted air-conditioning units. The advantage of casement windows, however, is that they tend to seal better when closed, they don't move around much when open, and when you look out of them you are looking through a single, unbroken pane of glass. At the same time, if you like the way it looks, you can order casement windows broken into panes.

Meanwhile, double-hung windows are great for most houses—they work well and look lovely, and the price is right. There are also real advantages to double-hung windows. They open up and down, so they don't take up any space when open.

TRICK OF THE TRADE: *Please remember that you cannot crack open a casement window. When you open it, you are opening it on three sides of the sash. If you live in a cold place and like to have your windows open just a smidge to let in air but keep the cold out, consider double-hung windows.*

96   Some window-purchasing tips

When ordering your windows, think about ordering screens and window safety guards at the same time. (See entry 408 for how to install window guards.) They don't come with the window, but they'll work better if they're made by the same company as the windows themselves. Also, take into account the window treatment—meaning the blinds, shades, curtains, and the like—that you are intending to use, and make sure the kind of window you order is compatible with the window treatment you want. For example, if you want to use blinds inside your house, don't order a casement window that opens inward—that just won't work. If you have exterior shutters, you'll have the same problem with a window that opens outward.

97   How to fix a window that's sticking

This issue is likely to come up in a house with wooden windows that you are just moving into or in a room that hasn't been used for a long time. Sometimes, windows just stick. The usual culprit here is old paint that has sealed the sash to the frame or built up to the point where the sash sticks. If this happens, do not under any circumstances try to force it open either by applying lots of pressure or by banging the window around. Why? There's glass in them there panes, and you don't want to break it, because that would mean replacing the entire window.

Before going any further, make sure the window is unlocked. If it isn't locked, you have a real problem. Take a hammer and a small

windows

block of wood. Hold the wood up to the window and lightly tap around the window sash and frame, using the wood to protect the window from hammer damage. That might loosen the sash. You can also take a utility or Spackle knife and score the perimeter of the window where the sash meets the frame. If that doesn't work, check to see if there is paint between the sash and the frame. If there is, you can try running a utility knife or a pizza cutter between the sash and the frame to break the seal. If you have a metal-frame double-hung window that's sticking, try removing the sashes from the frame (see entry 100) and adding some lubricant (see entry 110) to the channels. If you have a wooden window, you may need to remove the stop and take the sash out (see entry 115) and lubricate. If all of that fails, you may need professional help.

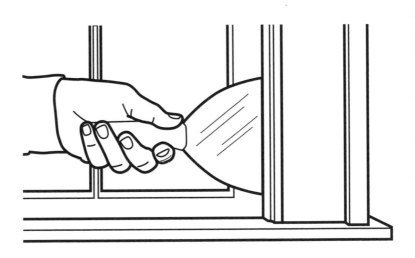

98 Double-Hung Windows:
THE DARK SIDE

When double-hung windows go bad, the spiral balance tube breaks, and the window will no longer stay up on its own. That's when you'll find yourself using all those other home repair books (the ones you no longer read because you have this one) to wedge under the window to keep it up. The spiral rod that goes up into the tube is held by a compression system. But when the compression system loosens, the rod falls out. There's no one reason that happens; mostly it is an issue of wear and tear. The spiral balance tube is kind of the Achilles' heel of the modern window. It's cheap, compact, and effective, but it breaks down easily. Fortunately, it is also easy to fix (see entry 100).

One thing that can and often does happen to windows is that panes occasionally break (say, if a baseball should happen to come through one). Since this is a double-paned system that will typically have gas or a vacuum between the two panes, you must call the manufacturer and order an entirely new sash.

Sometimes the seal around the sash will break down over time with changes in heat and cold. As a result, the double panes of glass will develop condensation between them, which will cause fogging that you can't get rid of. There is no fix for this other than ordering a new pane.

99 How double-hung windows stay in place

You'll notice that when you raise the sash on a double-hung window it will stay exactly where you've raised it to. Back in the day, sashes were attached to weights that hung on chains behind the frame of the window to either side of the sash. As the sash went up, the weight went down. The balance between the weight and the sash kept the window in place. It was a fine system for working a window—reliable, durable, and functional. The only problem with it was that the system made it impossible to properly insulate the window, because it meant the window frame was essentially a box that let cold and air in from the outside. Today's double-hung windows are controlled by what are called spiral balance tubes. The sash is attached to a spiraled metal coil, which sits on one side of the sash in the frame. As the window sash goes up, the coil goes up into a kind of tube, and there is a mechanism inside the tube that holds the coil in place. So when the sash goes up, it too stays in place.

100 Fixing a broken spiral balance

The first step is to order new spiral balance tubes. Each window manufacturer will make its own, so you need to know who made your window. If you can't figure that out, you can buy universal balance tubes through any window company and see if you can make them work. You have to measure the length and diameter of the balance tube in your window and buy one that is the same size. Since the cost of a universal balance tube is around fifteen dollars, it might be worth giving it a shot. Typically there will be two spiral balance

tubes in the window, one tube on each side of the sashes. Each tube will be attached to the window frame by a screw that you will find atop the frame. To replace the spiral balance tubes, you'll need to remove the bottom sash. Raise the sash an inch. At the upper side of the sash, you'll find two little levers, which you pull inward with your fingers while tilting the sash inside the house. Now you can angle the sash and take it out of the window frame. Then you can unscrew the spiral balance tubes, remove them, and screw the new ones right back in.

101 Fixing a wooden double-hung window

If you have a wooden double-hung window, chances are it will not have a spiral tubing system inside it. The reason is that wooden windows are much heavier than their vinyl and aluminum cousins and need a heavier system to operate properly. By and large, each manufacturer will have a slightly different system for operating its window. In general, the wooden double-hung window will be operated by nylon cords that are attached to something called a spring-tension mechanism box. The cord is held tense by the weight that is on it and the mechanism. As the window goes up, the cord goes up and is held in place by the tension, and the window stays put. The issue here is that you need a fine calibration for the weight of each individual window sash, and that is why they are all slightly different. In a wood window, really, the best thing to do if you have a broken weight system is to have the manufacturer come out and fix it. The warranties on these windows are typically twenty years.

102   How a casement window works

As we said before, there are various kinds of casement windows, but let's just take the simplest case, a normal casement window of one large sash that operates on a rotary arm system with a crank, which you'll find at the bottom of the window. The locking system for the casement window is typically on the side of the window. It holds the window in place wherever you leave it. No swinging back and forth. Casement windows are more expensive than double-hung not only because the hardware is more expensive to make but also because the casement unit, since it sticks out from your house, has to be heavier and have more durable hardware. In a casement window, the mechanism within the crank is connected to two rods that go from the window frame to the sash. When you turn the crank, one of the rods will push the window out and the other one will anchor the window so that it doesn't flap around in the wind.

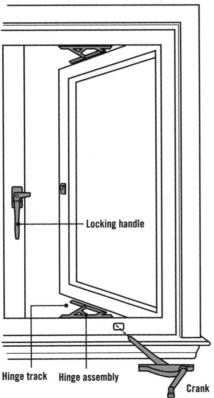

Locking handle

Hinge track   Hinge assembly

Crank

103 Casement Windows:
THE DARK SIDE

What tends to break on a casement window is the rotary mechanism. When you try to open the window, nothing will happen—it will just spin. When that happens, the crank is no longer attached to the rods that open and close the window, and that is why the crank will spin around uselessly. To fix the rotary crank, see entry 105.

The other thing that can happen with casement windows is that the windowpane itself can go wrong. The seal will break, and you'll see this cloudy fog between the two panes of glass. In this case, you would do exactly what you would do with a double-hung window in the same situation: order a replacement sash from the manufacturer.

104 How casement rotary systems work

The rotary mechanism is actually installed on the frame of the window. A small housing sits over it, and the mechanism itself is attached to the window by four screws. The two rods that run between the mechanism and the window are attached to the window sash by simple snap clips. If the rotary mechanism is broken, you'll have to order a new one from your window's manufacturer. A generic brand of mechanism may be available, but the problem is that the screws that line the mechanism into the frame may be in different locations, and that means having to drill new holes, which you don't want to do. Chances are the manufacturer's name and even the model number of the window will be found in the pane of glass down by the lower end of the sash. If you can't find your model and window maker, you are going to have to measure carefully, buy a generic brand, and see if you can make it work. Otherwise you'll need to call in a professional window contractor. Either way, have a new mechanism on hand before you attempt your fix.

105 Disassembling and fixing a rotary mechanism

You may need to take the rotary mechanism out to measure it before you start your fix if you cannot determine who the manufacturer is. As we said above, the mechanism sits in a casing and is screwed into the window frame. The first step is to pull the crank off. With most windows, the crank is meant to come off easily by hand, and you may not even have the crank on the mechanism all the time. Many households leave them off, because they stick out into window treatments such as drapes. The housing for the rotary mechanism will typically be attached by a snap system. You just pry it up by hand. If you are having a problem doing this, you can try a gentle nudge with a flat-head screwdriver. Detach the rods from the mechanism, which should be a self-explanatory process when you look at them. Then unscrew the screws attaching the rotary mechanism to the window and lift the mechanism up. Screw the new mechanism into the window frame, reattach the rods, snap the casing back over it, and test it with the crank.

TRICK OF THE TRADE: *Be sure to reassemble the window and wait for the replacement parts. Never leave a casement window disassembled, because it will flap around in the wind.*

106 Replacing broken rods in a casement window

There are two rods in a casement window. They are attached to the rotary mechanism and the window sash. One rod pushes the window open. The other rod pulls it closed and holds it in place wherever it is. The rods are attached to the rotary mechanism by a simple snap system. Detaching the rods should be a self-explanatory process when you look at them. The rods will be of different sizes, and you'll need to measure them. Once you've measured the rods, reassemble the window. (You do not want to leave a casement window without the rods attaching it to the frame; that is dangerous, because the window will be left to swing back and forth.) Then you can order new rods and replace the old ones.

windows

107 Mind your muntins

What's a muntin, you ask? Certainly not an old sheep. The explanation runs like this: in the old days, when large panes of glass were expensive and hard to make, most windows were composed of smaller glass panels held together in wooden frames. The muntins are the strips of wood (they come in metal too) that divide and sometimes hold the panels of glass together. Today the only reason to use a window with muntins is for the look. There's no practical reason. If you live in a Tudor-style home, you'll likely want muntins. If you live in a contemporary home, you probably won't. Muntins can be built into the window, just as they were in an earlier era, or you can use false muntins that snap over the windowpane and can be removed when you want to clean the window, because (let's face it) it's much easier to clean a single, large pane of glass than to rub your rag into six little squares of glass.

TRICK OF THE TRADE: *More like a warning. Muntins can be fragile. They are known to crack. Also, a wooden window with built-in muntins is going to set you back a pretty penny.*

108 How to apply sunscreen to your house

People are always going on and on and on about how much they love sunlight and how their house is bathed in the stuff. Well, you know what? Just as sunlight is bad for your skin, it is also bad for the things in your home. Sunlight will bleach the color out of carpeting and upholstery. It will fade family photos. It will lighten the color of wood and play havoc with fine paintings, prints, and drawings. One way to prevent this is to keep your blinds, shutters, and curtains closed. If you don't want to live in the dark, however, the other way is to have an ultraviolet-resistant film put on your windows. This is a sheet of see-through material that will block out the worst of the sun's rays. Make sure to read the label on the UV film, as it is called, because it has to be replaced every so often. There are also shades that have UV filters on them.

Maybe you have a bathroom window that you'd rather not have neighbors looking through. Before you go out and spend a lot of money on window treatments or on replacing the windowpane with a frosted-glass model, you can put the UV film on the window—it will simulate the look of a frosted pane of glass and offer you great privacy protection. Remember, however, you can use this film only on a double-paned window, because the cold leaking through a single-paned window will cause the frosted film to peel.

109 How and when should I check up on my windows?

Once a year, usually in autumn, you should walk around your house, inside and then outside, checking each window to make sure it is sound and there are no breaks in the caulking that seals the window into the house. You may find there are upper-story windows that you can't check so easily. If you can't actually get outside to take a look at an upper window, try a careful—and please be careful—lean out the window. Alternatively, if you happen to have any roofers or painters coming to work on the outside of your house, ask them to do a window check for you and give them a nice tip for their trouble. If you don't have any cooperative roofers around, take a good pair of binoculars and have a walk around the house. Another option is that your neighbors could let you into their houses to check your windows from their upper story. See what you can do.

110 Maintaining a window

This is a once-a-year checklist. Push up the window sashes and use your hand to clean out all the debris you find in the channels, both horizontal and vertical, that the window sashes sit in. Take a look around the window. The window frame is attached to the house by screws, and they will come loose. If you need to, tighten them up again, remembering not to overscrew. If you have double-hung windows, give your balance tubes a little silicone spray to keep them moving. Don't use any lubricant other than silicone for this job. Nonsilicone lubricants may have some water in them, and if you live in a cold-weather location, they may actually impede the working of your window if the water freezes. If you feel the need to lubricate the channels in your metal, double-hung window, a dry lubricant such as graphite will do the trick. If you have casement windows, you should try a little lubricant (like WD-40) on your crank mechanisms. On the exterior of the window, you should check for dried caulking around the frame of the window where it is attached to the structure of the house.

WOODEN WINDOWS

Some wooden windows are clad in aluminum on the outside. Those don't need much maintenance. Most people choose to have aluminum on the exterior side, but if you don't want to do that, or if you can't because of landmark issues, you will have a lot of maintenance to do. You'll need to paint the windows every four or five years. Think of it this way: your wood windows are like the hull of a boat. They need to keep you warm and dry, and the only thing protecting them from the elements is that layer of paint. The best time to paint windows is in the spring after the last of the bad weather. May is a great month—unless you are in the Southern Hemisphere (then reverse). Use a high-quality exterior paint and make sure you are buying paint that works in the weather conditions in your region. Tape off the glass with blue painter's tape and then paint the window.

111 Caulking a window

We are talking about caulking the seams where the window frame meets your house. (Do not caulk the window sashes shut.) You may not have to do this every year, but as we said previously, you should at least check your windows every year to see whether the caulking around them is dry. Caulking is a sealant that is used to fill in cracks in the façades of houses, or to fill in seams between different fixtures in houses that don't move, such as between windows and walls. There are many different kinds of caulks, but most of them dry out over time and loosen with the extremes of temperature. Modern caulks are supposed to do a better job than caulks did in the old days, but our experience is that you have to replace caulk around windows now and then. You may find that the entire window is in trouble, or that there are a few dry patches or holes that have appeared in the caulking. The repair is a simple one. Wait for a day when you are certain of having twenty-four hours without precipitation. Use a putty knife to scrape away any of the dried patches of caulk you find, or pull them up with your hands. The new caulk will come in a tube, and you can just squeeze a generous amount right into the area you are working with. Smooth the caulk into that area. If you want, you can then move around the perimeter of the window and add a new layer of caulking, just to be sure. The stuff isn't that expensive. Remove the excess caulking with a damp rag and wash your hands. Let the caulk dry.

windows

112 Cleaning a window

You can save yourself a lot of money by cleaning windows yourself. What's more, you will prolong the life of your windows by keeping them clean. How often you clean your windows depends very much on how clean you want your windows to be and how dirty windows get in the area where you live. But we recommend cleaning the windows at least every three or four months. Have paper towels and glass cleaner or a bucket of ammonia and warm water at the ready.

Casement windows are relatively easy to get at. You can wash the inside no problem, and the outside can be reached by a special latch that allows you to open the window at a 90-degree angle, gaining access to the outside pane by working around the window from both sides.

For double-hung windows, the process is a little more involved. Open the bottom sash around six inches. You'll find two latches at the top of the sash. Slide them in toward the center and pull the window in toward you and rest it against your leg or the lower sill of the window. Lower the top sash around ten inches. The latches for the top sash are sometimes on the face of the sash, but more often they are on top of the sash itself. Open the sash, pull it in, and rest it on the bottom sash. Take your window cleaning solution and give the glass a good spray. Let the solution sit for around twenty seconds, wipe clean, repeat the process, and close up the sash. Do the same for the bottom sash. You don't need a squeegee or any special tool. Just wipe the window using an easy, circular motion, as you would when cleaning a glass table.

113 How to weather-strip a window

Want to be more comfortable, block insects from getting into your house, and save money? Well, if you have double-hung windows you can add weather stripping to them for an added layer of protection. There are all different kinds of weather stripping, but the easiest to deal with is the variety that comes rolled up as an adhesive strip that you just attach right to the window. You can apply the stripping in the channels on either side of the sash, on the bottom of the lower sash, and on the inner face of the bottom of the frame of the upper sash. The easiest way to do this is to take a wet rag and clean the areas you want to apply the stripping to. Then measure them as accurately as you can. Cut the desired length of stripping. Raise or lower the sash in question a few inches. Leaving the backing alone, take the piece you want to put in the channel beside the sash and kind of work it up into the channel until it pops out the other side. Pull the backing off and press the stripping down. It's not as simple as it sounds, but with some experimentation you'll be able to make it work.

114 What goes around my newly installed window?

Once the window itself is in place, you'll need to build a trim around it. The trim is woodwork that creates a graceful transition between window and wall and keeps the window in place on the inside of the window. The trim consists of something called the stop, which goes around the inside of the window opening, from the window to the edge of the wall. There is also a casing, which runs around the frame of the window on the wall, like a frame around a painting. Trims come in various levels of complexity, but in the next three entries we're going to explain the simplest and easiest to create.

115 Project: Remove an Old Window and Install a New One

It's not for everybody, but if you are reasonably handy and patient enough, you can do it. Here's how:

1. Measure the height and width of the window opening in the wall, from brick to brick, as they say. Meaning you want to know the size of the opening of the wall in your house, *not* counting any woodwork around the old window. Measure once, then measure again, then do it a third and a fourth time until you get a consistent measurement.

2. Order the window. Await its arrival.

3. To remove the old window, put on goggles and a pair of construction gloves. Take a hammer or a small crowbar and remove the woodwork around the inside of the window, pulling the woodwork into the house. Save a section of the woodwork so you can match it when ordering new wood. Remove any screws and perimeter caulking.

4. Pull the window in toward you. If it is stuck, you can go outside your house and tap it loose with a hammer. You may want to make an X with adhesive tape on the pane to stabilize the glass.

5. Place the new window in the opening from the inside, until it abuts the existing exterior woodwork.

6. Square the window within the opening by measuring it diagonally from top left to bottom right, and from top right to bottom left, and then adjusting with shims, which are shingles of graduated thickness.

7. Use a level to make sure the window is plumb, meaning it hasn't been positioned at an angle leaning into the house or away from it.

8. Add a few more shims at the bottom of the window to wedge the window into the space tightly.

9. Jam strips of insulation (the kind of pink, rolled installation used in basements and attics) around the window to block any spaces where air might get in.

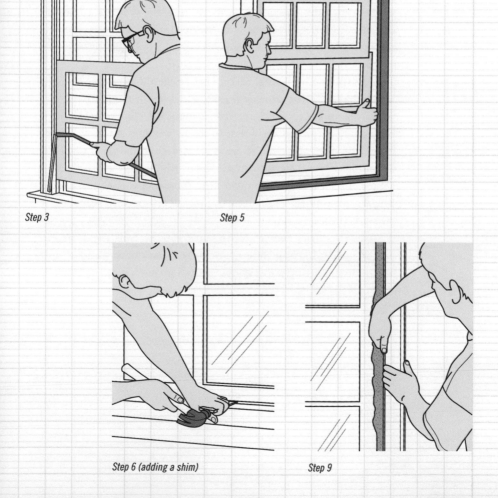

Step 3

Step 5

Step 6 (adding a shim)

Step 9

116 Creating and installing a window stop

The first step is to go to a lumberyard and get your wood cut. You'll need four pieces of wood for the stop. All four pieces should have a width that is equal to the distance from the window to the edge of the interior wall. You'll need a piece to go horizontally over the window, another to go horizontally beneath the window, and two pieces for the vertical sides. The top and bottom pieces should be the same length as the distance from the left side of the window opening to the right side. The side pieces should be the same length as the distance from the top of the window opening to the bottom of the window opening, minus the thickness of the two horizontal pieces of wood.

Take the top horizontal piece. Use a generous squiggly line of quick-drying yellow glue on one side and attach the piece to the upper opening. Leave a slight space, about the thickness of a quarter, between the stop and the window, so the window can move freely inside the stop. Once you've fixed your piece in the right place, use a hammer to tap a sixpenny nail two-thirds of the way in, at the center of the piece. Test to make sure the window can open and close properly behind the piece of wood. Install the bottom piece and the two side pieces the same way.

When you have everything in place, tap the nails all the way in and add nails, starting about 2 inches in from the very end of the wood piece, putting a nail about every 6 inches.

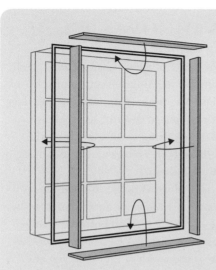

1. How the pieces will fit

2. Putting the last side piece in place

3. Hammering in nails every 6 inches

117   Creating a window casing

For the casing, you'll need four pieces of wood. Casings come in all sizes and styles. But chances are you're going to want to match—or at the bare minimum come close to—the existing window and door casings in the room. What we're going to describe here is how to make a totally plain, standard casing using stock wood from the lumberyard. If you need something more complex, take a drawing or a sample to the yard and work with them.

The big decision is what width of wood to use. A good idea is to measure the width of the existing window or door casings in the room and match that. As for length, the top and bottom pieces of the casing should be as long as the horizontal measurement of the window opening, plus two times the width of the wood you are using for the casing. The side pieces should be the height of the window opening, and that's that. (A quick way to decorate a simple frame is to buy wooden rosettes that can be glued onto the corners of the frame.)

118   Installing a window casing

The process for installing the casing is the same as for the stop, but you have to be careful to center the top and bottom pieces so that they overlap on both sides of the window equally. Start with the top piece. For this job it would be better if you bought something called paneling glue. It works with a caulking gun, is a touch stronger than yellow glue, and will hold better on a painted surface. Draw a generous squiggly line on one side of the wood and place it above the window (fig. 1). Measure with a ruler to make sure the wood overlaps the window the same distance on each side (fig. 2). Place a sixpenny nail in the dead center of the wood and tap it in just enough to hold the wood in place. If you need to, you can also put nails in the same way about 1½ inches in from the ends. Install the two side pieces the same way and make sure the pieces fit together evenly and levelly, creating a true rectangle. Install the bottom piece. Stand back and take a look. Measure. If it looks right, you can knock the nails in all the way and add nails about every 6 inches (fig. 3).

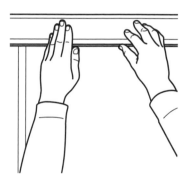

1. Place the first piece of wood on the wall.

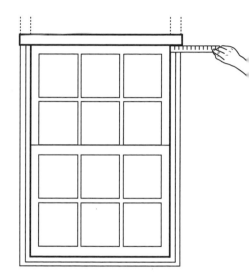

2. Measure the casing.

3. Hammer in the casing.

119 Repairing a damaged wooden windowsill

The sill is that little wooden overhang that sits just beneath your window on the exterior of your house. Sills come in as many different materials as houses are made of, but most homes will have wooden windowsills and those will deteriorate rapidly, especially if the paint begins to peel or degrade. To check the sill, take a sharp tool like a screwdriver and poke here and there around the sill. If the point penetrates the wood with ease, you have rot. If the entire sill is rotted out, you might consider hiring a carpenter to replace it. If you find bits of rot here and there, however, you can patch them yourself. Take a wood chisel or a utility knife and file away the rotted wood. Fill the area with wood putty. Wait twenty-four hours. Sand the area. Prime and paint it. If the rotted area is more than ½ inch, you will need to install a new piece of wood into the hole.

120 Installing a window shade

Shades are pieces of fabric or plastic, often opaque, which are wrapped around a spring-loaded rod. This rod is then installed on hardware that is mounted onto the inside of the window stop, which is the woodwork on the inside of the window opening that actually holds the window itself in place. The rod that holds the shade has metal pieces at either end that fit into slots on brackets that you install at either end of the window. Many shades come with installation instructions. If yours does, put this book down and follow them, and don't blame us if something goes wrong.

If you are replacing a used shade, measure the width of the old rod, including the metal pieces at either end. Then measure the length of the old shade when completely unrolled. That will give you the dimensions you'll need for the new shade. If you are installing a shade for the first time in that window, measure the inside of the window opening horizontally from one end to the other and then vertically. Subtract ⅛ inch for each measurement. The horizontal number gives the size of the rod you want, the vertical number the size of the shade.

To find the exact place you want the shade to go, hold it inside the window opening and mark where the brackets ought to be. Position one bracket over the spot you marked, and mark the spots where the nail holes are. With a screwdriver or other sharp implement, make starter holes. Holding one bracket in place, sink two brads, which are small nails, in to secure the bracket. When you have the bracket secure, place one end of the shade into it. Using a level and the rod, position the bracket on the other side so that the rod is perfectly level. Mark the spaces for the second set of brackets and make holes for them. Nail the second bracket to the wall. Insert the shade into the brackets.

121   Installing a blind

A window blind is typically made of slats of plastic, wood, or cloth that are pulled up and down on a pulley system. Blinds are mounted either inside the window opening on the window frame, as you would a shade, or on the face of the window casing, which is the wooden decoration that runs around the perimeter of the window opening. Blinds are mounted on boxlike, plastic brackets that snap closed over the blind. If you are mounting the blind inside the window frame, measure your distances as we described for a window shade (entry 120). If you are mounting the blind on the window

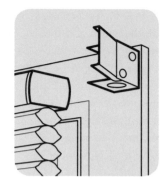

casing, you'll need to decide how wide you want the blind to be. Most people will want a blind that is approximately the width of the window opening, or that extends ½ inch on either side. Take your measurements and order the blind.

As we said regarding window shades, if there are instructions with the blinds, follow them. To install a blind, place the brackets on the blind and hold it up to where you want it on the window. Mark the locations where the brackets will go—keep in mind that there's a dedicated left bracket and a dedicated right bracket. Position the right bracket where you have marked, and mark the spaces where the screws will go. Use an awl to make small holes for the screws. You can use a regular screwdriver, but an electric screwdriver will make it much easier to mount the bracket. When you have the first bracket secure, place one end of the blind into it. Using a level and the blind, position the bracket on the other side so that the blind is perfectly level. Mark the spaces for the second set of brackets and make holes for them. Use a screwdriver to secure the second bracket. Insert the shade into the brackets.

122 What do I need to buy to install curtains?

Most curtains require a curtain rod, which is mounted on brackets on the window casing, or above the casing, onto the wall. If you are mounting a lightweight curtain onto the window casing, you can just follow the same instructions we gave you for mounting blinds. If, however, you are mounting a lightweight curtain onto the wall, or have a heavier curtain that comes with long screws that will go deep into the wall or through the casing and into the wall, you need to know what kind of walls you have: Sheetrock or plaster. If your house was built within the last sixty years, the walls are likely Sheetrock. If the house is older than that and hasn't had a major renovation, the walls are likely to be plaster. If you don't know the age of your house, tap on the wall. If it makes a hollow sound, it's probably Sheetrock. If it makes a solid sound, it's plaster. If it's Sheetrock, you'll be using screws with butterflies; if it's plaster, you'll need screws with anchors (see entry 24). Then you'll need to decide the dimensions of the curtain you are going to buy. Most curtain rods go a few inches past the window casing on each side, with a curtain that covers the window completely from side to side. As for the length of the curtain, some curtains fall to the windowsill and some go all the way to the floor.

TRICK OF THE TRADE: *If you decide to have a floor-length curtain, the traditional styling is to make it long enough so that the material drapes about an inch onto the floor, but if that is too much puddling for your taste, you can make it any length you want.*

123 Installing a curtain rod

Attach to the curtain rod both the curtain itself and the brackets that will hold the rod to the wall. Space the brackets out evenly at either end of the curtain rod. Place the rod above the window at the level that leaves the curtain hanging to the length you desire. Mark the spot beneath each bracket where you want that bracket to go. Or if you can see the screw holes in the bracket, put a pencil in the holes and mark the screw holes exactly. Screw one screw into the left bracket. Place the rod in that bracket. Then go to the right side of the rod and hold the right bracket over the spot where you marked it. Place a level on the rod and adjust the rod up and down until it is level. Mark again the spot where the right bracket should go so that the rod is level and the brackets evenly spaced. Remove the rod from the brackets. Screw in the brackets fully. Put the rod back.

124 How a window screen is put together

We said it before and we'll say it again: when you order new windows, make sure to order screens with them. The humble window screen is one of the greatest things in your house, because it allows you to have the benefit of fresh air during the warmer months without having your house fill with bugs. The screen is a simple object. It consists of a frame and an expanse of mesh. The mesh is just slightly larger than the frame, and the perimeter of the mesh is inserted into a small channel that runs around the frame and is secured by a spline, which is a rubber or metal tube that is pushed into the channel over the mesh. The screen itself is designed to fit snugly into the window opening and be secured by latches that push out when opened, to wedge the screen tightly into the opening.

125 Repairing and maintaining window screens

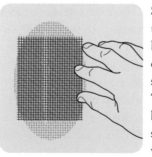

Screens are great. The bad news is, if there is one tiny hole in the screen, its bug-stopping powers will be greatly diminished. So you have to patch that screen or replace it. Patching is easy. They sell kits in hardware stores that basically involve using sections of screening mesh that you can literally weave into the existing screen by hand. The only downside is that the color of the new mesh will be different from that of the original screen and you'll see where the patches are.

Also, by their very nature, screens collect a lot of dirt and grime, and this can bleed onto your house in rainstorms, so keeping screens clean is an important task. Once in the spring and again sometime around the Fourth of July, take all the screens down and hose them off. If you don't have a hose, a bucket of soapy water and a sponge or a wire brush will do the trick.

126 Replacing the wire mesh on an existing window screen

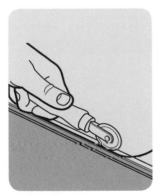

First, you have to remove the old screen. Take the screen out of the window and lay it on a worktable or on the ground. Using a screwdriver or a pair of pliers, pry the spline out of the channel that runs around the screen frame, and remove the old wire mesh from the frame. The spline is usually a rubber cord that fits into a channel in the frame, stuffing the ends of the mesh into the frame and securing them. Take that old spline to the hardware store and have them give you a matching spline in the same length. Please remember that if you live in an old house that has windows of differing sizes and you are repairing more than one screen, you'll need to mark which spline goes with which screen. When you are at the hardware store, also buy a roll of new mesh for the screen and something called a spline tool, which looks like a dull pizza cutter. Take the new screen mesh and lay a piece over the screen, cutting it so that you have a piece that covers the entire screen frame with a ¼-inch overlap. Take the spline and lay it around the perimeter of the frame. Then take the spline tool and run it over the spline, pushing it into the channel around the perimeter.

Plumbing

This is the chapter that can save you some real money. Plumbing problems often seem mysterious and difficult to the novice, and when a homeowner calls in a professional plumber, the plumber will, quite fairly, charge good money for the time and effort it takes him to visit your home, no matter how easy the repair is once he gets there. It turns out, however, that there are a number of plumbing issues that can easily be resolved by the homeowner long before he or she has to call in a plumber.

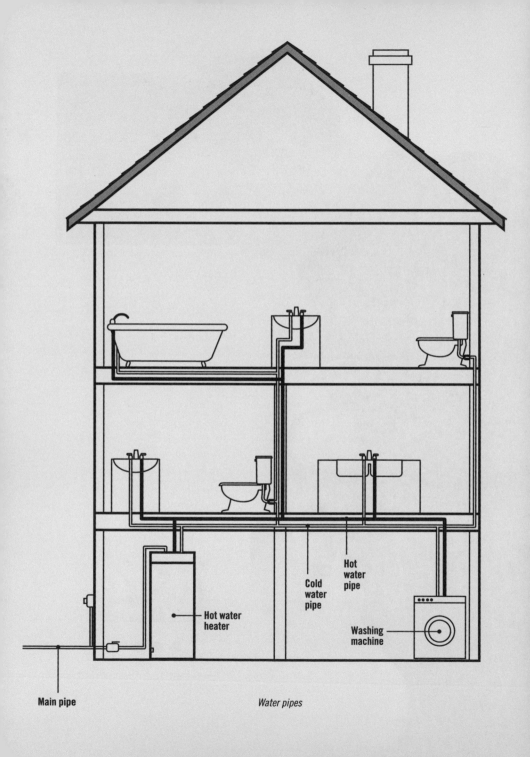

Hot water pipe

Cold water pipe

Hot water heater

Washing machine

Main pipe

Water pipes

127   How water pipes work

The water supply for most homes comes from a main pipe from the street. However, if you happen to live way out in the sticks, you may have a private well or rain cistern. That said, in most cases the water enters the house through a pipe that leads from the main water line under the street into your basement. Right at the spot where this pipe meets your house, you'll find a water meter, which is a machine that measures how much water is going into the house. Somewhere in the basement, right near the meter, will be a main valve that can shut off all water going to the house, closing the pipe that leads from the main water source in the street to your house. Near the main valve you should also find the risers, pipes that carry the water to the upper floors of the house. Most houses will have more than one set of risers. We say "set of risers," because one half of the riser is cold water, and the other half has gone through a heating system to provide hot water to the upper floors. From these risers the pipes will branch off to feed all the water sources in the home.

128   Which plumbing issues can I take care of myself?

Before you decide, think about your insurance policy. In the fine print of most homeowner's policies, it says you are obligated to use a licensed plumber for certain kinds of plumbing work. This is no joke. If you decide to do plumbing work that under your policy requires a licensed practitioner and something goes wrong, you may find yourself not being able to collect any insurance, because you didn't follow those guidelines. Of course, every policy is different, and we aren't exactly lawyers. Okay, we aren't lawyers. But, in general, most policies allow you to work with water pipes, the ones that take water to your house, and that's it. Waste pipes (the ones that take waste away from your house) and gas pipes (which provide natural gas to ovens, stoves, and central heating systems) are generally speaking off-limits to the weekend plumber. In this chapter, we will discuss some things you can think about doing with regard to waste pipes if you are willing to take the insurance risk. We're leaving gas pipes alone, however. Gas is not something you want to mess with. One false move with a gas pipe and kaboom!

129 How the waste pipes work

Now that we've talked about what's coming into the house, let's talk about how stuff goes out. The waste system has two parts: the pipes that drain away the fluids from your house, and a vent system that allows air into the pipes to carry away noxious smells and allow the fluids to drain properly. Every drain in your house, whether it leads from a sink, a toilet, an appliance, or a tub, is attached to something called a stack, which is a pipe that runs fluid down to the basement and has a vent that allows air to flow up to the roof. The fluids run down the stack, where they hit a pipe called a main sewer line that is pitched toward the street (where the main sewer line of the house meets the municipal sewer line) or toward your own private septic system. The pitch of your house's sewer line will be calculated so that for every foot the sewer line travels, it will slope down ¼ inch. Where the house's main sewage line meets the street, the sewer line hits a U-shaped pipe called a trap, which marks the transition from the house to the municipal sewer line. Please be aware that you may not see the trap or the sewer line, because they may be buried.

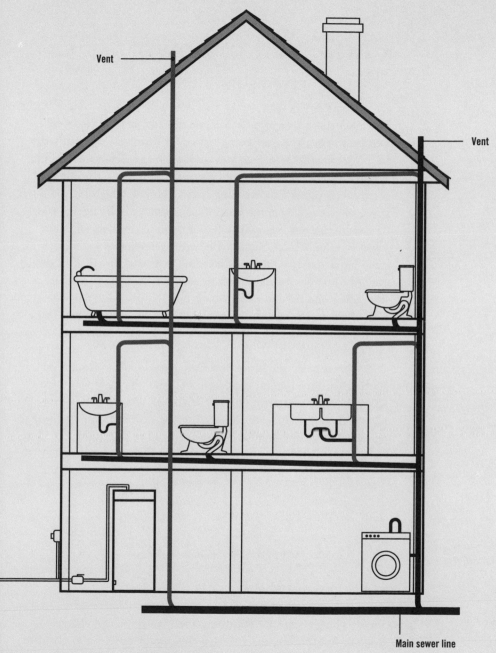

Vent

Vent

Main sewer line

*Waste pipes. When the main sewer line exits the house,
it runs to the municipal sewer line or to the septic system.*

130 Can I read my own water meter?

You don't really need to read your water meter, but did you ever wonder whether you were being ripped off when you saw your water bill? We sometimes do. So if you are the kind of person who likes to keep a handle on these kinds of expenses, you might try reading the water meter yourself and keeping track. Think how satisfied you'll feel if you can actually bust the water department for overcharging you.

Reading meters is easy. You'll find them in the basement or lower exterior of most houses, where the water comes in off the main municipal line. Meters are typically six dial, five dial, or single dial. Most meters measure in cubic feet, but some do in gallons. In the five- and six-dial meters, each dial records a different size measurement. Dial one will record 1,000 cubic feet, dial two 100 cubic feet, dial three 10 cubic feet, dial four single cubic feet . . . you get the idea.

So choose a day and write down the measurement of water use, starting with the biggest increment dial and moving down. That will give you your starting figure. Then wait a set length of time, say one month, and record the readings again. Your total use for that period is the second number minus the first one.

A single-dial meter is much easier. Just read the total number.

131 What you need to know about valves

We are going to do a lot of talking about valves in this chapter, so it is worth describing exactly what they are. A valve is a mechanism inside a pipe that closes off that pipe. There is a valve that shuts off the main water supply to the house, and every sink, toilet, or other water outlet in the house should have its own valve, although in some houses they don't. It's much better to have a valve for every water outlet, because the valve allows you to shut off that outlet specifically if something goes wrong, while still enjoying water in the rest of your house. If you don't have a valve on the pipe to a specific water source, think about having one installed. A plumber will have to do this, because installing a valve requires soldering, and you don't want to mess with that yourself. All valves are controlled by levers or handles on the outside.

132 How valves work on the inside

There are two main kinds of valves in terms of the way they operate.

1. The gate valve has a carrot-shaped piece that screws into the pipe, shutting the hole off.

2. The ball valve has a hole that goes right through it. When the ball valve turns, the hole faces the pipe and the water flows. When the ball valve turns again, the hole faces the wall of the pipe, and no water flows.

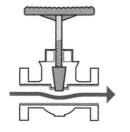

Gate valve (in the open position)

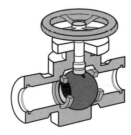

Ball valve

133 Locating the valves in your house

There are valves all over your house, and you should make it your business to know where each and every one of them is. Most faucets have two valves, one for hot water and one for cold, and they are typically located beneath the sink. (Garden hoses and toilets won't have hot water.) The valves for a shower and bathtub are located behind the wall in the mechanics of the shower itself, so you aren't messing much with them. Valves to dishwashers are almost always shared with the kitchen sink, as is the water to the fridge. A laundry room would have a valve down behind the washing machine. The main valve for your house is located right by the water meter in the basement. The valves that control the water supply to outdoor faucets and spigots are always accessible. Look for them somewhere in the basement. If you are having a hard time finding your valves, hire a plumber for an hour to come and give you a tour, and make sure to label the valves as you go along.

134 Testing your valves

There really isn't anything you can do to maintain your valves. They'll work until they stop working and then you'll need to replace them. But you should make sure to check your valves every so often so that you don't have any surprises when something goes wrong. Unless you test them, you'll have no idea whether your valves will shut the water off.

Start by finding where your valves are (see entry 133, above); then have a family meeting and make sure everyone (children included) knows where all the valves are located. As you go through the house to point them out, check that every valve works. Turn the valve off and make sure the water is shut off. Repeat once a year.

All of this is important, because shutting off a valve can mean the difference between a major flood and a minor incident. When you see the water rising in a toilet, when a faucet is running out of control, or when you see water pouring out of a wall or the ceiling, find where the water is coming from and shut the valve—or shut the main line off. With a flood, every second counts. Nothing bad will happen if you shut the main line down.

135 What's a check valve?

A check valve saves you from one of the most repulsive things that can happen to a homeowner. Think of it this way: the main waste pipe that travels down your street is the line that carries all of the toilet waste for your entire block. That's *all* the nasty stuff being produced by everyone in the area. This main waste line can be as much as 20 inches in diameter—which is one major pipe—and that major pipe can clog. The same thing can happen if you have a private septic system. When a clog occurs in the main waste line of a septic system line, the pressure will build up, and all that charming waste will back right up into your basement. In addition to being awful to deal with, this is an unsanitary situation that may cost you a lot of money in treatments to make your basement habitable again.

To avoid all of that, you can install a check valve on the outside of your house trap—remember, that's the U-shaped pipe that connects your main waste line to the municipal waste line or septic system—and that valve will prevent you from ever having waste back up into your house. When the waste begins to back up, the check valve will shut down, blocking the waste from your home and sending it along to your unfortunate neighbors. The kicker is, this little device costs no more than $100, and any competent plumber can install it for you.

136 How a tank toilet works

Tank toilets have, as you might expect, a tank of water located typically behind the seat. The tank fills up with water. When you pull the lever on the toilet to flush it, a valve opens, sending that water down into the toilet bowl, where it carries away whatever is in the bowl down into the piping. The toilet is serviced by three main components: a bowl-siphon, a flush valve, and a filler valve. The bowl-siphon is nothing fancier than a pipe molded into the porcelain of the toilet and shaped like a shepherd's crook or a question mark. It has no moving parts but is shaped so that standing water will stay in the bowl, but if pressure is exerted in the form of a flush, the water will go down the siphon. The flush valve, or flapper, is made of rubber and sits at the bottom of the tank. The handle of the toilet is attached to this valve by a chain. When you lift the chain, the valve opens and the right amount of water pours into the bowl.

The filler valve sits at the top of a tube that rises up from the bottom of the tank to just near the top of the tank. Attached to this tube, just below the filler valve, is something called the filler float. When the tank empties for a flush, the filler float falls, and this opens the filler valve, which releases water from the main piping system of the house into the tank. As the tank fills, the filler float rises, and when it gets to the top, the filler valve shuts off. There's a valve, usually somewhere near the base of the toilet, that shuts off the water supply to the appliance.

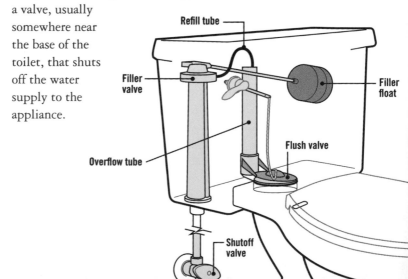

137 Using a plunger to fix a clogged toilet

A toilet clogs when something, usually a ball of toilet paper or some object that does not belong in a toilet, gets lodged in the siphon. When that happens you pull out the trusty old plunger. If you see that the water is low in the bowl, please don't flush again. You may end up with a nasty surprise overflowing on your floor. Just take the plunger, place it over the hole at the bottom of the bowl, and work it up and down and around without ever taking the plunger off the hole. There's a real technique to this, but it is hard to describe. The idea is to move the plunger up and down while creating and then maintaining a feeling of suction over the hole. Be careful not to splash yourself too much as you do this, especially if the bowl is full. But in reality you don't need a lot of violent motion to get this job done. Just apply gentle pressure. After a few seconds, remove the plunger. Hopefully, when you release the suction you've developed, whatever was in there will drain away down the siphon. Once you get the hang of it, the plunger is going to see you through most clogs. If plunging isn't working, your next option is to buy a toilet auger, otherwise known as a snake.

138 Using a toilet auger

This handy little device, which is sometimes called a closet auger (for water closet) or a snake, is a metal tube with a coiled metal cable inside it and a crank handle at one end. There are different kinds of augers, but in general you insert an auger into a clogged pipe, screw in the metal cable, and use it to break through whatever blockage is down there.

Before using an auger, turn off the water supply to the toilet. Crank the metal wire up inside the auger. Then insert the auger into the hole at the bottom of the bowl. The auger will have a slight curve at the inserted end, and you want to make sure you've pointed that curve up, into the siphon. Crank the cable down into the bowl siphon. If you feel resistance, you've likely reached the source of the blockage. Keep turning until you break through whatever it is and until the cable is fully extended. Then begin pulling the auger out of the toilet, continuing to turn the crank as you go. When the cable is fully withdrawn from the toilet, you will have likely broken up the obstruction, or, rather disgustingly, brought up whatever was down there. Wear gloves and have a garbage bag ready. Flush the toilet, then turn the water back on.

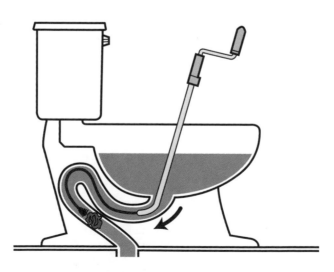

139 Fixing a tank toilet that is constantly running water

Replace the flush valve flapper.

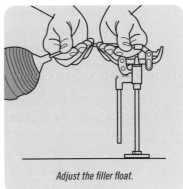
Adjust the filler float.

For all fixes of this nature, you are going to want to shut off the water supply to the toilet and flush it to remove all water. Always do that first. The cause of this problem is usually a faulty flush valve. The flush valve flapper could be rotted and not sealing the tank properly so that it never fills. This happens a lot. In most toilets, the flapper is attached to the base of the filler valve by two tabs on either side, and to the lever that you pull to flush the toilet by a hooked chain. You can simply remove the flapper from the chain and the filler valve and bring it to the hardware store to replace it. Remember, most flappers are specific to the brand of toilet you have, so you should bring the old one with you.

The second most common cause of a running toilet is a filler valve—usually it's not shutting off. This could be because the filler float isn't working properly; the float might be stuck for some reason. A little gentle fiddling with it might do the trick. If there is a larger problem, such as with the filler valve, it is going to have to be replaced, and that means removing the toilet tank. There are people who will tell you that you can do this, and you can, but don't. Hire a professional. The risk is that in attempting to remove the tank, you will crack it and have to replace the entire thing. It isn't worth it.

plumbing

140 Fixing a tank toilet that isn't getting enough water

If the water level in the tank is too low to properly flush out the toilet, you may have nothing more complex than a faulty filler float. Some filler floats are doughnuts that ride up and down the vertical pipe that supplies the water to the tank. Others are balls that sit at the ends of the metal arms. The doughnut variety can get stuck somehow on the pipe. A little fiddling may loosen it. The ball-and-metal-arm kind can become lodged against the wall of the tank, or the arm can bend. Here too a little light fiddling and a gentle bend to the arm might well resolve your issue.

The other thing that may be happening is that the small holes around the rim of the toilet bowl, which allow water from the tank to flush the bowl, can become clogged. Take a small mirror and look around the rim. You may see obstructions. Even if you don't, a gentle poke into each hole with a screwdriver may help the water flow.

141 Fixing a toilet that sweats or seeps

Toilets sweat not from too much use, but because the temperature of the water is markedly different from the air temperature, which causes condensation. In some cases a lot of water can run off that big bowl and pool on the floor. There's nothing actually unsanitary about this water—it's all on the outside of the bowl—but there is something yucky about it anyway. They do make pans that you can place underneath the bowl, and even little toilet sweaters that you can put over the bowl to sop up the moisture—although that is weird. Better still, you can reduce the problem quite nicely by installing a temperature valve, which allows a mixture of hot and cold water into the bowl, thus reducing the differential between the toilet temperature and the room temperature.

Water may also be seeping around the base of the bowl. This water is absolutely unsanitary, and you must do something about this seepage. The likely culprit here is the seal between the toilet and the drainage pipe. To install a temperature valve or to fix seepage, you are best off calling a plumber.

142 How a flushometer toilet works

The flushometer toilet has no tank. The water comes through the pipe and passes through a ball-shaped device, called the cartridge, which drives a given amount of water at high pressure into the toilet. Just so you know, the only shutoff in a flushometer is the valve on the pipe right before the cartridge, located where the pipe angles. The weak link in this kind of toilet is the cartridge itself. When the cartridge breaks down, there won't be enough water pressure when you flush. Replacing a cartridge is relatively easy in general terms, but the devil is in the details. You might think about calling in a professional to do this repair. But just begin by shutting off the water supply, remembering righty tighty, lefty loosey. The cartridge sits inside a ball-shaped space in the pipe, which has a lid. Using wrenches, open the outer cover, flip open the inner cover with a screwdriver, and remove the cartridge and take it to the hardware store. There are actually two kinds of cartridges, one that allows a flush of 3.2 gallons per second and one that allows a flush of 3.6 gallons per second. Purchase the correct cartridge for your toilet, take it home, place it in the pipe, and close the pipe up, and your toilet should work. That's the only flushometer fix you need.

143   Fixing a loose toilet seat

We hate those rattling toilet seats. The toilet seat is attached to the bowl with a screw and a nut. The nut is on the underside, and the screw is on the top. It might make sense to tighten these screws once a year. You may need a wrench, but if you can hold the nut with your fingers, use any slotted screwdriver (or a quarter, if you have one in your pocket) and tighten the screws. The toilet itself is attached to the floor with two bolts called Johnny bolts. They don't usually come loose, but we did want to remind you that it looks a little more finished if you put small pieces on top of these called Johnny bolt covers. There's only one size, so just match the color you want.

144   Fixing a clogged sink with an auger

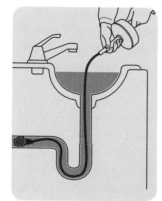

Bathroom drains clog because hair gets stuck inside them, along with residue from all the creams and powders and other stuff people use to make themselves beautiful. You can unclog a bathroom drain in two ways. The first is to use an auger, just like you did with the toilet (see entry 138). Except that you shouldn't use a toilet auger on a sink. You should use something called a drain auger, which is like a toilet auger, only narrower and longer to deal with the kinds of pipes and blockages you'll find in sinks. If you are going to snake your sink, the first thing you'll have to do is remove the stopper. Some stoppers will simply lift out. If that doesn't work, look under the sink. There are different ways the stoppers are attached, but you'll see some kind of lever or bar that connects the stopper to the handle that operates it on the sink. Usually there's a nut attaching the stopper to the lever, and you can unscrew that and then pull the stopper out.

TRICK OF THE TRADE: *Our advice is, don't use those liquid or crystal de-cloggers—it is much more effective to clear the clog directly.*

145 Fixing a clogged sink by going into the pipes

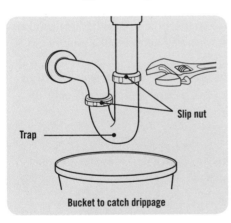

Slip nut

Trap

Bucket to catch drippage

What you need to do here is unscrew the trap. The trap is the U-shaped pipe below your sink. First shut off the hot and cold water valves beneath the sink. Go underneath the sink and open up the nuts at either end of the trap. (It is a good idea to place a bucket underneath the trap as you do your work, in order to catch whatever falls out of the pipe.) You should be able to do this by hand. If you can't get the job done manually, dig into the tool kit for a pair of pliers, but be very careful and very gentle. Use one hand to brace the pipe, and turn the nut with caution, because these pipes will crack very easily under the kind of force you are exerting on them. Once you have the trap removed, flush it out with water in a garden sink if you have one. Use a garden hose if you need a lot of pressure. If you can't flush it out, you have two options: buy a new trap or call a plumber. If you clean out the trap and the sink still fails to drain properly, then you have a clog deeper down in your pipes. At that stage you'll need to try an auger. If that fails, call a plumber. You have something big, sticky, or ugly trapped down there. Be afraid—it may be alive.

146 Dealing with a clogged tub

Chances are you're going to need to call a plumber to fix a clogged tub, because the clog will be so deep down in the pipes that you'll need specialized tools to reach it. You may be able to deal with the problem yourself with an auger. But first you are going to have to remove the tub stopper, the hardware that stops the drain and allows the tub to fill with water. There's almost always a lever on the tub, usually located underneath the spout. This lever controls the rod that opens and closes the drain stopper, and it's usually attached to the face of the tub with two screws. Unscrew those screws and remove the rod slowly and gently. When it comes up, you may find a nice hairball at the end of it. If you remove this hairball, you can put the rod back down the hole, screw in the lever, and see whether the tub drains. If it doesn't drain, you can open the stopper up again and try an auger. If that doesn't work, then you have to call a plumber.

TRICK OF THE TRADE: *Don't use your toilet auger on a bathtub. For this job you need a specialized drain auger, which is longer and shaped differently. See entry 144.*

147 Maintaining pipes and preventing nasty smells

Once a month, pour a cup of regular bleach down each sink and tub drain. The bleach will break down hair, congealed toothpaste, shampoo, and soap buildup without damaging your pipes in any way. If you have a dishwasher, run it empty once a month. The hot water will flush out the pipes within the machine and the pipes that lead from the dishwasher to the drain system of your house.

A more professional form of maintenance is having the waste pipes in your house water-jetted. A company will come and insert a pipe into your waste line and flush it out with high-pressure water. This will clean away buildup and debris. If you are hard on your pipes—meaning you flush down the toilet material that doesn't dissolve or are in the habit of pouring grease and other clogging materials down your sink—you might think about getting your pipes water-jetted once a year. If you are easier on your pipes, every four or five years is just fine.

148 How to insulate pipes

If you live in a place that gets cold, you should think about insulating your pipes. When water freezes it expands, and if there's water in pipes that are exposed to cold air, they will fill up with ice and crack. The pipes you'll need to insulate are any that are abutting an exterior wall or that are in spaces like garages that aren't heated. Measure the length and diameter of any pipe you want to insulate. Go to the hardware store and ask for pipe insulation in the correct size. Pipe insulation is typically made of foam or fiberglass and comes in a tube shape with a slit on it. Cut it and place it around the pipe. Using pipe insulation will not only protect your pipes from all but the most severe cold but will also prevent children from touching any hot piping. You can also apply heating tape to pipes.

149 Adding heating tape to pipes

Heating tape is basically an insulated electric coil that you wrap around pipes. It will heat up when the weather turns cold, keeping the pipes warm.

Before you begin to add heating tape to pipes, focus on this obvious, but important, caution. When you are doing this job, you are working with electricity and water, two elements that mix together in a rather dangerous way. So the first thing you need to do is check whether there are any leaks anywhere along the piping you are intending to add heating tape to. If there are, fix them before going any further. Do not risk electrocution. Also, you want to buy top-quality heating tape. You want the kind that turns on automatically at a certain temperature, not the kind that stays hot all the time. You also want the type of heating tape that has thick rubber insulation, to make sure you never have electricity and water coming together.

Each brand of heating tape will attach to the pipe in a different way, so follow the instructions on the packet. Begin your installation from the power outlet. Remember that all heating tape must be plugged directly—never, ever use an extension cord—into a type of plug called a ground fault circuit interrupter. If you don't have a GFCI at hand, you are going to have to install one (see entry 189). After installing the heating tape, you'll need to cover the pipe in insulation (see entry 148).

150 Fixing a leaky pipe

To properly fix a leaky pipe you are going to need a professional plumber, but if you master a few simple skills you can patch leaking

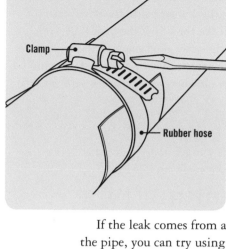

Clamp

Rubber hose

pipes and forestall the day when you have to call in the expensive cavalry. If the leak is occurring where two pipes are threaded together (this is known as a joint in the business), then try tightening the joint—gently, to avoid cracking a pipe. Use a pipe wrench, which is a kind of adjustable wrench designed for use on pipes, and turn the pipe into the other one. Be aware that some older forms of pipes are not threaded into one another and may be soldered together. If they are, call a plumber.

If the leak comes from a small hole somewhere along the length of the pipe, you can try using a patch. Pick up a premade pipe patching kit in the hardware store or rig one yourself using something called a hose clamp and a piece of plastic hose. The hose clamp can be two convex pieces that clamp together with screws, or a kind of metal strap with a screw at one end. Either way, the clamp is designed to go around the pipe at the leak. You place a section of rubber hose over the leak, then clamp it firmly to the pipe, and that may leave you trouble free for some time.

151 The importance of Teflon tape

Teflon tape is superstrong tape that will give you an extra seal when you screw a threaded pipe or valve into another pipe or valve. Using it is important because no matter how well you screw one pipe into another, there is always a small space here or there where water or steam can escape (water and steam being two substances that love to leak out all over the place). The Teflon tape will keep that from happening. Before you screw the one pipe into the other, take the Teflon tape and roll it around the threads of the male pipe, which is the one that is going into the other pipe, counterclockwise three times. It is vital to do this counterclockwise, because if you go clockwise, the tape will come off when you screw one pipe into the other.

152 Fixing a clanking pipe

In some houses the pipes clank when the water is turned on. This can be caused by a variety of things, but generally what you've got is a loose pipe somewhere that is banging against another pipe, a wall, or whatever is holding it in place. The fix for any of these situations is to stop the pipe from moving. There are many ways you can do this. If the pipe is held down by a hose clamp, or something of that nature, tighten the clamp a little. Failing that, you can wedge something dampening, like a piece of roofing felt or a section of hose, behind the pipe.

If two pipes are banging together, you can try putting something dampening between them. Otherwise, have someone trained come in and solder the pipes together.

You can wrap pipes in insulation. If you have a pipe that is banging inside a wall, see if you can find where it emerges from the wall and place some buffering in the space between the pipe and the wall.

TRICK OF THE TRADE: *Please remember, with all of these fixes, do not wedge the pipe in question too tightly. Pipes do need to expand and contract a little, and if you don't give them anywhere to go, they are going to break.*

153 Fixing water hammer

Water hammer is a specific condition that occurs within pipes. It is caused by an imbalance between the liquid and the air in the pipes. When a pipe works properly, both air and water are present. When you turn on a pipe and then shut it off, the water in the pipe is stopped all of a sudden. As long as there's a sufficient quantity of air in the pipe, that air will kind of cushion the water and stop it from slamming into the pipe. If there isn't enough air, you will get a water hammer, which sounds like a single wallop—bam!—and doesn't sound like any other kind of pipe noise. The fix for this is a simple one. You find the pipe in question, drain it of all fluid, close it, and fill up the system again with water. The hard part about it is that you need to know where the problem is, and that can be difficult to determine. There are also special pressure valves that you can install to pipes or systems that are prone to this kind of problem; these will keep the air and water regulated. Installing the pressure valve may be a job for a plumber, but he should charge you less if you have found the problem yourself.

154 How do I fix a loose sink faucet?

Just to be clear, you'll find faucets on sinks and tubs. The faucet is the place where the water comes out, and it comprises the hot and cold handles and the spout. Some faucets come as a one-piece unit. Others are installed in three different pieces, and there are faucets that have a single handle for hot and cold. With normal use, faucets can come loose from where they are attached to the body of the sink with nuts that are mounted underneath the sink. The simplest way to tighten the nuts is to work with a friend. One person will hold the

plumbing

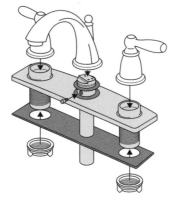

faucet while the other tightens the nut with her hands. If you can't tighten the nut with your hand, you'll need a tool called a basin wrench, which is a curved wrench that allows you to reach into tight spaces.

155   How to fix a leaky faucet

When you have a leak in a faucet, you have a problem with something called a cartridge. We talked about cartridges in toilets, but this is a different animal. It is a circular piece with a hole drilled through it. In faucets with two handles, there's one cartridge each for hot and cold. In a single-handled faucet (as shown), there's just one cartridge. When the faucet is shut off, the cartridge is turned so that the hole faces the wall of the pipe and the pipe is closed off. When the faucet is on, the hole faces the pipe, and the water flows through it. When you have a leak, the problem is that the cartridge is not turned fully to close off the hole. What happens is that over time the connected pieces within the mechanism become stripped and no longer turn properly. When that occurs, you need to replace the cartridge.

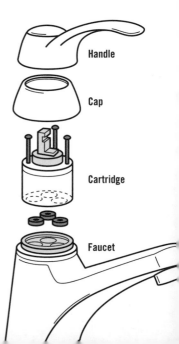

Handle

Cap

Cartridge

Faucet

Here's how to do it: turn off the valves. Somewhere on the handle, you'll find a screw. This may be hidden underneath a plastic cap. If you can't find the screw easily, look up the model of your faucet on the Internet, or call the manufacturer in order to find out where that screw is. Unscrew the handle and pull it off. Underneath there you'll find the cartridge, which looks rather like the head of a bolt. Using a pair of pliers, loosen the bolt and lift out the cartridge. Take it to a plumbing supply store, because you probably won't find it at your local hardware store. Buy a new one, screw it into place, and reattach the handle.

156 What's a pop-up?

The pop-up is just that little handle behind your faucet that closes off your sink so you can fill it with water. Over time these things come loose and no longer function, but they are really easy to fix. Look underneath the sink. You'll see that the handle has a rod coming down out of it, which is hooked onto a shorter, horizontal rod. The pop-up stops working when the two rods become detached from each other. The fix is to reattach them. Doing this is self-explanatory. The vertical rod, the one attached to the handle, has a series of holes in it. Hook the horizontal rod to it. Choose the hole that leaves your handle sitting at the height you would like. Sometimes the pop-up will be loose, even when the vertical rod has slipped down on the horizontal rod. You can fix it by just moving it farther up the horizontal rod.

157 Why do I have low water pressure in my house?

The first question you need to ask is, do I have low pressure in the entire house, or do I have it in certain select areas, or in just one area? If the pressure is low throughout, check with your neighbors. There may be a problem in your area or, if you live in an apartment, in the whole building. If so, you need to contact the local water authority or building management and get them involved. If the problem is just in your house, but it is happening throughout the house, then you likely have an issue with the pipe that is supplying water to your home from the municipal pipe. That pipe has become clogged, and you are going to need professional help. The same is true if you have low pressure in one section of your house. Chances are the pipes in there are old and have become clogged with mineral deposits and other material, and you are going to need to change them out. This is more properly done by a professional. You may, however, discover that you are only having an issue with one sink or shower. In that case, there's an easy fix.

158 Getting more water pressure

Water pressure regulator

Let's say you live in a place where there's low water pressure. You've called the local water authority a million times, you've shouted and cajoled, but nothing works. In that case, you can install something called a water pressure regulator. This is a valve that can be installed at the point where the water comes into your home from the street. It can adjust the water pressure in your house, keeping it not too low and not too high either (too much pressure is also a bad thing), but just right. Most water pressure regulators have dials that you can use to control the pressure. A good rule of thumb is that forty pounds per square inch of pressure is in that just-right zone. But you might want to consult with a plumber or other professional before fiddling too much with the dials of your regulator.

159 How to fix a faucet or showerhead that is losing water pressure

Over time you may notice that you are getting less pressure in your sink or shower. Fixing that is simple.

THE FAUCET

There's a screen at the end of the faucet that over time gets gunked up with minerals found in your local water supply. You should be able to unscrew the screen and clean it with water from your faucet. That should take care of the problem.

THE SHOWERHEAD

You'll find a nut just above the showerhead that you should be able to unscrew by hand. Once you have the showerhead off, run some hot water over it, or pour some bleach through it. Put it back on. If that fix doesn't work, you may have a bigger problem: a leak inside the piping. Or you may be the sort of person who doesn't enjoy living in the modern, water-conserving era. You see, for the past ten years or so, showerheads have been designed to limit the amount of water that they spray on you. These limitations are mandated by federal law to around 2½ gallons per minute maximum, and in some places local ordinances make that number lower.

TRICK OF THE TRADE: *If the pressure in an individual sink or shower diminishes suddenly (and not over time, as we said above), check its intake valve. Someone might have tightened it by accident.*

160 How to, ahem, personalize your showerhead

Do not write us letters. Do not send angry e-mails. For the record, we both use conforming showerheads in our homes and have no issue with the important and valuable efforts our government is making to preserve the life of this planet. We don't waste water, and we don't advocate water wastage. However, we are in the information business, and we'd be derelict in our duty if we did not tell you that you can—if you really want to—make your modern, conforming showerhead into a nonconforming, water-blasting, old-style showerhead. Every brand of showerhead is different, but most are designed with a little washer, or piece of plastic, that blocks the water. All you need to do is take your showerhead down, open it up, and pop that little bad boy out, and you are going to have the most popular bathroom in the neighborhood. Not that you ever should, under any circumstance, do that. But that is how you could—not that you would, or should.

161 Getting to know your shower

When plumbers talk about a shower, they typically refer to the "shower body." This is all the piping that sits behind your wall. Essentially, the shower body is like the system that delivers water to a sink faucet. You have pipes carrying hot and cold water and valves connected to the handles to turn them on and off. That's the basic model. There are two upgrades. The first is something you'll find on all showers these days, and that's a "check valve." This cuts the shower off from feeding hot or cold water to a toilet or sink that's operated during the shower, thus preventing dramatic changes in temperature and screams from the bathroom. The second is a thermostat and volume control valve. Built into the body, the thermostat allows you to set the temperature you want, and the volume control combines the control for hot and cold water into a single knob that you use to turn the system on and off.

162 Fixing a leaky shower

1. Remove the handle.

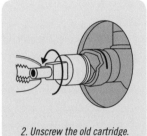

2. Unscrew the old cartridge.

3. Install the new cartridge.

The most common problem with showers is that they drip. The fix for this is exactly what you would do if you were fixing a leaky faucet on a sink. Except in this case the cartridge is located within the hot and cold water handles. Of course, first you need to shut off the water supply. Most likely you'll need to go to your basement and shut off the main valve. Then go to the lowest point where you have a water faucet and open up the hot and cold water flow until there's no more water. To remove the handle in your shower, find the screw that holds it into the wall. This will usually be behind a plastic cap on the handle that has the name of the manufacturer or a symbol for hot and cold on it. Pop the cap and unscrew the screw that is behind it and remove the handle (fig. 1). The cartridge will be a small bolt sticking out of the wall. You can screw it out of the wall by using an

plumbing

145

adjustable wrench (fig. 2), then bring the cartridge to your plumbing supply store and get a new one. Back home, screw the cartridge into the wall (fig. 3), and then turn the water supply back on in your basement. Wait a few minutes to let the water pressure build up before you check your shower. If it isn't dripping, you can screw the handle back on and you're done.

163 Why is there water damage near the bathroom?

If there's a water stain or dripping in the ceiling of the room beneath the bathroom, chances are it's caused by one of four issues. The first is the grout between the bath tiles coming loose. When this happens, you'll get water pooling behind the wall and seeping into the ceiling below. The second is water getting into the wall because the shower or tub spout handles are not sealed correctly or tight enough against the wall. The third is a leak in the piping in your shower, toilet, or sink. The fourth is a problem that occurs only with stand-up showers. Underneath the stand-up shower is a membrane made out of lead, copper, or vinyl called the pan. Pans wear out, and when they do, they spring leaks.

164 Where is that bathroom leak coming from?

The best way to figure out where a leak in your bathroom is coming from is to start with the grout. Just eyeball it. If you see that grout is missing, replace it, wait a few days, and see if you are still getting the leak. (To learn how to replace grout, go to chapter 9 and the section on tiles.) If you still have a leak after you've fixed the grout, you have plumbing issues. Go to the hardware store and buy three different-colored dyes. Essentially, you sprinkle a different colored dye in the tub, toilet, and sink and go to the floor below and see which color is leaking through. If you have a leak in the plumbing, you need to call a plumber. The fix may involve opening a wall and other issues that you can't address yourself.

165 When water comes up around the base of a sink handle

If you see water pooling at the base of the hot and cold water handles of your sink, you have a problem with one of two things: either the cartridge, which is what controls the flow of the water, or the rubber gasket that sits at the base of the handle. The handle is attached to the water pipe with a screw; that screw is usually located underneath a cap that has the brand name of the faucet or the symbol for hot or cold on it. You can flip that cap off with a flat-head screwdriver. In the pipe is the cartridge, and at the base of the cartridge is the rubber gasket.

Before you attempt any fix, turn off the valve that sends water to the handle. Unscrew the handle. You'll see the pipe, with the cartridge in it and a nut at its top and the gasket at its base. Try tightening the nut, which will increase the pressure between the counter and the handle and cut off the water flow. Turn the water back on. If you still see leakage, you probably have a rotted gasket. Now you have to loosen the cartridge again by loosening the nut you just tightened. Remove the cartridge, and the gasket will be sitting there at the base. Remove the gasket and take it to your local hardware store and match it to what is available there. Gaskets are generic, and you don't need to worry about brands. Back home, place the new gasket at the base, screw the cartridge back in, and turn on the water.

166 Dealing with pipe stinks around the house

Now and then you'll smell a kind of rotten egg scent coming out of your sinks and tubs. It comes from the buildup of material in the drains. There's a quick home remedy for this. Boil a big pot of water and pour it down the drain. Don't think the hot water from the faucet or shower is going to get the job done. It isn't hot enough. You need a rolling boil. The intense heat will break up what's in there. If one pot doesn't work, try a few more. Eventually the smell ought to go away.

You may also detect bad smells in the basement, particularly after someone flushes the toilet. The culprit in this case could be a few different things. Most likely you have a loose cap on the main sewer trap to the house. As you'll recall, the main sewer trap is usually located in your basement in the front of your house where your sewer line goes to your septic tank or city waste line. There is a cap on top of this trap that is designed to be opened and closed. Find the cap and tighten it with your hands. If you are still getting a smell, it may be because you have a blockage somewhere in the system. Call a plumber.

TRICK OF THE TRADE: *Whatever you do, if you think you have a blockage in the system, don't unscrew the cap. If you do, you may get a rather unpleasant spray in your face. If the cause isn't a loose cap or a blockage, you may have a cracked pipe. In any event, you'll need to call your plumber.*

167 How does my septic system work?

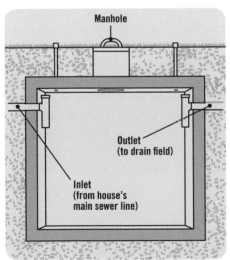

Manhole

Outlet
(to drain field)

Inlet
(from house's
main sewer line)

If a house isn't connected to a municipal sewer line, its plumbing is attached to a septic system. A septic system is a tank that is typically buried beneath the lawn. The tank holds the waste and disperses it slowly into the dirt. As nasty as this sounds, it works really well and can work well for decades. But you do need to pump the septic system out now and then. There's a large concrete cap at the top of the tank. Sometimes it is buried. A licensed pro will come to your house, open the tank, attach a pipe, and pump out the tank. If your home is new, you can get away with pumping the tank every two years. If you have an older home, you'll want to do this every year. In fact, any homeowner should think about pumping his or her septic system once a year. For the price of a few restaurant dinners, you'll save yourself a lot of heartache. When a septic system gets too full, it will back up into your lawn. Then you will be the most unpopular person on your block. Everyone will smell it, and you'll see mushy spots on the lawn and bad things in your basement.

168 Dealing with washing machine issues

In effect the washing machine is like a sink or a tub, with hot water and cold water lines going into it, and a drain line coming out of it. But the water pipes from the wall travel to the machine by way of flexible piping that enters the washing machine through a kind of box that is there to allow for a smooth transition. The biggest problem with washing machines isn't about plumbing but about the functioning of the machine itself. A washing machine works by filling up with water. There is a sensor within the machine that tells it when the machine is full and is ready to drain. Now and then this sensor will malfunction, and the washing machine will keeping filling and overflowing until a person in the house realizes this is happening and stops the process. That can take a while. There is, however, a simple fix for this. There's something called a flood stopper, which is a sensor and valve system that attaches to the washing machine and will shut off the water flow when there's a flood.

169 How to connect a flood sensor to a washing machine

Yes, you can do this yourself. It's not that hard. A flood sensor consists of two valves, each with a wire connecting it to an alarm and another wire going from the alarm box to a sensor, which is a flat piece of plastic with metal lines running through it. The flood sensor will come with its own instructions. In general, however, to connect the flood sensor you shut off the water, attach the valves to the hot and cold pipes that run into the washing machine box, and then place the sensor underneath the washing machine. The flood sensor can be plugged into a jack or run off of battery power. Turn it on. If the washing machine floods, the sensor will detect water underneath it and the valves will close, shutting the water supply to the machine.

Electricity

The electrical system in your house is remarkably simple. The current comes in, flows into your appliances through wires and connections of various sorts, and flows out. A good, professionally wired electrical system should function well and last for quite some time. However, it never hurts to check your electrical system. The issue with electricity is that when it goes wrong, you can have fires, and that is no joke. On the other hand, most of us use electricity every day without any major mishaps. If you treat electricity with respect, then you should have no problems.

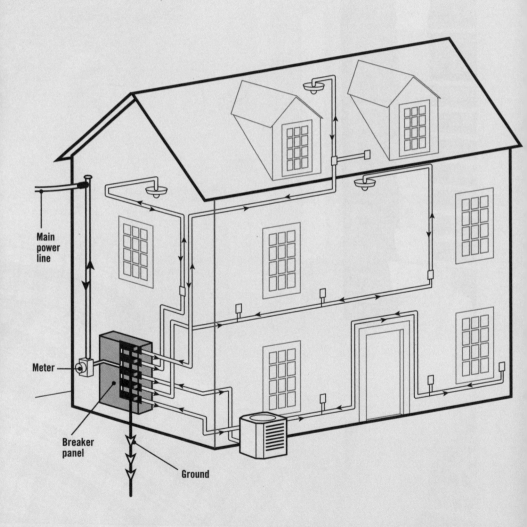

Main power line

Meter

Breaker panel

Ground

170 How is electricity delivered throughout a house?

There are two ways electricity comes to your home from the local utility: overhead wires or underground wires. Either way, the power enters your house through a main pair of hot and neutral wires that come from the utility and pass through a meter, which reads the amount of energy usage in the home, and then on to an end box, which makes the transition from the main power line into the wires from your home. From the end box, the main hot and neutral wires go into the circuit breaker panel. From the panel, the electricity delivered by the main hot wire is distributed throughout the house and the returning electricity from the home's neutral wires is delivered back to the utility.

One pair of main wires comes into the circuit breaker panel, and from there a series of pairs of wires branches out through the house. Each pair of wires consists of a hot wire sheathed in black rubber and a neutral wire sheathed in white. These are grouped together in two kinds of tubing: metal-sheathed wiring is usually referred to by electricians as BX cable but is technically known as AC or armored cable; plastic-sheathed cable is usually referred to by electricians as Romex cable, which is a brand name, but it is technically called NM cable. Most newer homes will be wired with the plastic-sheathed Romex cable, although some localities demand BX cable—it all depends. Whatever they are sheathed in, these wires bring the electricity directly to outlets, light switches, and the major appliances, which then take their own dedicated wiring.

171 When is it all right for me to make an electrical fix?

The short answer to this question is never. There is something called the National Electric Code. It isn't a law itself—it's produced by a nongovernmental body called the National Fire Protection Association. But use of its standards is mandated by law in many places. Under this code, homeowners are prohibited from undertaking any electrical repairs or projects at all. That means that unless you are a licensed electrician, you aren't allowed to touch your electrical system. The reason for this is that if you mess up an electrical repair or installation, you are literally playing with fire or you could receive a life-threatening electric shock. So this chapter is unique in this book, because the information we are giving you here is meant solely to help you understand how your house works. That said, many homeowners do undertake simple electrical fixes. We aren't recommending that you work with your electrical system. It's your choice, but if you do decide to undertake repairs, always treat the work with the utmost care for your safety.

172 Electricity: the basics

You plug a radio into an outlet, turn it on, and it works! Well, how does that happen? Without going into all the gritty details, let's run through the general concept. At its most basic level, to make an electric device work you need a pair of wires. Wires always work in pairs and come in pairs. You never have a single wire going to a device. The two wires in the pair are a hot wire, usually sheathed in black rubber, which delivers electricity to the device, and a neutral wire, usually sheathed in white rubber, which takes the electricity away and sends it back to the utility, where it is dissipated into the earth somewhere. All wiring, all electricity in the house, all outlets, and all electric devices in the house are based on this dual form of wiring. The hot wire brings the electricity in, and the neutral wire takes it away again. If you keep that in mind as we go forward, then electricity, which can sometimes seem like magic, will actually come to seem quite simple.

You may also see a green wire. Be patient. We'll get to it.

173   Reading your electric meter

You don't need to read your electric meter any more than you do your water meter. But as we said before, knowledge is power, and there is no reason that you can't keep track of your electricity usage if you want to and check to make sure the local utility is charging you a fair price. Electric meters measure electricity in kilowatt-hours. A handy way to think about it is that a one-hundred-watt lightbulb burning for ten hours uses one kilowatt-hour. There are two common kinds of meters, the dial and the digital, and neither is that hard to understand. Digital meters are easy to read. Just take down the numbers as you would on an automobile odometer and you are done.

The dial meter has five dials. Each dial will have zero to nine arranged around it like a clock and a single hand that is spinning, however slowly. From left to right the dials represent tens of thousands, thousands, hundreds, tens, and ones respectively. Don't be thrown by the fact that some dials are going clockwise and some counterclockwise. Just start from left to right and take down the number closest to the hand. You should end up with a five-digit number. Wait a set amount of time—say, twenty-four hours, a week, or a month—and take down the new number. Subtract the old number from the new number and you have your energy usage for that time period. Or consult your power bill.

174 Measuring the energy in your house

When we speak about electricity in the home, we tend to use two units of measurement: amps (short for amperes) and watts. One amp equals around ninety watts. Each outlet in the house (and each wire that services that outlet) is designed to deal with a certain amount of energy. For example, most outlets and light fixtures are serviced by wires rated to carry either fifteen or twenty amps. This is more than adequate to deal with the amount of energy required by most appliances that would be plugged into an outlet or most lights that would be attached to a light fixture. However, some appliances require more power. A great example is an electric oven, which might need fifty amps and would have to be serviced by a dedicated wire designed to carry that much power.

TRICK OF THE TRADE: *An unlikely appliance that often needs a lot of power is the electric hair dryer. What makes this even more of a problem is that hair dryers are typically plugged into regular outlets that do not provide enough electricity to make the dryer work. When that happens you get an overload, the circuit breaker kicks in, and your hair stays wet.*

175 How a circuit breaker works

The circuit breaker panel is a metal box with two rows of toggles in it that look like basic light switches turned on their sides so that they run horizontally. You might find the main breaker panel in a one-family house located in the basement. The circuit breaker is really a simple thing. It acts like a traffic cop that directs the energy

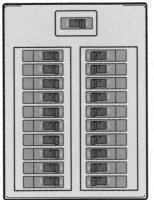

coming into the house from the local utility, dividing that energy into smaller parcels and sending it to each power source in the home in just the right amount. The main wire goes into the breaker from the utility, and a series of smaller wires snake out from it to the house. The breaker panel will have a top toggle or a set of two or three toggles that can shut down the whole house in one flick of a switch. Each of the other toggles on the panel controls the flow of energy to a single hot wire. That wire may deliver energy to a series of outlets, light fixtures, and appliances—say, all in one room—or it may go to a single outlet, light, or major appliance. For a variety of reasons, the wire in question might overheat. When that happens, the breaker senses this and shuts off the power to that wire.

176 Navigating a circuit breaker

Before you go near your circuit breaker, keep in mind these four points:

1. Never touch a circuit breaker with both hands.
2. Always wear rubber-soled shoes.
3. Never stand on wet or damp ground.
4. If possible, stand on a rubber mat.

As long as you stick to these rules, you should avoid receiving a shock from the breaker. As we said, each of the toggles on the breaker deals with the electricity running through a single wire that goes to a series of outlets, lights, or an appliance. The appliances that require a dedicated line in your circuit breaker include things

electricity

like microwaves, toaster ovens, and coffeemakers. Some larger appliances, like refrigerators and dishwashers, actually don't need their own lines, although it is preferable that they have them. Good rule of thumb: if more than twenty amps are needed, then you might consider a dedicated line. In any event, it is vital for the homeowner to know which toggle on the panel goes with which part of the house. Imagine being at home and seeing a fire start in an outlet. Wouldn't you like to know which breaker to switch off? For this reason, in many places it's the law that each breaker toggle must be properly marked. To label your breaker panel, do what the pros do. Grab an assistant. One person stands at the breaker, shutting off each toggle in turn, while the other person calls down to say what part of the house shut off with that toggle. Then the person at the panel takes some tape and labels each toggle.

177 How to open, shut, and reset a breaker

A circuit breaker will usually have two columns of toggles. The toggles will often, but not always, be marked ON and OFF. The ON position is always inside, and the OFF position is outside—in other words, the two columns are mirror images of each other. However, each toggle may have a third position in the center that is unmarked. In all cases, when the toggle is on, it will point inward toward the inside of the panel, and electricity will flow to the wire. In a panel with toggles that have just two positions, when the breaker breaks, the toggle will point outward, away from the center of the panel, to OFF. In a panel that has three positions, however, when the breaker is broken, the toggle points straight up in an intermediary position between ON and OFF. If you want to reset a breaker that has broken in order to get energy flowing again through that breaker, move the toggle in question all the way first to the outside (past pointing straight up in some cases), then to the inside. If that breaker should happen to break again right after you have reset it, you can assume you have a problem on that wire. Either it is consistently being asked to deliver too much energy, or you have a short circuit and you will need to fix the situation before using that wire again.

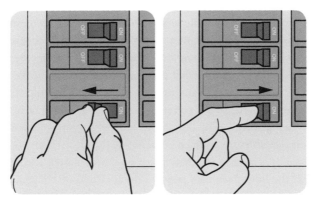

1. Push the lever fully OFF.   2. Then push it fully to the ON position.

WHY A BREAKER BREAKS

An overloaded wire is easy to understand. You have a wire that is designed to carry a given amount of electricity, and you ask it to carry more than it is designed for, because you are either using multiple appliances simultaneously on a single line or using a single appliance that requires more energy all at once than the wire can manage easily. As we mentioned, the biggest culprit for this second kind of overload is the hair dryer, a small but energy-sucking device that has caused many a breaker to trip.

The other main reason a breaker will break is a short circuit. A short is caused by a bare wire coming in contact with another bare wire or with a metal object in the wall, like an air duct.

178 Why is there more than one breaker panel in my house?

You will find this in larger homes that have too many wires in them for one panel to handle or in homes that are, or were, multiple-unit dwellings. If you live in a condo, say, that has three apartments in one building, each apartment should have its own panel. You may also find a second breaker panel on a higher floor of the house, usually near a kitchen, a bathroom, or a major appliance like a washer/dryer. The reason for this is convenience. Let's say a new or updated kitchen is being installed in a house. Instead of running six or seven new power cables up from the basement, the electrician will run one big line up, attach it to a new panel at the site of the kitchen, and branch off the lines from that panel. This is also more convenient for the homeowner, because it allows him or her to cut off the power right on the spot, instead of having to go down into the basement.

TRICK OF THE TRADE: *If a secondary panel is installed, the breaker in the basement will have a group of two or three toggles next to one another that will shut down the entire secondary panel.*

179 Do I have enough power in my house?

The question of whether you have enough power comes up a lot when you purchase a new home, but it can raise its head anytime. The circuit breaker panel places a limitation on the amount of power coming into your house. Each house is different, and each family uses power in a different way, so there is no answer to the question "How much power should I have coming to my house?" That said, there are ways you can tell if you have too little power coming in. There is really no such thing as too much power. If you have more power than you need coming into your breaker, then you'll use what you need and forget the rest.

But if you have too little power coming in, you will notice. Your main breaker will be tripping a lot, meaning that more than a few times a year it will shut down and have to be reset. In an adequately wired house, the circuit breakers shouldn't ever break. If a breaker is tripping when you use a certain appliance, you don't have enough power on that breaker for that appliance. A normal house will have a total of around one hundred amps of available power. That is just a rule of thumb. If you think you might be underserved power-wise, you can hire an electrician to come in and do a test to determine how much power you have and how much you need.

180   Doing a power upgrade in your house . . . or not

This is a major job and needs to be done by a licensed pro. He will have to replace the meter, which is rated for a certain amount of amperage, replace the end box, replace or upgrade the panel of toggles on the circuit breaker, and replace all the wiring from the utility to the circuit breaker. In most parts of the country this will cost thousands of dollars.

There is, however, another choice: live within the amperage you have. Don't run powerful devices at the same time. When buying new appliances, make sure you go for the ones that are rated as energy efficient. This is really no different from living in a house where there isn't enough hot water for two people to shower at the same time. Some people in the house may have to wait. It isn't the end of the world. The only thing you need to be careful of is that you don't have a situation that will create endless overloads, like a kitchen with a microwave and an electric oven that use the same wiring.

181 Dealing with a fuse box

Some readers may find they have a panel in their basement with little glass-covered gizmos inside. These are fuses. Fuses were the old-fashioned system that circuit breakers replaced. They look somewhat like stubby lightbulbs, with a lightbulb base and a glass-encased top with a copper wire in it. The fuse plays the same role as a breaker. When too much power goes over the wire, the fuse burns out, and when that happens, power is shut off to the wire in question. Fuses are also like lightbulbs in that you simply unscrew the burnt-out fuse and screw in a new one. If you have a panel of fuse boxes instead of breakers in your house, you should replace it. Breaker panels are just safer. Also, if you have a fuse-box panel, it is probably old, and if the panel is old, then the wiring behind it is old, and those wires are a likely fire hazard. Fuses are also inconvenient, because when they burn out, you need to go to the store and buy new ones of the same amperage. Whatever you decide to do, if you have a fuse that is overloading a lot, do not—under any circumstance—resort to the old ploy of replacing the fuse with a coin or other piece of metal. This is asking for a fire.

182 How a house is wired

The wires that run throughout your house begin at the circuit breaker panel. From there they are snaked throughout the house behind walls and between floors and ceilings. Let's take as an example a second-floor living room. A fifteen- or twenty-amp BX wire will be snaked up inside the wall until it arrives in one corner of the room. There it will be attached to the first outlet. From there, the wires can be looped from outlet to outlet around the room. Just to recapitulate, all of these outlets are connected to a single BX wire and through that wire down to a single circuit breaker in the panel in the basement.

In a kitchen, there will be a series of wires snaked up from the basement, including one wire for the outlets, another for a microwave, and another for a fridge. The most difficult aspect of rewiring a house or fixing bad wiring in a house, therefore, is gaining access to the wires. Often this will involve breaking into walls and baseboards and ceilings. The difficulty increases in older homes that have plaster walls. Sheetrock walls are easier to break into and get behind.

183 Wires: THE DARK SIDE

There are two reasons wiring will break down.

When wires are overloaded, they heat up. This is why wiring is such a fire hazard. If a wire is repeatedly overloaded over time, the constant heat and cooling will effect changes in the metal that will degrade it and its ability to carry electricity.

The other thing that happens is the insulation around the wiring wears away. This can be due to melting caused by overheating, but believe it or not, the most common way this happens is critters. We don't like to think about it, but many houses, even superclean ones, will have rodents in them. Mice and sometimes rats and squirrels will get into the spaces between walls from time to time and chew on wires. When this happens you can get short circuits, meaning two live wires touching each other, or the wire will simply become severed, ending the connection. The wiring will have to be replaced; as we have said before, the big headache with this is gaining access to the wiring itself, which may require opening walls and ceilings.

184 Outlets and why they go bad

Hot slot

Neutral slot

Ground

An electrical outlet (electricians actually call them receptacles, but no one else does) is one of those little plastic or metal rectangles with holes in them that you see all around the baseboards of your home and elsewhere. The holes or slots in outlets come in different shapes around the world, but in North America, an outlet consists of a faceplate that holds either one set or a series of sets of slits. These sets of slits come in pairs, with two parallel vertical slits, or in threes, with two vertical slits above a single circular hole.

Remember what we said before about all wiring including a hot wire for delivering electricity and a neutral wire for taking it away? The outlet forms a bridge between the wiring of the home and an electronic device. The left-hand slit in the pair is connected to the neutral wire. The right-hand slit is connected to the hot wire. Often the slit for the neutral wire will be longer than the slit for the hot wire. When a device is plugged into the outlet, the right-hand, hot-wire slit will deliver electricity; the left-hand, neutral slit will allow the used electricity to pass away, out of the house. The third, circular hole is the grounding. It acts as a second route out of the home for used electricity, but instead of delivering the electricity back to the utility, it sends it away from the house and out into the earth, where it is dissipated. Outlets break when they are worn away from use. Plugs going in and out of the outlet will loosen the slits over time. The other thing that happens is the connection between the outlet and the wiring behind it comes loose, for whatever reason.

electricity

167

185 How to test an outlet or a wire

There's a simple little tool called a voltage circuit tester that can help you determine whether an outlet, a wire, or a breaker panel is functioning as it should. Do not use your fingers, please. Voltage circuit testers are cheap and easy to use, and they could save your life if you are working with electricity, or save you a lot of money if you are trying to figure out whether to call an electrician. Typically the tester consists of a metal tip, or two metal tips, attached to a body that has a light on it. Make sure the tester itself is working properly and has live batteries in it. Take the metal tip and insert it into each of the slits of an outlet, or hold it along a wire. Depending on the model, the tester will light up, beep, or flash if there is electricity flowing properly through the wire or through the outlet. It is an excellent idea, even a crucial one, to have a tester on hand while doing any electrical work and use it, even after you have shut power down at the breaker panel, to double-check that there's no live electricity anywhere near you when you are working.

HOW TO TEST AN OUTLET OR AN ELECTRONIC DEVICE WITHOUT A VOLTAGE CIRCUIT TESTER

If you don't have a voltage circuit tester handy, you can use an electronic device as a tester, and you can even use the outlets to test a device. If you have an outlet you are worried about, take a device, such as a lamp, that is working when it is plugged into a *different* outlet. Plug it into the outlet that you are worried about and see whether it works. If it doesn't work on that outlet, there is no electricity flowing there. Simple. If it is the device you are worried about, you can check it in reverse. Make sure you have an outlet that is working. Plug the device in question into that outlet, turn it on properly, and see whether anything happens. If the device doesn't work, you probably have a problem with the device.

TRICK OF THE TRADE: *Make sure to buy a tester that is rated for at least five hundred volts.*

186   Removing an outlet

We are talking here about a single-receptacle outlet, meaning it has just one set of slits. Before making any electrical repair, you need to go to the circuit breaker panel and shut off the power to the place where you are making the repair. It is also a good idea to mark the toggle in question PERSON WORKING, or something like that. You should also use a voltage tester to double-check that there's no electrical flow. The outlet sits in a faceplate, which is there simply to cover up the mechanics behind the outlet. Unscrew the faceplate. You will now see that the outlet itself is screwed into a metal box, which is called a junction box. The junction box is just there to hold the outlet in place and create a shield for the wires to keep them from burning down the house if they overheat, or from being attacked by vermin.

Unscrew the outlet from the box. You will now see that the outlet has a black wire and a white wire attached to it, with each wire going into one side of the box. The black wire is typically connected to a gold-colored screw and the white wire to a silver-colored screw. In most cases, you will also find a ground wire, which either is sheathed in green plastic or is just a bare copper. It will be attached to a green screw, which is at the bottom of the outlet. The wires are made out of copper and are rather stiff, so they are usually looped just once around the screw. Loosen the screws and pull the wires off, or unravel them with needle-nose pliers. You have now removed the old outlet.

187   Replacing an outlet

All outlets are essentially the same, so you can just go to a hardware store and buy a replacement. Again, we are speaking here about a single-receptacle outlet. First, shut off the power. Always begin with the white or neutral wire. Then connect the ground wire, and finally connect the black or hot wire. Take the white wire and loop it around the silver screw and tighten the screw. Take the green or copper wire and loop it around the green screw and tighten it. Finally, take the black wire, loop it around the gold screw, and tighten the screw. Before you push the outlet back into the box, take a little electrical tape, which is a special kind of tape you can buy at a hardware store, and wrap some tape around the outside of the outlet so that you cover the three metal screws. This will help prevent shorts when you push the outlet back into the junction box. Now push the outlet back into the junction box. Screw it in. Close the faceplate. Go and turn the circuit breaker back on. Test the outlet.

188 Removing and installing a duplex outlet

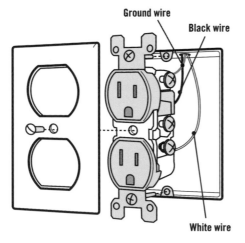

Ground wire

Black wire

White wire

As always, shut off the power to the area in which you are working and use a voltage circuit tester to make sure all the power is off. The idea behind the wiring of a duplex outlet—one with two sets of slots—is exactly the same as the wiring of a single outlet. There are ground, neutral, and hot wires, and they need to be connected from the wall to the outlet. The only complication is that you may have more than one set of wires going into a duplex outlet, depending on how the electrician chose to wire it and whether it is one in the middle of a series of outlets all wired together, or the last in a line. Once you have removed the faceplate and unscrewed the outlet from the junction box, take a good look at it and sketch a diagram of all the wires on a piece of paper so you'll be sure which wires go to which connection. You may find two sets of wires connected to the outlet, or you may see just one. Remove the wires and attach the new outlet to the box in exactly the same way the old outlet was attached.

189 What is a GFI outlet, and why do I need one?

Reset button

Test button

Actually the proper acronym should be GFCI, which stands for ground fault circuit interrupter, but most electricians just call them GFIs. The GFI is an outlet that has its own circuit breaker built in, almost. It isn't quite the same as a circuit breaker because the breaker in the GFI is right on-site and will trip immediately if the wire starts to overheat. You've seen this kind of outlet in bathrooms, where you often find them, or in kitchens, or outdoors. They look like double-receptacle outlets, with two buttons in between them. You need GFIs in places where you have water, because, as you know, water and electricity are a combustible mix. GFIs are also a good idea in places where there are plugged-in appliances like blow dryers or toasters, which may require more electricity than the outlet can handle. If you don't have GFIs in your house in kitchens, bathrooms, and outdoor areas, you should replace the regular outlets with GFIs.

171

190   How to use the GFI

The GFI has two buttons on it, one to test the unit and the other to reset it in case of a real incident. In theory, you should check your GFIs once a month. Nobody does this. But really, you should check them as often as possible. Do the best you can; it's for your own safety. To test the unit, press the test button down. When you do this, the GFI should trip instantaneously. If it doesn't, you need to replace the unit. If you are using a hair dryer, let's say, and the GFI trips, you'll hear a click, and the reset button will pop out. You can push the button back in to reset it and resume drying. Here's the deal: sometimes GFIs click for no good reason. If the GFI clicks again, then you may have a real problem with the blow dryer, the GFI, or the amount of amperage you are using on the wire. At this point you might want to switch your blow dryer to another GFI outlet, just to be safe. You might also test the first GFI outlet by plugging a different appliance into it and using that.

191   Replacing a GFI

A GFI is an outlet, plain and simple, and will go wrong much the same way a regular outlet will. It will stop delivering electricity. When that happens, you need to check the wiring and perhaps replace the GFI. Changing a GFI is the same as changing a regular outlet. Shut off the power. Remove the faceplate. Unscrew the outlet from the junction box. Detach the wires from the screws on the GFI. Buy a new one, and install it. The only added issue is that there's a breaker switch that may fail and not allow you to reset it. Before you replace the entire GFI, go to the main breaker panel and make sure the breaker is not tripped. If it is tripped, the GFI will not reset. If the problem isn't at the panel, then you do need to replace the GFI.

192   Splicing electrical wires

You will need to know something about splicing wires in order to deal with electrical fixtures. Splicing is a way of connecting two wires. As always, the first step is to turn off the electricity. You may have to strip the plastic sheathing off the wires you are going to splice. There is a tool for this called a wire stripper. This is a pliers-type device that has little circles in it for different gauges, or widths, of wire. To splice a wire, you need to expose about an inch of wire, removing the sheathing to that depth. You remove the sheathing by placing the wire in the wire stripper, pressing down gently at the point you want to remove the plastic, and then pulling the plastic off. Take your two stripped wires side by side and use a pair of regular pliers to twist them together until they're essentially braided together. Finish the job by screwing a wire cap over the splice. A wire cap looks like a plastic thimble with threading inside it. You place it over the braided wires and screw it down, and this holds the wires together and shields you from any electricity.

193   How do light fixtures work?

A light fixture is the electrician's term for a light that sits on the wall or ceiling and is hardwired to your house's power. The fixture is connected to the main wiring of the house through a junction box (sometimes a light fixture's junction box is round, but it is still called a "box"). A light fixture will have the ground, hot, and neutral

electricity

173

wires, just as you would have in an electrical outlet. From the fixture, a hot and a neutral wire will run to the socket. The socket is a short porcelain or plastic tube with grooved metal on the inside. This is where the lightbulb will sit. The socket is wired much the same way an outlet is: hot and neutral wires are screwed into it, or soldered onto it. Sockets do not typically have a ground wire connected to them. Look inside the empty socket. You'll see a gold metal strip at the bottom. That is where the electricity comes into the socket. The grooved metal around the sides is where the used electricity feeds out to the neutral wire.

194　How to fix a loose light fixture

When a light is loose, it isn't really an electrical problem. You'll probably notice that the fixture is loose when you try to replace a lightbulb. These fixtures usually have coverings like glass bowls or glass shades. As you spin the glass bowl to remove it, the fixture itself will rattle around on the ceiling. It shouldn't do that. The fixture should be tight and in no danger of falling down and breaking. The fix for this is easy. Turn off the power to the fixture at the breaker panel. Remove whatever form of covering there is over the lightbulb(s). You will now see that the fixture is attached to the ceiling or wall with screws. Tighten those screws. Replace the covering. Turn the power back on at the breaker panel.

195 Fixing a malfunctioning light fixture

If your light fixture is flickering or not turning on at all, you probably have a faulty socket or a loose connection between wires at the junction box. To make sure the problem isn't a bulb, replace all bulbs with new ones and try the light again. If you are still having difficulties, you may need to make a repair. The first step is to check that the wires are properly spliced. There are many different kinds of fixtures, but one way or the other you'll need to unscrew the fixture from the wall or ceiling. As always, first shut off the power. When you remove the fixture, you'll see the hot wires and the neutral wires spliced to their counterparts from the wall. Take a look at the neutral wires, and screw the wire cap on a little tighter; pull on the wires to make sure they are attached firmly. Do the same for the hot wire, and you are done. Before you put the fixture back on, go to the breaker panel and restore the power. If the light is now functioning well, you have made the repair. If it is still flickering, you may have a socket problem (see entry 198).

196 Replacing a ceiling fixture

In some ways the hardest thing about replacing a ceiling fixture may be dealing with the fixture itself, which can be heavy, fragile, and unwieldy. The electrical part of the equation is relatively easy. For the best results, think about having someone help you. He or she may be able to help hold the fixture up while you work on the wiring. If not, you may find yourself dropping a valuable light, or, worse, falling off the ladder and hurting yourself.

Shut off the power to the fixture. Remove any lightbulb covers and lightbulbs from the fixture. Unscrew the fixture from the junction box. Remove the caps that are holding the spliced wires together. As always, you'll see three wires: white, black, and green. Splice the wires into the wires of the new fixture. Screw the fixture into the wall. You are done.

197   Installing a ceiling fan

Assuming you already have an electrical outlet in place in the ceiling that is attached to the main wiring of the house, you can accomplish this wiring job much as you would for a light fixture. If you need to create a junction box for the fan to sit in, hire a professional. Also, be aware that because fans are heavy and in motion, there are strict requirements about what kind of box they can be attached to. (The box is the metal or plastic container that sits in the ceiling, or wall for that matter, and provides space to attach the light fixture or fan to the ceiling.) First, shut off the power. Detach the existing wires from the existing junction box and remove the box. Chances are you'll need to install a hanger bar for the fan. This is a metal bar that the fan will hang off of. The bar is typically pushed through the hole in the ceiling and screwed into the joists behind the ceiling. Hang the new box off the bar and attach the wiring from the house. Then you'll need to assemble the fan, following the manufacturer's instructions, and wire it to the main wires of the house.

198 Fixing a socket

To fix a socket, start by shutting off the power to the fixture at the breaker panel. Unscrew and remove the lightbulb. Look into the bottom of the socket. If you don't see a screw down there, it's likely that the socket has been soldered into the fixture. The bad news, in that case, is that if there is a problem, the light is probably done for; the good news is that lights constructed this way are usually somewhat cheap and more disposable. If the socket is of the screwed-in variety, make sure, again, that all power to the fixture is off and unscrew it. Pull the socket down, and you'll see the wires connected to it—they may also be either screwed or soldered. If the wires are soldered to the socket, cut them loose with a wire cutter, keeping track of which wire is which. If they are screwed, unscrew them. Always label your wires to remind you which is which (you can use Post-it notes). Sockets come in three basic sizes: small, medium, and large. Take yours down to the hardware store and buy a replacement of the right size. Make sure to buy a socket that can be wired by screwing the wires in, since you don't want to be messing with soldering. There are also sockets that can be spliced in, but the screw-in kind is the simplest. Attach the wires by screwing them down. Most sockets will have a gold screw for the hot wire and a silver screw for the neutral wire. Attach your wires, screw the socket itself into the fixture, and attach a bulb.

199 Lightbulbs: THE DARK SIDE

Sometimes lightbulbs get stuck in their sockets. The best way to prevent this is to make sure not to tighten them too hard when you are screwing them in. The only thing you can do when a bulb gets stuck in the socket is put on some construction gloves and try to unscrew the bulb with more force. Eventually the glass is going to break in your hand. A lightbulb is not like the bolt on a car tire. You must be gentle with it. But fear not: if the glass of the bulb breaks with the bulb in the socket, you can remove the bulb using a pair of needle-nose pliers. Make sure to shut off the power to the light fixture. Take your pliers, grip into the bulb, and turn it to the left carefully. Eventually the bulb will come out.

TRICK OF THE TRADE: *There's another cool fix for unscrewing a broken lightbulb. Use a raw potato. Cut it in half and shove it down on the broken lightbulb and turn it. The sharp edges of the broken bulb will bite into the potato, allowing you to twist the bulb out of the socket. Of course, you must first always turn off the power to the fixture or lamp. And don't eat the potato afterward.*

200 How do I fix a lamp?

There are two differences between a lamp and a light fixture. The lamp derives its power from being plugged into an outlet, and the lamp will typically have an ON/OFF switch attached to it. As always, begin by replacing the bulb. Then check the socket. Also, make sure the problem isn't with the outlet by plugging the lamp into a new socket. Most lamps will have sockets that are screwed into them. Unscrew the socket and check to see whether the wiring to the socket is proper. These wires can be screwed or soldered, depending on the lamp. If the socket is soldered and the wiring has come loose, throw it out or take it to a pro. If it is screwed, tighten the screws and carefully test the light. If it still doesn't work, you can replace the socket, much as you would in a light fixture. Unscrew it, buy a new one at the hardware store, and screw the new one in. Be aware that most lamps have sockets that have switches attached. So when you buy a new one, you'll need to buy one with a switch. Luckily, that means there's no installation for the switch.

201 What are the different kinds of lightbulbs?

Lightbulbs come in many different shapes and sizes, but the following are the most common.

Incandescent: the standard bulb most people are familiar with. Works with a metal wire called a filament that heats up and gives off light. Hot. To increase energy efficiency, these are being phased out in 2012 in Canada and by 2014 in the United States.

Fluorescent: works by passing a current through a chamber filled with various gasses. Long lasting and cool.

electricity

Compact fluorescent: like fluorescent bulbs, but in a smaller package, these are the bulbs that people are using as a more efficient replacement for the standard incandescent bulbs.

Halogen: a variant of the incandescent bulb that uses a different set of chemicals to produce a slightly more efficient form of light. Very hot.

LED: this stands for light-emitting diodes. They last a very long time and are cool and energy efficient, but they do not produce as much light as incandescent bulbs.

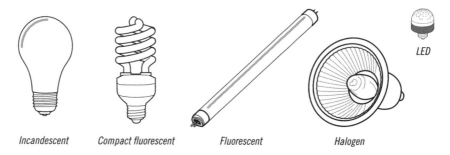

LED

Incandescent   Compact fluorescent   Fluorescent   Halogen

202 How an incandescent lightbulb works

Although they're being phased out, incandescent lightbulbs are still the most common variety, so we thought we'd explain how they operate. The lightbulb is actually a small electrical appliance in and of itself. Like any other electrical appliance, the lightbulb works when energy is sent through it on a hot wire and carried away from it on a neutral wire. But instead of being plugged into an outlet, the way most appliances are, the bulb is screwed into a socket. The small metal nipple at the base of the bulb touches the golden strip at the bottom of the socket, which is itself wired to the hot wire. The metal grooves around the base of the lightbulb fit into the metal grooves in the socket, which are wired to the neutral wire. Two wires inside the bulb are attached to the nipple and the grooves, respectively, and these run up into the filament, which is that small wire you can see suspended between two other wires inside the bulb. When you plug in the bulb and turn on the light, electricity runs into the filament, and the bulb lights up. Incandescent bulbs also give off a lot of heat, which is why they are inefficient in comparison to compact fluorescents, because incandescent bulbs convert a lot of the energy put into them into useless heat rather than light.

203 How a basic light switch works

Please note that we are talking here about a single-pole light switch—a single switch that is dedicated to controlling a single light fixture. (There are so-called three-way switches, which are systems where multiple switches are attached to a single light, as well as dimmer switches, which can make the light brighter or dimmer.) Like the breaker panel, the light switch is the traffic cop that allows energy to flow from the main power supply to a light fixture (or prevents it from flowing).

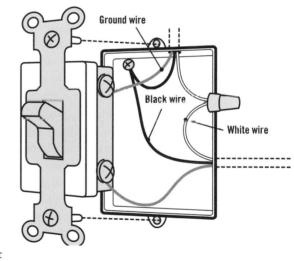

If you pull the panel off a light switch, you will see something very similar to what is inside an outlet. There will be a metal or plastic box with wires running into it: black for the hot wire, white for the neutral wire, and green or copper for the ground wire. The two white wires will be spliced together. These are the neutral wires from the main electrical line and from the light fixtures. The two black wires will be screwed into the apparatus of the switch itself. Those two wires connect the fixture to the main power. When the switch is turned off, the connection is broken, and no energy runs into the fixture. When the switch is turned on, energy flows, and the light turns on.

204 How a dimmer switch works

A dimmer is an ON/OFF switch that has something called a resistor, which doesn't shut off the entire flow of energy to the bulb but allows less energy to go into the bulb. The resistor is within a closed, factory-sealed box. If a dimmer switch goes bad—and they do blow out—you must replace the whole dimmer switch. The good news is that a switch with a dimmer is usually wired exactly the same way as a standard switch, and replacing it is exactly the same.

However, you may find some dimmer switches where instead of two screws on the switch, there are two wires. In that case you need to splice the wires. First, turn off the electricity to the switch. You then take the wire from the main house line and splice it to the wire leading into the switch; then take the wire leading out of the switch and splice that to the wire going to the fixture; finally, put wire caps on each splice. Sometimes the dimmer will come with an instruction book explaining which wire goes in and which wire goes out.

205 Light Switches:
THE DARK SIDE

Light switches almost never stop working. When they do, it is because the wiring has come loose. The other problem that can arise is that too many lights are connected to one switch and the switch overloads and burns out.

To replace a switch, turn off the electricity to the switch. Unscrew the plate from the wall and pull the switch out. There is usually 6 to 8 inches of slack on the wires, so you can get them pretty far out. Make a clear map of where the wires go. Unscrew and unsplice the wires connected to the switch and pull the wires away from the switch. Remove the switch and buy a new one. All basic switches are the same; the only difference among them is aesthetic. Screw the wires into the switch, making sure the wires are screwed in very tightly. Put the switch back in the wall and screw the plate back in.

TRICK OF THE TRADE: *It is always a good idea to use a little electrical tape over the screws to prevent shock or shorts when you are putting a switch into or taking one out of the wall.*

206 Fixing a buzzing lightbulb or dimmer switch

This is a very common problem. It is very rare that a lightbulb will hum when it is on a basic switch. Most of the bulbs that buzz do so when the switch is connected to a dimmer and the light is slightly dimmed. There are two ways to fix this. First, you can replace an older bulb that may still be working, but is buzzing, with a new one. There may be a piece inside the older bulb that has loosened, and once the bulb is turned on, this loose piece starts vibrating, causing the humming. The second problem can be with the dimmer switch. There are times when the dimmer switch is not compatible with the bulb you are using. If that is the case, call an electrician, who can come and give you advice on exactly which bulb you need to use.

207 How and when to clean the appliances in your home

The main message here is that you should be cleaning your appliances regularly. Besides the obvious aesthetic and hygiene issues involved, if you have caked dirt on an appliance, there's probably also dirt that's worked its way into the mechanics of that appliance, and when that happens you are on your way to a costly repair. Each appliance will have its own special needs, but generally you'll want to have a look at each machine in the house at the bare minimum once a month, and for most kitchen appliances that you use regularly, once a week. For machines with stainless steel exteriors, buy a cleaner made specifically for stainless appliances. Any widely available glass cleaner will work for glass surfaces, and good old soap and warm water will do for most other jobs.

208   Cleaning an oven

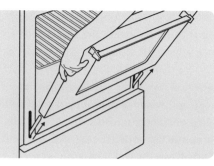

We're assuming now that you actually use your oven, because we know plenty of people who never turn their ovens on. If you do use this appliance, you should clean it once a month. This is back-straining work, and you can make your life easier by lifting the oven door off its hinges for easier access. Be aware, however, that oven doors are very heavy, and you should consider having a friend help you if you decide to lift the door off. That said, the door should come off its hinges fairly easily and simply slide back onto them when you are ready to put it back on. For most oven cleaning jobs, you can use soap and warm water. For caked-on dirt, try a mildly abrasive cleanser or a soap-filled pad, but be gentle with these.

Self-cleaning ovens are ovens that will heat up to a high temperature, which has the effect of burning away the old food in the oven. If you have a self-cleaning oven, you should use that function once a month. If you are using a self-cleaning oven, you should clean it with soap and water once in a while too. But don't clean it with household spray cleaners or other abrasive cleaners, because they will ruin the porcelain interior. Oven grates can be taken out and soaked in warm water and soap for easy cleaning.

209   Cleaning and maintaining a cooktop

There are three different kinds of cooktops found in most homes: gas burners over a porcelain or glass top; electric burners with a smooth, ceramic top; and electric coils above a porcelain surface. Back in the day, you could lift most cooktops and clean underneath them, but these days most cooktops are sealed. If you should happen to have a stove with a top that opens, you should clean underneath it about once a month, using a wet rag to wipe up grease and stains. Be very gentle and careful not to knock any of the electric or gas connections out of place.

For a glass cooktop with a sealed top, make sure you clean after every time you cook, using soap and water to pick up any food spills and grease before they get caked on. There is also a chance that the burner holes, where the flame comes out, can get clogged, and when that happens you won't have any flame, or you'll have an erratic flame. You can try to unclog the burners by using a toothpick; if that doesn't work, you are going to need a repairman. The metal grates that sit over gas cooktops get dulled by the flames. You can quickly fix this by cleaning them with a paper towel dipped in olive oil. They will look like new. For a smooth, ceramic-topped electric cooktop, you can buy products specifically designed for cleaning this kind of surface. For electric coils above a porcelain top, just use some soapy water and elbow grease. If there is anything caked on, use a single-edged razor blade to carefully scratch it off.

210 Cleaning a range hood

A range hood is an appliance that sits above your cooktop and is designed to remove greasy air, smells, and fumes from the kitchen and expel them outside the house. Whenever you clean your oven, clean your range hood as well. A range hood may have two elements that you need to clean: the filter and the body of the hood itself. If the filter is removable, you can take it out, give it a good soak in warm soapy water, and scrub it. If the filter is beyond dirty, you can see whether you can buy a new one and replace it. For the body of the range hood, you should clean it with soap and water too, unless

the range hood is stainless steel—in that case, use a stainless steel cleaner. If you have grease caked onto your range hood, you can try carefully nudging it off with a sharp razor. You can also try using a very weak solution of ammonia in warm water, maybe four-fifths water to one-fifth ammonia, and use a sponge or a paper towel to see whether you can loosen the grease. Then clean with stainless steel cleaner or soap and water. Be careful when cleaning the range hood not to knock it off the wall. Some range hoods are installed more delicately than you might think.

211 Cleaning and maintaining a microwave

If you have an old microwave—let's say, more than ten years old—think about replacing it. The older a microwave oven gets, the greater its propensity to allow radiation leakage, usually through a faulty seal in the door. Although the type of radiation generated by microwave ovens has not been shown to be harmful to human beings, except at levels far higher than the average microwave oven can produce, why bother with it? Get a new one.

Ideally a microwave should be attached to its own outlet with a dedicated power line. These appliances require some serious amperage, and your microwave will run better and your house will be in less danger of an electrical fire if each microwave has its own power source. If your microwave breaks down, do not attempt to fix it yourself. Take it to a professional. Clean the interior after every use with soap and water, making sure to remove all caked-on bits of food.

electricity

212 Cleaning and maintaining a dishwasher

Most people neglect to clean the inside of their dishwashers, but it's an important thing to do. Give the interior a washing once a month, or at least a few times a year. The best soap to use for cleaning the inside of a dishwasher is the detergent you are using in that appliance to clean your dishes. Use a sponge to clean out the inside of the machine and then run it once with just water to wash it out. If you use any other kind of soap, you'll create a buildup of unwanted suds that may clog your machine. Make sure that the baskets by the drain, which are at the bottom of the unit, are kept clear and free of debris. Run your dishwasher at least once a week to keep the seals around the door moist and to make sure oil is flowing through the motor. Clean the outside of a dishwasher at least once a week with a soft damp cloth and mild detergent or stainless steel cleaner, depending on what the surface of the dishwasher is.

213 Cleaning a refrigerator

We're not talking about cleaning the inside of the fridge, although that is also a good thing to do. We are talking about cleaning the machinery of the appliance. The most important thing you can do to keep your fridge in good running order is to keep the condenser coils clean and free of dust. These coils are what help make the refrigerator cold, and they work best if they are clean. You should clean the coils at least once a year, although once every six months would be ideal. In most models, the coils are located at the bottom of the unit with a plastic grille in front of them. You should remove the grille, which will usually be screwed in, and gently vacuum the coils or use a feather duster on them. In some of the pricier units and those that are custom made for a particular kitchen, you'll find the grille and the coils atop the unit. Again, the same process applies. Unscrew the grille and give the coils a gentle dusting or vacuuming.

214 Cleaning and maintaining clothes washers and dryers

Washing machines will work best if you take the time to run them empty at least once a month with the same detergent and bleach you would use for your clothes. For dryers, clean the lint screen carefully after every single load. You should also clean your vent line, the tube or duct that sends the air from the dryer to outside your house, at least twice a year. This is important because if lint gets trapped in the line, it can cause a fire. If you have a relatively short line, you can get away with using a long-handled, stiff-bristled brush dryer duct cleaning brush, which you can buy at the hardware store. Just open up the line and give it a good scrubbing. Opening up the line should be self-explanatory. Depending on the model, you would either unscrew it or pop it out. If you have a longer vent line, you will need to attach the brush to a length of electrical fish tape, which is the wire that electricians use to snake electrical wires through houses. This will allow you to feed the brush through the length of the vent.

Heating and Cooling

In many homes the heating and cooling systems are unrelated mechanically. There's a boiler to provide heat and either window air conditioners or some kind of central air system to provide cooling. In other homes heating and cooling are parts of a unified system. One way or the other, we are going to talk about heating and cooling in the same chapter, because they provide the same essential function, which is making the home more comfortable.

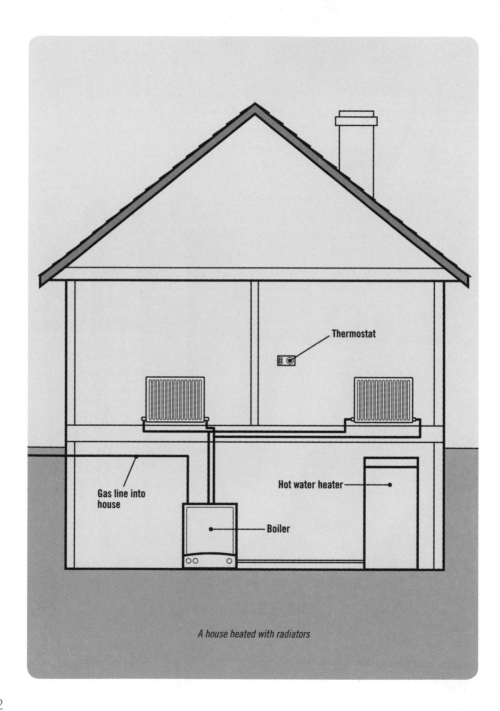

Thermostat

Gas line into house

Hot water heater

Boiler

A house heated with radiators

215   How is my home heated?

The beginning of all heat in the home is a boiler. The boiler—also
known as a furnace—is essentially an oven. It consists of a box with
a fire source at the bottom. If the boiler is powered by gas, there
will be a series of small flames, like you might have on a cooktop.
If the boiler is powered by oil, there will be a sealed chamber where
the oil is ignited into a single larger flame. The boiler may also be
connected to the water supply of the house.

If you have radiators, the boiler will heat water and send hot
water or steam to the radiators. If you have baseboard heating
radiators, the boiler will send hot water to them. If you have a forced
air system, the boiler will heat water, and air will be passed over it
and go into your house through a duct system.

Some houses may also have rooms heated with something called
radiant heat, which is a system where heating coils are installed
beneath the flooring. In some radiant heat systems the coils will be
heated with hot water from the boiler, or from a dedicated heater. In
other radiant systems the heat will come from electrical coils.

216   How to shut your boiler down

Almost all boilers have two emergency switches, typically one on the
boiler and one at the top of the stairs to the basement. They look like
old-fashioned light switches but are colored red. If you think there's a
problem with your boiler—for example, if you smell smoke or soot or
if the boiler just isn't working—shut it off. Better safe than sorry, and
you may prevent a fire or a smoke disaster in your home. Also, there
is no harm in turning off your boiler. You can shut it down and then
turn it on again without fear of damaging the boiler or the pipes.

217 Why to get a service contract for a boiler

When something goes wrong with your boiler, shut it down right away. Your next step is to call a local boiler maintenance company. Whatever else you do in life, sign up for a boiler maintenance contract. For an annual charge that equals what most people pay for cable television and telephone service for one month, you will have year-round twenty-four-hour service if something goes wrong. And here's the thing: something *always* goes wrong with boilers, and something usually goes wrong with boilers when it's really cold out, and, although this isn't scientific, a lot of the time these problems seem to occur late at night and on weekends, moments when almost no one will answer your call except a company you have a contract with. Chances are if you have oil heat, you'll be offered a boiler service contract by the company that provides you with the oil. If you have gas heat, you'll have to find a plumber or a boiler maintenance company.

218 Maintaining a boiler

Have your service company come and do an annual service at the end of the summer or in early autumn, right before the prime central heating season. Otherwise, there's only one thing you have to do directly to the boiler. If your heating system involves water or steam going up into the house, you'll have to flush your boiler. At the side of the boiler you'll see a valve, a glass tube partly filled with water, and a spigot. Once a week during the winter and once every two weeks during the summer, place a bucket underneath the spigot and release the valve to flush water out of the boiler. Be careful, because this water will be scalding hot. You'll typically see a slightly dirty flow, followed by a really dirty flow, followed by cleaner water. When you see the cleaner water, close the valve. You will now need to add some water back into the boiler. The level of water in the glass tube tells you how much you'll need to add. For most systems you'll want to keep the tube a third to half filled. You can have your boiler service guy mark the tube where he thinks the water should go. The truth is that the system will be more efficient with slightly less water in it. You let the water into the boiler via a small valve that will usually be located somewhere on top of the boiler. If you can't find this valve, call your service provider.

219 How does hot water work?

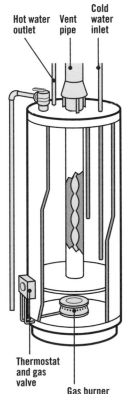

Hot water outlet **Vent pipe** **Cold water inlet**

Thermostat and gas valve

Gas burner

The hot water in most homes comes from a large tank, which is kept warm all the time. The water in the tank is heated one of three ways. If the home is heated with oil, the water tank is heated directly off the boiler. If the home is heated by gas, the hot water tank will have its own built-in burner, powered by gas or electricity (in remote areas, by propane). All three hot water systems are inefficient because the water is kept hot all the time, whether it is needed or not.

Recently, on-demand hot water systems have come on the market that are more efficient because they heat the water only when it is needed rather than keeping it hot all the time. This kind of system has no tank to heat. The cold water passes through an electric or gas coil that heats the water when you need it. The people who make these systems swear they create enough hot water to meet the needs of most families. If you are skeptical, and worry that your home will run out of hot water if two or more people shower in a row, then try to find someone who has such a system. Ask how well it works and compare your hot water usage with that household's.

220 Maintaining your hot water tank

Hot water tanks go bad in two ways. The first thing that can happen to them is that they will rust or even crack at the bottom and begin leaking. This is caused by minerals and other substances in the water that are breaking down the viability of the tank itself. If that occurs, you'll need to buy a new tank.

The other thing that can happen is that the flame within the boiler has died. At the bottom of the heater you'll see a small door, with a space behind it. This is where the flame should be. If it isn't there, you have a problem. Now, don't worry too much. There's no gas flowing into your home. There's something called a gas regulator within the tank that will shut down the gas if there is no flame. The thing to do in this case is to try to relight the flame yourself. It's not very dangerous. There's a red button that overrides the gas regulator and lets the gas out again. Push this button and light the flame with a utility match. Some systems have a self-lighting mechanism within them and will go back on at the flick of a button.

221 Fixing a gas burner that won't stay lit

If this occurs, chances are you have a problem with something called the thermal (or thermo) coupling. But before we get into that, you should check to see that there's no lint or dust clogging the hole that lets the gas out. Try cleaning that area and then relighting the flame. If this doesn't work, you'll need to replace the thermal coupling. This is a small metal piece that sits above the flame and is attached to a coiled wire that runs up to the gas regulator. This device tells the gas regulator when there is heat present. It is attached to the regulator with a small nut. Unscrew the nut manually and carefully pull out the thermal coupling, unspooling the wire. Go to the hardware store and buy a new one. All thermal couplings will work in all water heaters. To install the new one, place the small metal piece above where the flame will be. Unspool the wire and run the nut up to the gas regulator and screw in the thermal coupling.

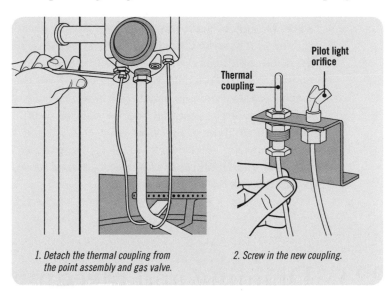

1. Detach the thermal coupling from the point assembly and gas valve.

2. Screw in the new coupling.

222 Why old radiators are best

There are two basic kinds of radiators: the old-fashioned ones (often called cast-iron radiators), which look like small pieces of furniture, with a series of pipes running up and down, and the more modern variety, which run along the side of the wall at the baseboard.

Cast-iron radiators work with either steam or hot water. When it comes down to it, these radiators will keep your home warmer than any other heating system, and they're relatively maintenance free. There are two ways cast-iron radiators work: with one pipe or two pipes. In a one-pipe system the steam comes up from the boiler, goes into the radiator, cools, and condenses into water, which travels back down the same pipe the steam traveled up in. In a two-pipe system steam or hot water goes up the first pipe, through the radiator, and down a second pipe at the other end.

A one-pipe system will have two valves. The first is called the radiator valve. This valve is usually a handle somewhere on the floor where the pipe is, and it allows you to adjust the level of steam coming in. The second is called the air valve. It looks like a large medicine capsule and sits at one end of the radiator about halfway up from the floor. You don't control it, but it allows the excess steam to blow out. In a two-pipe system you have a radiator valve and something called a steam trap, which cycles the steam back to the pipe that leads down to the boiler.

TRICK OF THE TRADE: *Never paint radiators. It makes them less efficient, because it reduces their ability to conduct heat.*

223 Draining and bleeding a radiator

Before you attempt any fix on your radiator system, you will have to drain and bleed it. This isn't that hard to do. Draining the system is easy. Go down to the boiler. Open the valve that you use to flush your boiler and let it go until no more water comes out. Remember to put a bucket under there. This will not hurt your system, but you will have to pump the air out and the water back into the system before it will be operational. Then you have to go up to your radiators and bleed them of air.

To do this you use something called a bleed key. Most radiators should work with a bleed key, which tends to look like a notched fork. But let's face it—you probably won't have a bleed key around, so go to the hardware store and buy one. At the top of the radiator is a valve designed to work with this key. It is called a bleed valve. Turn the key in the valve and listen for the hissing sound. Open up the valve and let the air hiss out of it. No hissing, no more air. Please note, however, that some radiators are designed to be bled with a plain old screwdriver. In that case, instead of seeing a bolt that would work with a bleed key, you'll see a slotted screw. To bleed this kind of radiator, simply turn the screw.

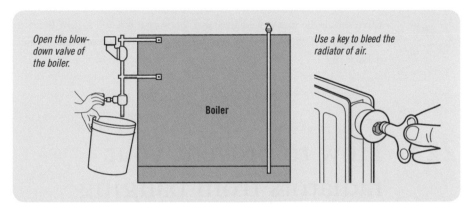

Open the blow-down valve of the boiler.

Boiler

Use a key to bleed the radiator of air.

224 How to fix radiator problems

Now and then, the radiator valve or the air valve breaks down. When the radiator valve breaks down it will leak, and you won't be able to shut the heat off. When the air valve breaks, it will hiss as it leaks air. Before attempting any fix, drain and bleed the radiator system and shut off the boiler (see entries 223 and 216). The radiator valve is an L-shaped or straight tube attached to the radiator and to the pipe that comes from the boiler. Each side of the tube has a nut on it. You'll need to unscrew these nuts to remove the valve. The nut that attaches the valve to the radiator can be easily unscrewed using a wrench. To disassemble the valve and the pipe from the boiler, you'll need two wrenches. Use one in one hand to hold the pipe in place and prevent damage to the piping that goes downstairs. The other unscrews the nut.

Once you've removed the valve, you will also need to unscrew the little pipe that runs from the nut on the valve to the radiator itself. This can also be done with a wrench. Take the small pipe and the valve to the hardware store and buy a new valve. A small pipe will come with it. Reverse the process to install, and remember to use Teflon tape on the threads of the male pipe (see entry 151). The air valve should be unscrewed by hand, because a wrench might bend it or break it off. All air valves are the same. Buy a new one and screw it back in.

225 How to prevent your radiators from banging

More often than not, old-fashioned radiators bang and clang when the heat comes up. This is caused by water that gets stuck in the pipes. The water is supposed to drain away, but if there is water sitting in the radiator, it will pop and sizzle when the boiler heats the radiator up again. Then you'll get a phenomenon that someone once described to us as being similar to the popping sound you hear when you pour cold water into a hot pan. This sounds like the banging in a radiator. There are a few fixes for this. The radiator must be pitched properly so that it drains the water into the drain pipe. You can raise one side of the radiator with shims to drain the water into the pipe (see the photograph on page 191). You may also have a radiator that is banging against the wall as it expands and contracts with the heat. To fix this, make sure the radiator is attached to the wall securely.

226 How baseboard radiators work

The baseboard type of radiator is a simple machine. It's a copper tube with aluminum fins coming off it. Hot water goes into the tube and heats the fins, which disperse the heat. The fins are so thin that they heat up quickly and cool down just as fast. There are no valves in this system. You control it with the thermostat. The problem with baseboard systems is that people take off the covers or the covers fall off, and the fins, which are fragile, are easily bent, and when they are bent, they no longer give off heat as effectively. When that happens, you'll need to call a plumber and replace that section of piping.

227 What air-conditioning system should I buy?

There are three common air-conditioning systems: window units, ducted HVAC, and ductless HVAC. Most people use window units, those air conditioners that sit in the window frame, because they are relatively cheap to buy and relatively cheap to run and because they allow you to control the temperature in one room at a time. The downside to window units is that they block up windows, are loud, and tend to provide extremes of cooling rather than an even cool.

heating and cooling

HVAC stands for heating, ventilation, and air-conditioning. A ducted HVAC system will have an air-conditioning unit (either all in one piece or split into two) attached to a series of ducts that are run throughout the house. Ducted HVAC systems are quiet, you don't see them, and they provide an even cool. But it is expensive to install and run a ducted HVAC, and the homeowner must install a separate HVAC unit for each room that he or she wants individually cooled. A ducted HVAC system that runs throughout the house cannot be used to cool one room at a time but will always cool the entire area where it is installed.

Ductless HVAC has an outdoor unit connected to a series of indoor units, which sit on the wall. These systems are quiet, provide even cooling, and can be easily installed to cool one room at a time, without ripping up the walls to install ducts. The downside to ductless HVAC is that it is much more expensive than window units, and you do see the HVAC units on the walls.

Which type of system to choose? Well, if expense is not an issue, comfort is a priority, and you would rather not block up your windows, a ducted system is the one for you. If you want the comfort of a ducted system but also the ability to cool a single room, a ductless system is the way to go. If ease of installation and lower initial costs are important, choose a window unit.

228 How air-conditioning works

Air conditioners, like refrigerators, make a space cool not by adding colder air to the space, as most people imagine, but by removing heat from the space. The secret to this is evaporation, a process that removes heat and humidity.

An air-conditioning system will have a compressor, a condenser, an evaporator, a thermostat, fans, and metal fins. The compressor is filled with a refrigerant, which is a chemical, often Freon. The refrigerant enters the compressor as a cool gas. The compressor squeezes that gas down, and as the gas's molecules are compressed they heat up. This hot gas is passed through the condenser, which is a series of coils on the outside of the air conditioner. Inside these coils, the refrigerant's heat dissipates, and the hot gas condenses into a cool liquid. This cool liquid is forced through a narrow valve into another set of coils called the evaporator, which is on the inside of the room. As this occurs the refrigerant begins to evaporate, and because it evaporates at a significantly lower temperature than water, it draws both the heat and the moisture out of the surrounding air and into the coils. It is this action that cools the room. The refrigerant is now a cold gas once again and is pumped back into the compressor, where the cycle begins again. The thermostat regulates the cooling action of the air conditioner, the fans help blow hotter and cooler air over the coils, and the metal fins help dissipate outside the house the heat the air conditioner has collected.

229 How a ducted or ductless HVAC is installed

This installation will be done by a professional HVAC company. The main air-conditioning unit for a ducted system can be located inside your house in a garage or machine room, or anywhere on the outside of the house. The ducts themselves are rectangular boxes made of metal and other materials and will vary in size, depending on the size of the space that is being cooled. The ducts can be run either inside walls, ceilings, and floors; in soffits (drywall boxes built around the duct); or in dropped ceilings. A main duct will be run from the unit, and then ducts will branch off that unit to deliver air to individual rooms. It is also important to install return air ducts here and there, which will take the hot air away from the house.

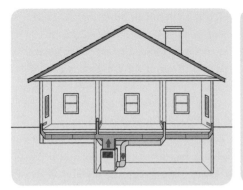

Ducted system   Ductless system

In a ductless HVAC system, the compressor unit will be located outside of the house. It will be attached by relatively narrow wires and tubes to one or a series of rectangular fan units that are mounted on the walls of each room that is being cooled.

230 Can an HVAC system provide heat?

Yes. Let's say you took the air-conditioning process and reversed it. Then you would have a system that heated your house instead of cooling it. Thus, with the addition of a heat pump, you can have an HVAC system that heats as well as cools. A heat pump has a valve that allows the HVAC to move forward or in reverse, so to speak, toggling between being an AC and a heater. This can be an efficient way to heat a house or a room, especially at slightly higher temperatures, as long as the air temperature outside remains above 20° Fahrenheit. At temperatures of 20° and above, the HVAC may be more efficient than burning gas or oil in a boiler, because at slightly warmer temperatures you may not need or want to heat your entire home, and many HVAC systems are targeted to a specific area of the house. If the temperature drops below 20°, however, you should switch to your main boiler and heat the entire home. HVAC units can also be installed in such a way that they humidify the air in winter (which keeps the house warmer and fights against the drying effects of radiator heat) and work as air purification systems as well.

231 Maintaining a ducted or ductless HVAC

With these systems the best thing you can do—frankly, you have no choice—is to have a service contract with an HVAC company, perhaps the same people who installed your system. For the annual cost of around two meals for two at a nice restaurant, the pros will come between two and four times a year and keep your HVAC running well. This is not something you can do yourself.

Having said that, there is some maintenance a homeowner can do a few times a year to keep the system running well. Please remember to shut off all power to any AC unit you are working on before you touch it. Dirt and debris can build up inside an HVAC condenser, especially one that is outside. Remove the cover. You'll observe a fan and a coil. Remove all debris and clean the machinery with a dry rag. You can also use some condenser coil cleaner, which you can find in hardware stores. Do not use water, which can turn the dirt into mud and make things worse. You may or may not be able to get at your evaporator. If you can, use a vacuum cleaner with a brush attachment to sweep away any dirt you find there.

232 Choosing a window-unit air conditioner

AC units are rated by their capacity in British thermal units, or BTUs. A good rule of thumb is that twelve thousand BTUs will cool between 400 and 500 square feet. ACs are also given an energy efficiency rating, or EER. The higher the EER the better, since that means the unit uses less electricity. Most air conditioners are rated between eight and eleven EER. Window-unit air conditioners are designed to be installed in double-hung windows. That means windows with two sashes, one above the other. If you have a room with casement or other kinds of windows, you cannot use a window unit. (You can purchase so-called portable air conditioners that are freestanding in the middle of the room.) Choose a window with an electrical outlet near it and make sure you know what the voltage of that outlet is. Measure your window. Buy an air conditioner of the appropriate size and shape to cool the room and fit in the window you have chosen.

233 Installing a window unit

Any homeowner can install a window AC unit. Think about having a friend along to help you hold the air conditioner in the window—otherwise, you do risk dropping it out when you are installing it. The AC will come with all the hardware needed to install it. Follow the manufacturer's directions. Generally, screw the mounting brackets into the window frame. Open the window. Carefully slide the AC unit over the windowsill and into the mounting brackets. Close the window onto the AC unit. The air conditioner will come with extensions at either side. Pull these out until they touch the sides of the window. Drill small holes in the window sash above the

AC and screw the extensions into the sash. Use a strip of insulation (like a foam) to seal up the gap where the two sashes meet. Tilt the AC slightly so that the back of the unit is angled toward the ground; this will ensure that the water drains properly out of the unit. (If you don't angle the unit properly, you may end up with dirty water dripping into your room and, even worse, a small flood on days of torrential rain.) Caulk around the AC. (If you wish to remove the air conditioner, you can easily remove the caulking.) Plug it in.

234 Maintaining a window unit

You should clean and condition your AC unit at least twice a year, in spring and in autumn if you live in a place where you have hot summers and cool or cold winters. If you use your AC year-round, you might think about doing this once every three months. Regular maintenance of your AC unit is important. Failure to maintain the unit will result in its working inefficiently and breaking down. There are two things you need to do: clean the filter, and clean the coils. Every air conditioner has a filter that cleans the air as it passes through the machine. Unplug the AC. Follow the manufacturer's instructions on how to remove the filter. (Typically, there's a grille that has to be unscrewed or removed, with the filter behind it.)

Remove the filter. Soak it in warm, soapy water for around ten minutes. Rinse the filter and let it dry. Reinstall.

To clean the coils, your best bet is to take the AC unit out of the window, remove the casing that surrounds

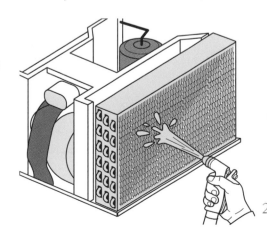

the AC, and spray the coils lightly with water, perhaps adding and rinsing off with an all-purpose cleaner. We realize this is a bit extreme for most homeowners, but that is the proper way to go. If you can't or won't do this, you can try taking the front off the unit and running a vacuum over the coils as best you can.

235   Keeping efficiency in mind

The key to keeping any heating or cooling system efficient is not to shut it down during a day when you know you are going to use it again, but to leave it running at a lower level. For example, it's a hot summer morning and you have had the thermostat in your bedroom at 72° Fahrenheit all night but are now going off for a day of work. Do not shut the central air off. It is better to turn it up to 78° or 80° and maintain a certain level of humidity throughout the day. (This does not work for window-unit air conditioners.) The same would be true of heating. What you don't want is temperature swings of more than 5 or 6 degrees throughout the day, because it costs more energy for the heating or cooling system to bring the temperature back to the point you want it with a large swing than it does to maintain the temperature at a reasonably steady rate throughout the day.

236　Air-conditioning:
THE DARK SIDE

There are so many ways an AC system can break down that it would be impossible to deal with them all here. So we'll give you some of the more common ones and their solutions.

If the system isn't turning on at all, you may have tripped a breaker on your breaker panel. The power switch for the unit may be off. On hot days you should also check the compressor. Compressors have a tendency to shut down, and you may have to press the reset button, typically located near the compressor.

If the system is clearly running but not cooling, you may have a clogged filter, or the condenser may have become gunked with dirt and debris, or someone may have fiddled with the thermostat, changing it from cooling to heating, for example.

Finally, you may have a broken thermostat that is not registering the right air temperature. If that is the case, you will have to have a new one installed. You may also see frost buildup on various parts of your HVAC system, and that is always a bad sign.

TRICK OF THE TRADE: *You should not have frost anywhere on the HVAC system. If you see frost, call your maintenance company and have them come and take a look.*

Household Carpentry

This is a big chapter, and there's a simple reason for that. When you come right down to it, apart from plumbing and electrical, home repair and maintenance is all about carpentry. For the most part, our homes are framed in wood, have wood floors and wooden stairs, and are filled with wood furniture. But the coolest part about carpentry is making new things for your home. If you can master wood, you can not only maintain your house but also begin to add on to it in various ways.

237 All woodworking can be divided into three parts

The three levels of woodworking are carpentry, cabinetmaking, and furniture making. Carpentry is the simplest. It deals with rough framing for walls and low-level fixes around the house. Cabinetmaking has to do with building the boxes that are used for storage as kitchen cabinets, bookshelves, and closet partitions. Many cabinets are built in, meaning they are custom designed to fit a specific place in your home and do not move. Furniture making, by contrast, is where woodworking becomes an art. It involves creating pieces of furniture that are more than just simple boxes and include decorative elements, curved pieces, and other complex forms of woodcraft. In terms of difficulty, the novice homeowner can first tackle smaller carpentry projects before graduating to more involved cabinetmaking tasks. If you master those skills, you might develop enough confidence to try your hand at basic furniture making. The good news is that with woodworking the most useful projects are often the simplest, and a general knowledge of carpentry is all most homeowners will ever need.

238 How is a wood surface finished?

Wood is great stuff. It's beautiful and durable, but only when properly protected. If you don't paint, stain, or finish wood, it will degrade over time. This is because wood is a porous material that absorbs moisture and expands and contracts, depending on the humidity in the air. Finishing wood helps protect it from moisture. The process is relatively simple. First, the surface is sanded to smooth it and open it up to bond with the stain or paint. Then the finishing material of your choice is applied. If the wood is painted, the paint will act as a barrier between the wood and the elements. But if the wood is stained, the stained surface needs to be sanded again and then a finisher such as urethane, lacquer, or wax is applied on top of the stained surface to seal it.

TRICK OF THE TRADE: *When applying any kind of stain or sealant, or when stripping a wood surface with solvent, always wear rubber gloves.*

239 How to talk sandpaper

Sandpaper comes in various "grits," and we don't mean the stuff you see on your breakfast plate in the South. When you are talking sandpaper, the grit represents the number of abrasive particles per inch of paper. A lower-numbered grit will be rougher than a higher-numbered grit, meaning it will create a rougher, more abraded surface than a finer grit sandpaper. As a rule of thumb, with wood, you would use a 40- to 60-grit paper for the heavy sanding at the beginning, an 80- to 120-grit for smoothing the surface, and a 150- to 180-grit paper for a sanding job right before using a urethane finisher. If you want to go all the way, you can also buy a 220- to 240-grit paper, which you can use for a light sand between applications of stain or sealer.

240 Sanding a wood surface

To sand any kind of flat surface by hand, you'll be better off placing the sandpaper on a sanding block. A sanding block is a piece of wood or plastic that is the right size to fit in the hand you'll use to run the sandpaper over whatever you are working with. You can buy sanding blocks from the hardware store or make one yourself out of a block of scrap wood. Attach the sandpaper to the block with a few small nails and, gripping the block, run the sandpaper over the wood in long, even strokes, applying gentle pressure and following the grain. Do not sand back and forth—sand with the grain. Applying too much pressure will create an uneven job. Begin sanding with sandpaper that is coarser and then move to finer-grit paper.

For curved areas of wood, you can use a smaller strip of sandpaper in your fingers or place a sheet of sandpaper over a sponge or other malleable substance. When you are done sanding, use tack cloth—a sticky, but not too sticky, material available in stores—to wipe away the dust and particles that have built up on the wood's surface during sanding. As you sand, make sure to tap the wood dust off the sandpaper and replace the paper as it wears and becomes smooth.

TRICK OF THE TRADE: *For larger surfaces, like floors, you should use an electric sander. Electric sanders come in two varieties: a belt sander has a strip on it to which you attach sandpaper and the belt rotates; a radial sander has a circular piece that rotates, and you place the flat end of the circle down on the wood. Either one will work just fine, although we are partial to belt sanders.*

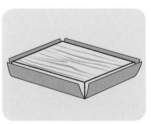
Sandpaper on a block

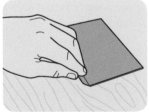
Sandpaper held with fingers

241 Staining a wood surface

Stain is a kind of ink designed to color wood. Unlike paint, which sits on the surface of wood, stain will sink into the fibers, especially when the wood has been sanded. The key to staining is not to apply too much of it. The best thing to do is buy cheesecloth, like you use for cooking, or use a rag that does not give off lint. Put the cloth in the tin of stain and then just wipe it gently across whatever you are staining (see the photograph on page 211). The issue with staining is to get an even coat. Keep your hand moving at all times, and try to avoid puddling the stain in certain spots, because if you do that, you will create unsightly dark patches on the stained object. If you want the object to be a darker color overall than the one you have achieved with your first layer of stain, by all means add a second, third, fourth, or fifth layer. You can apply coats of stain one after the other, but after each coat, let it dry for a night. If you create any darker areas or blotches, you will have to sand them down and start over.

Remember to wear rubber gloves.

242 How do I choose the right finish for a stained surface?

As we said before, paint seals the wood. Stain does not. Stained wood must be finished with a sealant. There are a variety of sealants that are commonly used, including urethane, lacquer, shellac, and wax. Lacquers and shellacs are more likely to be used by professionals, so we won't deal with them here. Wax is an old-fashioned finish, more likely to be found on older wooden objects and on furniture and smaller items. Most floors will be finished with an oil- or water-based urethane, so that is the finish we are going to concentrate on.

household carpentry

The two issues with urethanes are choosing between oil and water and choosing the right sheen. We recommend choosing the water-based or latex urethanes. Oil-based products smell terrible, take a day to dry, and yellow over time. Latex-based urethanes are more expensive, but they don't yellow and they dry in a few hours with little smell. Urethane sheens range from flat to matte, satin, semigloss, gloss, and finally high gloss. The glossier the finish, the more durable it is, but any imperfections in the wood will be more obvious. Nine out of ten professionals will use satin as the final coat, which is a good compromise.

TRICK OF THE TRADE: *If you want more durability but less sheen to the finish of your wood, apply a layer of glossier urethane first and then a matte or satin layer over that. What your eye will see is the sheen of the final layer of urethane applied.*

243   Finishing a stained surface

Before applying urethane to finish the surface, take some fine steel wool or fine sandpaper and wipe away any grit or residue from the staining job. Use a good paintbrush, and apply a coat of the urethane. You want to apply an even, thin layer, using light, careful brushstrokes. Let the urethane dry for at least an hour if you are using latex. Once there's no more stickiness to the touch, sand the surface with the steel wool or sandpaper. Apply a second coat of urethane. Let this coat cure overnight. If you want the job to be perfect, you can now use something called a buffing pad, which is a power tool you can rent or buy, and buff the job to a fine finish.

244 Removing a wood stain

A stained surface can be sanded off. There are two ways to do this: manually with sandpaper, which will take forever, or with a radial sander equipped with a few belts, which you can buy or rent (see Trick of the Trade, page 214). You may also need steel wool brushes to get into nooks and crannies. Always apply your sander with care. Keep it moving. Never stay in one place for more than a second and continually stop to see how far you have gone. If you are dealing with solid wood, make sure you aren't creating valleys and dips in the wood.

If you have a veneered surface, remember that it is the thickness of a quarter, or less—once you sand through that veneer, it's over. You'll see the lighter spot where the veneer has worn away, revealing the wood below. If you do go too far, you may be able to hide your error with a darker stain.

245 Painting a wood surface

To learn more about different kinds of paints and paintbrushes, as well as how to apply paints and other painting facts, please see chapter 9 (pages 308–20). In general, painting wood is a four-step process that includes priming, filling in nail and screw holes, applying one coat of paint, and then adding a second coat of paint. The biggest mistake people make is not beginning with a primer. This is a sealant that works to prevent the piece of wood from expanding and contracting with changes in the atmosphere.

Once you've primed, you need to take care of any possible nail or screw holes. Prime first, so that the primer goes into the holes. Let the primer dry. Fill the holes with wood putty, leaving excess putty. Sand the filled holes flush with the surface. Apply the first coat of paint. Let the paint dry. Then apply a second coat.

household carpentry

TRICK OF THE TRADE: *If you are using paint of a darker hue over white primer, you may need as many as four coats of paint for everything to look just right. One way you can potentially decrease the number of coats of darker paint you'll need to use is by adding some of the dark paint to the primer before you prime the walls. Don't add too much, just enough to ever so slightly color the primer.*

246 How to remove a painted surface from wood

Get yourself some paste solvent. There are many solvents out there, so go to the hardware store and see what they recommend. These solvents are designed to eat the paint away, and they smell terrible. So be sure to also buy gloves, goggles, and a dust mask and to wear long sleeves while you work. Apply the solvent onto the painted wood with a sponge applicator. Let it sit for two to six hours (depending on the product—check the directions—and how much time you have). Then take a Spackle knife, place the edge of it onto the painted surface, and push the paint off the wood. Older pieces of wood, such as door frames in antique homes, may have many layers of paint on them. You aren't going to be able to strip that surface with solvent. The only way to remove multiple layers of paint is to painstakingly strip them off, one layer at a time. Realize that you are in for a long, drawn-out campaign.

247 What's the best way to tighten loose fasteners?

If you have something with a nut, a bolt, or a screw in it, then that thing is going to loosen. It's like death and taxes.

There's no way we can go through all the scenarios that come up when something loose needs to be tightened, because they are as varied as the furniture, fixtures, and machines you have in your house. But when you are faced with a loose screw or bolt of some sort, first choose the right tool. Take a look at the fastener and see what tool is required. The most common will be a Phillips-head or slot-head screwdriver, or something like an Allen wrench.

When you tighten something, do it with care, turning the fastener until you begin meeting some real resistance. Then stop. This is especially important for screws in wood. Remember that if you turn a screw too much into wood, you will have ruined the fastening power of that screw. Please try not to give in to the temptation to give the screw just one more turn. Don't do it. For more advice on screwing in screws, see entry 17.

248 How is a wood floor installed?

The average homeowner will not want to install a wood floor. This is a job for the professionals. However, it does pay to understand how a wood floor works.

In an apartment building, wood flooring will usually be laid directly atop the concrete floor. In a private home, the wood flooring will be installed onto a plywood subfloor that is attached to the joists of the house. (A joist is a horizontal wooden beam that supports the flooring of a structure.) There are two types of wood flooring: parquet and plank. Parquet is a pattern formed by five or six small wood strips laid down to form a square, and the entire floor is composed of these squares. Plank floors are made up of larger strips. These planks can vary in width from around 2 inches to around 8 inches. The wider the plank, the more expensive it is. They vary in length from around 2 feet to around 6 feet.

Installing a parquet floor

Installing a plank floor

A FEW SPECIAL POINTS ABOUT PLANK FLOORING

Plank floors are almost always installed with an extra layer that goes between the plywood subfloor and the planks. That layer is made of resin paper, which is a red-colored building paper, or something like a roofing felt. The resin paper or roofing felt acts as a barrier that prevents dust and moisture from getting into the areas between the planks, and it is a form of sound insulation that guards against squeaks and other sounds that loose floorboards make. The planks of a wood floor also tend to connect to one another using a tongue-and-groove system. The tongue is a small notch that runs along one side of the plank, and the groove is a small indentation on the other. The tongues fit into the grooves, like an interlocking puzzle.

249 How do I fix a squeaky plank?

There are two reasons a floor plank squeaks and creaks. Either the board is loose (see entry 250), or the resin paper underneath it has worn away over time.

If the problem is the resin paper, you have four choices.

1. **Live with it.**
2. **Knock in a few nails.**
3. **Lay down a carpet.**
4. **Hire a floor man to rip up that section of flooring and replace the resin paper.**

You might think about ripping up that section of the floor yourself, but we don't recommend it. If you tear out a section of floor, you'll most likely have to replace it with new planks, and those new planks, even if they are sanded and refinished, are not going to look like the rest of the floor. You can sand and refinish the entire floor, but that is a big task. And that assumes you haven't done serious damage to the entire floor when trying to rip up one section of it. With the typical tongue-and-groove floor, every plank is interconnected. If you're unlucky, the rest of the floor is going to come up with the plank you are attempting to lift. Now you are in for a major renovation, and when it is over, you'll end up with a floor that's a different shade from the other floors in your house. So before you decide to fix a squeaky plank yourself, consider that things can easily spiral out of control.

250 How to fix a loose plank

If the squeak is caused by a loose plank, you have a much simpler situation. You need to put a few nails into the plank. The issue here is picking the right nail. Assuming you don't know how thick your floor is, you can reckon, for example, that the plank is ¾ inch thick, and so is the plywood subfloor beneath it, so now you are dealing with 1½ inches. The best nail for this is 1¼ inches long, so you'll probably want a fourpenny finishing nail. A finishing nail is designed with a small head that is meant to be hammered all the way into the wood. Use a countersink (see entry 251) to hammer the nail in.

251 When do I use a countersink?

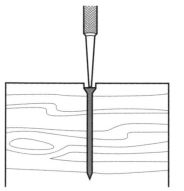

A countersink is a tapered spike that ends at the same diameter as the nail head. This little gizmo is one of the most useful items you can buy for carpentry of all sorts, but especially when you are repairing floors. Countersinks are made for use with finishing nails, which are designed with small heads so that they can be hammered all the way into the wood. This method allows the nail head to disappear beneath the surface of the wood, creating a smooth appearance and avoiding the possibility of dangerous little bits of nail sticking out from the surface. But while it is often advantageous to have the nail disappear into the wood, you don't want to be striking the wood with a hammer. That's where the countersink comes in. First, tap the nail directly into the wood with a hammer, so that the nail is still standing up. Place the countersink on the nail head, and then hit the countersink into the nail, rather than using the hammer on the nail directly. By using the countersink you don't damage or dent the wood flooring by pounding the hammer head into it. With the countersink, you can get the nail all the way into the wood without making a dent in the wood itself.

252 Can I hammer a finishing nail without a countersink?

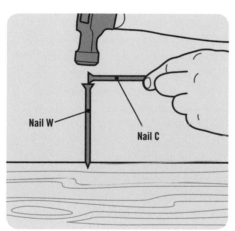

Nail W

Nail C

If you don't have a countersink or can't be bothered to go buy one, you can use another nail. This might get a little confusing, so let's just say Nail W is the nail that is going into the wood, and Nail C is the nail being used as a countersink. Take Nail W and tap it into the wood so that it is standing up. Then take Nail C and hold it perpendicular over Nail W, so that Nail C's head is over Nail W's head. Then you can strike Nail C gently until you get Nail W almost sunk into the wood. At this point you are going to want to turn Nail C around and point its tip right into the head of Nail W. Most nails will have a small indentation in the head, and you'll be able to situate the point of Nail C in that indentation. Now tap nail C until Nail W disappears into the wood. This is very important. The nail must go *beneath* the wood's surface. Otherwise you are going to have a generation of damaged socks and feet in your house.

253 How to finish a wood floor, in two parts .

Plenty of people decide they want to save money by finishing a floor themselves. This is one of the easiest ways you can cut corners on a home renovation and not kill yourself or ruin your home. And the saving is huge.

1. The first step to finishing a floor is sanding it. Remember, this is only going to work if you have solid wood floors. A veneered floor is too easy to mess up. (If you want to refinish a veneered floor, call a pro.) You can rent a sander, and the easier one to use is the radial version (see Trick of the Trade, page 214). When you rent the machine, ask for a 110-volt type that can be plugged directly into most home outlets. You'll want a heavy-duty sandpaper for a rough sanding and a finer sandpaper for the fine sanding. Use the sander like a vacuum. Just push it gently across the floor, using even movements, and don't stay in one spot for too long, or you'll oversand one area. Start at one end and go up and down the room as though you were mowing a lawn.

2. After sanding, it's time to stain. Think about wearing knee pads for this job, because you are going to spend a lot of time kneeling. Begin by sweeping the floor to remove excess sawdust. Then do a test spot, so you can see what the stain will look like—do not go by the chart in the store. If you feel the floor is too light in color, you can do a second coat. Each coat will make the floor about 10 percent darker. Remember that the color will lighten as the floor dries, but darken again when you put on the urethane finish. When you are applying urethane to a floor, you must start at one end, working your way to the door where you will finish, because you cannot walk on urethane until it dries. Apply it with a sponge on a stick, because it has to be put on quickly. Don't use a roller. It will leave marks. You must let the urethane dry before putting on another layer. If you use a water-based urethane, it will dry in a

half hour. Every coat of oil-based urethane needs a night of drying, and it really smells. As we said before, you need at least four coats of water-based urethane and two coats of the oil-based type.

For in-depth information on staining and finishing wood, see entries 241 through 243.

254 Maintaining a finished wood floor

There are many products out there designed to clean wood, but they cost money and are sometimes filled with chemicals you don't really want to breathe in. If you want to go green, save money, and do something good for the air you breathe, take a bucket and fill it with two parts white vinegar and eight parts lukewarm water. You apply this mixture with a mop or with a loose rag. There are people who do this every week. Some people do it every day. The important thing is that when you are mopping the floor, don't make the floor too wet. You just want to dampen it. If you soak the floor, there's a danger the water is going to sink down between the floorboards, and then you'll get buckling. If you see the urethane coming off the finished floor, then you might want to do another application. One layer will do, but as long as you are going to the trouble, do two.

255 How do I fix a scratch or a ding in a wood floor?

If you see a white line in your floor, the truth is you probably haven't scratched your floor; you have scratched the stain. Even if you have scratched your wood a little, you should try to live with it. Scratched floors are a fact of life. You don't want to do a major repair just because of a scratch here or there. What you do want to do is go to the hardware store and purchase a special floor pen in the same color as your stain. Most stain companies make these.

Alternatively, you might have a container of the stain you used. In that case, take a cotton swab, dip it in the stain, and just use your swab or pen to fill in the line. Then take a rag and wipe off the excess.

Whether you use a floor pen or stain, you won't be removing the scratch, exactly, but you'll darken it in so that you don't see it. Think of it as akin to using makeup to correct a slight wrinkle or blemish on an otherwise pretty face.

If you have a ding, our advice is to color it in, as you would a scratch, and leave it alone. The only real fix for a ding is to sand and refinish, and sanding a ding can leave you with an unsightly valley in your floor. Just walk away. If you can't stand it, get a pro to come in and replace the piece of wood.

256 How laminate flooring is installed

Many homeowners are now choosing laminate flooring instead of solid, wood planks. Laminate is usually made of some kind of synthetic material with a layer on top designed to look like wood. Laminate is cheaper and easier to install, and it gives you the kind of uniform appearance that wood never can. It is durable and works well in high-traffic areas. That said, laminate floors will suffer damage, and when they do, you can't do with them what you would do with wood floors, which is to sand and refinish them. Each brand of laminate floor has its own system of installation, but in general the flooring is installed over plywood or concrete, with a buffering padded layer of some sort in between. The floor itself works like a puzzle, with the pieces fitting into one another. You lay the pieces out over the floor and install spacers, which are little shims, to keep the pieces evenly spaced. Baseboards around the perimeter of the floor hold the laminate flooring in place. Some laminate systems are glued down, but most essentially float unconnected to the floor by either glue or nails. In fact, they're known as floating floors.

257 How to repair a damaged laminate floor

Inevitably, you are going to get nicks, scratches, and indentations in your laminate floor. Most types of flooring will have patch-up kits available. These include putties, crayons, and pens especially matched to your floor so that you can do some light cosmetic surgery. If you have to go so far as to replace an entire plank, hope that your floor isn't glued down. If it isn't glued down, you take up the baseboard molding near the affected area and remove all the boards leading to the one you want. Slide the new board into place and then replace the molding.

If you have a glued-down system, you are going to have to rip the floor out, using a crowbar, and start over. Not fun.

You may also have laminate planks that are kind of bowing upward. This is caused by an increase in tension in the floor, which might be due to the house shifting or changes in humidity and temperature. If you have this, take up the baseboard molding and replace your spacers (see entry 256) with smaller spacers. On the other hand, if you are seeing spaces between laminate boards, lift up the baseboard molding and add larger spacers.

258 How baseboard moldings are installed

A baseboard molding is a long, usually thin, piece of wood—often of pine or poplar, though it could be made of vinyl—which sits in the crook between the wall and the floor. Moldings were first used for the purpose of covering the imperfections at the base of walls and for blocking rodents and bugs from entering the house.

The proper way to install a baseboard molding is to glue it down with white glue on an unfinished wall, or, if the wall is painted, with construction adhesive. Then nail it in with small finishing nails. However, builders often don't bother to glue the molding down. They just nail it.

No matter how moldings are installed, they have a tendency to separate from the wall. Houses move. They shift and settle, and an unglued baseboard can be dislodged as a result. The other issue is that baseboards don't come in continuous strips. The longest piece of stock molding is 16 feet—they don't make them longer. It is always best to create a molding out of a single piece of wood. If you have a long wall, the moldings will have to be made of multiple wood pieces, but you will also see breaks in the molding of walls that are shorter than 16 feet, because the carpenter couldn't be bothered to do the math and cut the moldings on each wall out of a single length.

TRICK OF THE TRADE: *If you have an uneven floor, you can use a flat or rounded strip of wood called a shoe molding that will help bridge the gap between the bottom of the molding and the uneven floor.*

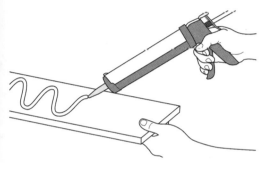

Apply glue to back of molding.

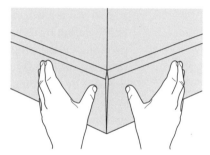

Install molding on the wall.

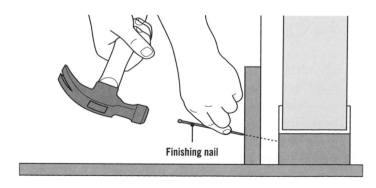

Finishing nail

Secure molding with nails.

259 Fixing a loose molding

If you see a place where the baseboard molding is loosening, take a crowbar, *gently* pry the loose molding a little farther from the wall, and see if you can get some white glue down there. Seriously, you can use your children's paper glue for this. But make sure you have a wet rag handy to wipe off the excess. Moreover, you should add a few nails. You will always want ½ inch of nail to go into the second surface you are nailing into. So with most ¾-inch-thick moldings, a fourpenny finishing nail will do the trick. If the molding is a little larger, go with the sixpenny nail. You will be hammering the nail perpendicular to the wall, with a slight hint of an angle down. (The angled nail is a better fastener than the straight one.) Again, you'll finish nailing by using a countersink (see entry 251). If you start to pry away the molding and it begins to come off, just take the entire thing off and start over. Once you've taken the molding out, remove the nails by punching them out gently with a hammer, or pulling them with a pair of pliers. Run a bead of glue across the center of the molding, replace the molding, and starting from 1½ inches from the end, hammer in nails every 8 to 12 inches.

260 Fixing any kind of molding

The advice we just gave you is applicable to any other kind of molding you have in your house. This would work for door frames, for crown moldings on the ceiling, or for any kind of molding around a window, etc. But the molding you are repairing may be made of two pieces for one length. If so, you want to put the glue not only on the back of the molding, but also on both ends of the thick side. When the two pieces touch each other they will bond, and that is something you want. Make sure you line up the pieces evenly. If when the molding is finished you see a little difference in how the pieces are lined up, you can sand down the difference by hand with a rough sandpaper.

261   How are wooden stairs constructed?

At its most basic, a set of wooden stairs is composed of stringers, risers, and treads. The stringers are two wood planks laid at an angle to form the frame of the stair. Right-angled cuts are made into the stringers at even intervals to provide spaces for the treads and the risers. The treads are the horizontal planks that you actually step on. The risers are the vertical planks that bridge the gap from tread to tread. The treads are usually 10 to 12 inches deep. The risers are of varying heights, depending on the amount of upward movement desired on the stair and on how comfortable it is for people to walk up and down. The handrail runs parallel to the stringer and provides something for people to hold on to as they pass up and down. The rail is secured at both ends by vertical posts called newel posts, which are typically secured to the house joists for greater stability. The vertical posts between the two newel posts are called balusters or spindles, and they are usually secured to the treads and to the handrail.

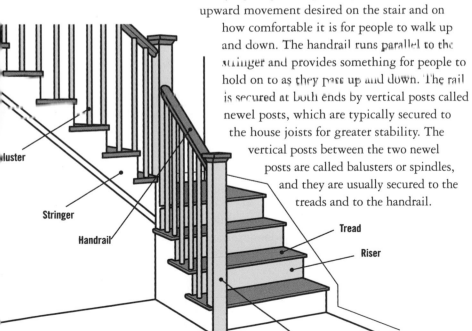

Baluster

Stringer

Handrail

Tread

Riser

Newel post

262 Deciding when to undertake a stair repair

The average homeowner is not going to rebuild the structure of a staircase. If the integrity of the staircase in its entirety is in question—meaning one or two of the stringers are starting to sink, the stringers are pulling away from the wall, or the stringers are rotted or infested with termites—you will need to call a professional carpenter or stair builder. The issue with a stair that is starting to collapse is that it is dangerous to deal with. Working with a staircase in this condition could result in you and the stairs taking quite a nasty fall. Generally, however, a homeowner can safely learn to fix loose treads, cracked risers, loose balusters, and loose handrails.

263 How do I fix a loose tread?

Chances are the tread is glued and nailed to the stringers and the riser beneath it. If the tread is loose, as you step on it you will feel the tread move. Take a closer look at it and move it around with your hand to see where it is loose. If it doesn't move with your hand, kneel on it and move around, and look down or ask someone to step on it and eyeball it. When you've found the place where it is loose, take a few sixpenny to eightpenny nails and knock them into the perimeter of the tread, paying special attention to the area that is loose. You will have to use a countersink to put the nail beneath the surface of the wood (see entry 251), so you don't hurt yourself when walking or mar the look of the staircase. If the step continues to be loose, add a few more nails. Keep doing this until you achieve your goal.

264 Can I replace a broken tread?

Yes. Of course, for most cracks you don't need to do anything, but if the crack is making the wood unstable, then you'll want to replace the entire tread. The first thing to do is go out and buy a replacement tread. Measure the tread horizontally from stringer to stringer and vertically from the riser above it to the front end of the tread. You will also need to measure the thickness of the tread, which may be hard if the front edge of the tread is rounded. The trick to measuring a rounded edge is to place a flat, solid object, such as a hardcover book, overhanging the tread. From underneath, measure from the bottom face of the book to the bottom of the rounded tread, and you have your number. Bring your length, width, and thickness measurements to the lumberyard, along with a photo of the rounding of the edge. They'll cut and sand the piece you need (most treads are oak), or they may have ready-made treads. Also pick up a stain color chart and a wood chisel.

Now take the old tread out. Place the chisel into the split, if it is close to the middle of the tread, and strike it with a hammer until the tread splits in two (fig. 1). Then you can jam the chisel into the crack and pry up one half of the tread (fig. 2). Next, pry up the other half. Place wood glue on the riser and the stringers, wiping off excess glue with a wet rag. Place the new tread in (fig. 3) and knock in 6- to 8-inch penny nails every 5 inches, using a countersink. Using

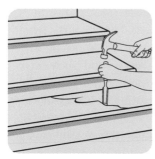

1. Hammer on the chisel to split the tread.

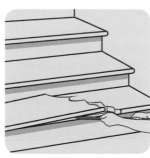

2. Pry up the tread.

3. Position the new tread.

the stain chart, choose the right color stain, take the chart to the hardware store, buy the stain and urethane in the right finish—you'll have to eyeball it—and stain and urethane the new tread.

265 How do I fix a cracked riser?

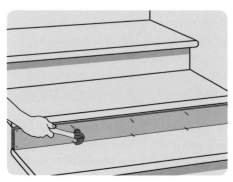

Here you may get lucky. Most risers are painted, not stained. So if you develop a slight crack in a riser that isn't jeopardizing the integrity of the riser, you may have a quick fix available to you. You'll need wood putty, a Spackle knife, rough sandpaper, and a paint color wheel. Apply an ample amount of putty over the crack. Leave it to dry overnight and sand it flush. Now the crack is gone. Buy paint that matches the riser and paint over the riser. If you have a bigger crack, or maybe a hole punched from years of shoe toes knocking into the risers, you'll need to do a larger repair. But remember, since the riser doesn't play a structural role in the stair, you can just put a patch right over the entire riser. Measure the riser from stringer to stringer and from the bottom of the tread above to the top of the tread beneath, then subtract ⅛ inch on the width and the height. Take that to the lumberyard and get them to cut you a ⅜-inch stock lumber piece. Place dots of glue around the new piece of wood, lean it up against the existing riser, and knock a few fourpenny nails on an angle into the new piece of wood. Patch the nail holes—you have to patch these because you are painting, not staining—and you now have your patch. Paint it.

266 Fixing a loose baluster

One of the most common problems you'll find on a staircase is a loose baluster. Fixing these spindles that run from the riser to the handrail is simple. Typically the baluster will be loose either at the top or the bottom. Figure out which end is loose. Replace the baluster to the exact position you want it in. Using a power drill with a bit that is narrower than a fourpenny nail, drill a pilot hole at the center of the baluster, less than ½ inch away from the top or bottom, at a 45-degree angle toward the handrail or tread, depending on where the problem arises. It is important that you don't drill all the way through the spindle into the handrail or tread—no more than ½ inch. Take a hammer and a fourpenny nail and knock the nail in, using a countersink at the end. If you don't want to paint the entire baluster, just live with the pinhole. If you can't live with the pinhole, patch with wood putty and paint.

267 Gluing a cracked baluster back together

If the crack is really small, then putty it, sand it, and paint it, as we explained in entry 265. If the crack is bigger, you'll need a more involved fix. Some of you might be saying, "Wait a minute, why don't you just buy a new baluster and replace it?" While you might be able to match the baluster, especially in a home built in the past twenty years, older homes will have balusters that just don't exist anymore. There is also the small point that removing one baluster and replacing it can involve taking off the entire handrail, which is not something you want to have to do. So you're better off repairing the baluster in place without removing it. For this job you'll need a couple of dry rags, one wet rag, white glue, and a few clamps (any kind of clamp will do). If the crack is small, pry it open and put as much glue in there as you can get. Pour it in. Wipe off the excess glue with the wet rag. Take the dry rag and place it between the clamp and the wood. Clamp the cracked wood down. If you need to clamp it in more than one place, do so. Generally, you'll place a clamp every 2 to 4 inches. Wipe off the excess glue with the wet rag. Let this sit for twenty-four hours. After the twenty-four hours, remove the clamps. Sand down any bits of glue or rags. Paint or stain.

268 How do I remove an entire baluster?

If the baluster is just so blown out you can't patch it back together in situ, or you are actually replacing the entire thing, the most common way to deal with the situation is to remove the old baluster from the handrail by taking the entire handrail from all the balusters and lifting out the baluster you want to fix. We are not going to recommend you do this. If you are really contemplating removing the entire handrail, you should probably call a carpenter. You are going to do some major damage to your stairs unless you have real skill. There's a great cheat for this, however, although you may risk trashing a saw or two. You'll need a hand saw and a hacksaw. Start by placing the hand saw in the joint between the baluster and the handrail. Saw away until you begin to feel you are hitting a nail (fig. 1). Stop. Take the hacksaw and cut through the nail (fig. 2). Stop. Start in again with the hand saw until you hit another nail. Repeat this until you are through. Now you can angle the baluster a little bit and pull it out. Introduce the new baluster on an angle, wedge it underneath the handrail, and nail it as described in entry 266 (fig. 3).

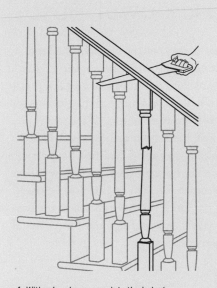

1. With a hand saw, saw into the baluster.

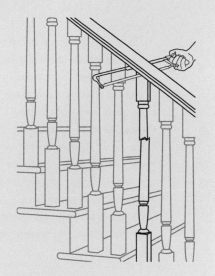

2. Once you reach the nail, switch to a hacksaw.

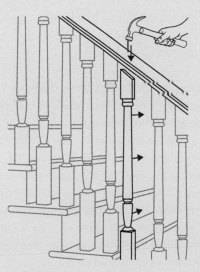

3. After inserting the new baluster,
nail it to the handrail.

269 Fixing a loose newel post

The newel post is the big vertical post at the foot and the head of the stairs that holds the handrail and the balusters together. In old houses, these were actually sunk into the steps like a jigsaw puzzle and covered by a molding. In newer construction, they are anchored into the joists of the house with straps or screws. If the newel post on your stair comes loose, think hard about calling a pro. Here's the deal: in order to get to where the post is attached to the stair or the floor, you are going to have to do some damage. You will have to either break in from underneath the floor or cut into the riser somehow. Neither is easy to do. Once you have gotten to the base of the post, if it's a new house, you'll tighten the screws and bolts; if it's an old house, you might want to sink a few screws in there.

270 How to make a wood box for a cabinet

The construction of a wood box is the basic unit of cabinetmaking. With this skill you can make all manner of cabinets, bookshelves, or any other storage unit you need.

Cabinet frames are generally made from ¾-inch plywood. Solid wood is too expensive and too irregular. You will want to think about buying plywood with finished surfaces, like a veneer or a factory paint finish. If you buy unfinished plywood, you'll eventually want to paint it. The backs of base cabinets, those that sit on the floor, are made of ¼-inch plywood. The backs of hanging cabinets are made from ½-inch plywood, because you need more support when you are hanging the cabinet on a wall.

The process for putting a cabinet together is simple. You use four pieces of wood to form two right angles, and then you glue and nail the two right angles together using white glue and sixpenny finishing nails, countersinking the nails (see entry 251). Please note that the horizontal pieces will always sit between the vertical pieces and that the nails are driven through the vertical pieces into the horizontal pieces. The tricky part is making sure the frame is squared. You check that after you have nailed the two right angles together but before you have installed the backing. Measure diagonally from the upper-right to the bottom-left corner and then upper left to bottom right. If those measurements are equal, you are squared. If they aren't square, you can push or shift the box into shape. Then you nail in the backing, using a short, squat type of nail called a blue-head nail, and you have your cabinet.

TRICK OF THE TRADE: *Before you put in all of your blue nails, check one last time to make sure that the cabinet is squared.*

271 How do I create adjustable supports for shelving?

The shelving in a cabinet is held up by shelf rests, which are small metal pins that go in holes along the vertical sides of the cabinet frame. You'll need to create those holes in two sets of parallel rows, each set on one of the vertical pieces. (Do this before you put the cabinet together.) You can measure the places to make those holes with a pencil. But it is easier to cut yourself a guide out of ¼-inch plywood that is 3 inches wide and a few inches short of the cabinet height. Make a center pencil line on the plywood guide and make crossing lines, starting at 8 inches up from the bottom and then every 1½ inches until you are 8 inches from the top.

Now you have to decide whether you want to use ³⁄₁₆-inch or ¼-inch shelf rests. Go to the store and buy the ones you want. Then

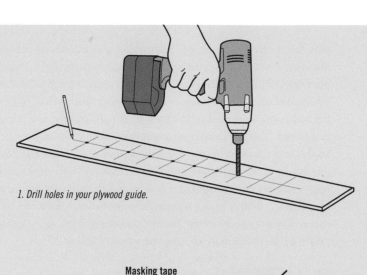

1. Drill holes in your plywood guide.

Masking tape

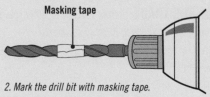

2. Mark the drill bit with masking tape.

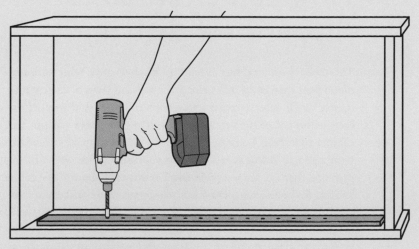

3. Lay the guide on the cabinet and drill the hole.

use the appropriate wood drill bit with your power drill to create your holes. Nail the marked guide on some junk wood. Using a hammer and a nail, make a small indentation at each pencil cross. Then place your drill bit in each hole and drill (fig. 1). Now you have your guide. Sand your guide to make it ready.

But you'll also need to measure the depth you want to go on your drill bit. Measure ¾ inch on your bit and mark that with masking tape (fig. 2). Three-quarters inch of drill will take you through your guide and ½ inch into the wood of the cabinet. Lay the cabinet down on some junk wood, on its vertical side. Take the drill guide and place it flush with the outer edge of the vertical side of the cabinet and nail the guide partially into the wood with two wire nails. Make sure that from the edge of the cabinet to the center of your plywood guide is 1½ inches. Drill the holes to the depth that you have marked (fig. 3). Drill slowly to avoid splintering and going too far into the wood. Then place the guide against the backing at the other end of the cabinet, nail the guide in there, and drill those holes. Do the same with the other vertical piece.

272 Making a cabinet shelf

The key to making a shelf is measuring correctly. Take the inner dimensions of your cabinet and subtract ¼ inch in depth from back to front and ³⁄₁₆ inch in width from side to side. This way the shelving will fit nicely into the interior of the cabinet. Don't make the shelves flush; you need to leave a little room to allow for the natural expansion of the wood in humid conditions. Most likely you'll be using a ¾-inch piece of plywood for the shelf. Take your shelf pins or shelf rests and put them in the cabinet at the height you have chosen for the shelf. Slide the shelf into the cabinet and place it atop the pins. You now have made a shelf. How many shelves do you need? Well, that is an individual preference, but a cabinetmaker will tell you that a shelf height of 10 to 12 inches is about standard.

273 How to veneer the edges of a cabinet

Now that you have your cabinet, you are going to want to give it a nicer look than just plywood. For the edges—not the faces of the cabinets but the narrow edges in the pieces of wood that frame the faces of the cabinets—you can buy a product called veneer tape. This is essentially a roll of tape on one side and a finished surface on the other side. The finish will look like paint, or like veneer, which is a thin strip of wood placed onto a piece of furniture to improve its appearance. You should purchase veneer tape that is slightly wider than the piece of wood you are finishing. Once you have your tape, lay your cabinet down on its back and roll the tape onto the surface you want to cover. Mostly we are talking about covering the edges of the wood, which will be facing out as the cabinet sits up against the wall. Start with the vertical pieces of wood. Take an iron and iron the veneer onto the surface. The heat of the iron will melt the adhesive on the strip. Use a block of wood to press the veneer down. Then take a tool called an edge trimmer and trim the edges. Cut the veneer tape off. Do the same with each surface of the cabinet.

274 Fixing a broken cabinet hinge

There are many different kinds of doors and hinges, but all cabinet doors are attached to the cabinet with hinges that are screwed into the cabinet and the door. When a cabinet's doors loosen, it is because either the hinge mechanism has broken down or the screws have loosened. If you have a door that has come loose, first inspect the screws. Take a handheld screwdriver and tighten the screws (remember not to tighten them too far, just a few turns). You may also find that a screw is missing. If you do, pull one of the remaining screws out and take it to the hardware store to find an exact match. Don't just use whatever screws you have in a jar somewhere—chances are you'll end up ruining the screw hole that is already there. Once you've determined that the screws are tight, then the problem could be a faulty mechanism. Now you have to take the entire hinge off and take it to the hardware store and match it, or go online and buy another one from the manufacturer.

275 Fixing a broken drawer slide

Drawers run on tracks. One set of tracks is screwed into the cabinet and the other into the drawer. Tracks are mounted on the sides of the drawer or on the bottom. The tracks on the drawer and the cabinet interlock, either directly with each other or with a slide mechanism between them. When a drawer breaks, what usually happens is that the screws loosen, causing the drawer to drop and bump against the drawer below or against the cabinet frame. The screw holes for the drawer tracks are oval shaped so that the screw can be moved up and down within them just a little to make adjustments. You may be able to fix the drawer by gently jamming it up a little with your hand and tightening the screws you can see, which are the ones on the drawer itself. If that doesn't work, you'll want to pull the drawer out from the cabinet. Every drawer is removable. Each manufacturer will be different, so you may have to experiment.

Sometimes you'll just need to lift the drawer up a little. Other times you'll find a release system you can press in order to get the drawer out. Once you have the drawer out, check the screws on the tracks.

household carpentry

243

276 Fixing a drawer that is falling apart

Sometimes you may think your drawer is coming loose when in fact it is falling apart. Some drawers are constructed with faceplates that are screwed onto the main box of the drawer. If the faceplate comes loose, it may appear that the entire drawer is off its tracks, but you may just need to tighten the faceplate. If the whole drawer is falling apart, remove it and try some white glue and some fourpenny finish nails. The most important thing is that the drawer must be squared. After you've put your nails in, measure both sides of the X formed by going from one corner to its diagonal opposite and then the other corner. If the measurements are equal, you're square. If they aren't equal, you need to do a little adjusting. If the bottom goes loose, use some glue and sink a few blue-head nails in to tighten it up.

277 How do I fix broken veneer on a cabinet?

Okay, you can't really fix broken veneer if it is coming off the faces of the cabinet. But you can do a few things. If it's a tiny scratch, you can use a number 2 lead pencil to darken the crack. If it's a small crack, you can try to ply it back, use some white glue underneath it, and put masking tape over it to let it dry. If you have a large crack, you can try finding the same veneer for sale or ordering a piece of plywood with veneer on it, ⅜ inch thick, then glue it onto the cabinet and tap in a few wire finishing nails. If the crack is on the door, you can have it replaced. But if the problem is on the edges, meaning the narrow widths of the wood that face out, you can make a fix. You'll do the reverse of what we described in entry 273 for veneering a cabinet. Run a hot iron over the edge of the cabinet to melt the veneer, then pull it off. Clean the surface with sandpaper, and you can then install new veneer tape as we explained previously.

278 How to put a door on a cabinet (our way)

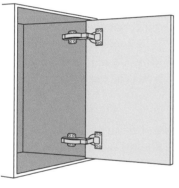

Before you make your door, decide how far out you'll want it to swing. The choice is usually either to a 90- or 180-degree angle. Then decide whether you want to see the hinges when the door is closed or have the hinges concealed. You may not care about this, but in general the visible hinges give you a more country look; the concealed hinges are more modern and are easier to install. Finally, decide whether your doors fit inside the front opening of the cabinet (inlay), or on top (overlay). This isn't a book about cabinetmaking, so we're not going to describe all the different ways this can be done. We'll outline the basic installation, which is a face-frame concealed hinge on two inlay doors. The basic trick is to measure the doors properly. You'll need to cut doors that are ⅛ inch smaller on the outside perimeter, ⅛ inch smaller on the upper and lower perimeters, and ¹⁄₁₆ inch smaller on the inside perimeter, which sits next to the other door. Then you'll screw two hinges onto the inside face of each door and onto the frame of the cabinet. The hinges will go about 3 inches from the upper and lower edges of the door. Drill handles into the door and finish the surface.

279 **Project:** Retrofit a Cabinet or a Bookshelf for a Flat-screen Television

Let's say you have an entertainment center of some kind that was designed for one of those super-deep, old-fashioned television sets. Now you've bought a thin flat-screen and you don't want to see all that space behind it. All you have to do is install a dummy panel.

1. Measure the opening you are going to fill and cut a piece of wood of the same type as the cabinet, but ⅛ inch smaller all the way around than the opening, meaning ¹⁄₁₆ inch on each side. This will be the dummy panel. Use ¾-inch-thick wood and think about painting it black so that it doesn't distract the eye when you are looking at the television.

2. Drill a 1½-inch hole in the base of the shelf on which the TV will sit, somewhere in front of where the dummy panel will sit, for wires.

3. Buy two strips of 1½-inch-wide wood that are three-quarters the height of the opening. Those strips are called cleats. The cleats will sit behind the panel and help attach the panel to the cabinet.

4. Mark off how far back you want the panel in the opening and glue and screw down one cleat to one side of the opening and the other cleat to the other side. How far back should the panel be? This will depend on whether the television will be on a stand or mounted. If it's on a stand, take the depth of the stand plus at least 2 inches. For a mounted TV, take the width of the television plus 1 inch for a stationary bracket and at least 3 inches for an articulating bracket.

5. Glue and screw down the panel to the cleats, effectively closing up the space.

6. Either place the television on the stand in front of the panel or attach the bracket to the backing, being careful to position it properly within the space.

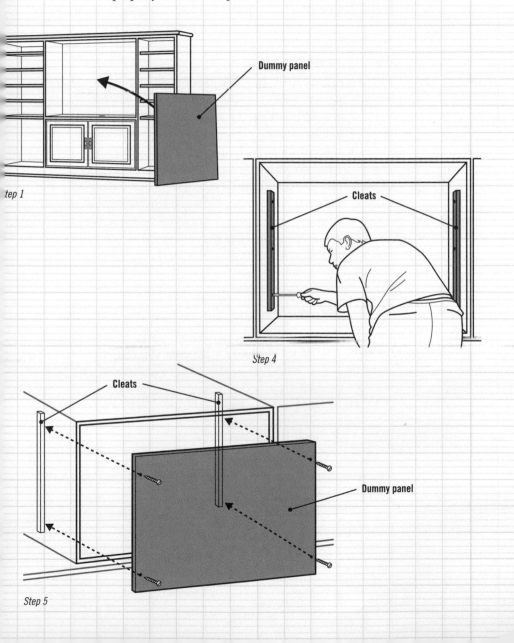

Dummy panel

Step 1

Cleats

Step 4

Cleats

Dummy panel

Step 5

280 How to fix dings in cabinets

If your cabinet is painted, you can use something called auto-body repair compound. It's a pink cement you have to mix yourself that is used to fix dents in cars. If you have a ding, you will put the compound into the ding, wipe away the excess, and let it dry for a few hours. Sand it with a 60- to 80-grit sandpaper until it is even with the cabinet. Then paint. Remember, you are going to paint the entire surface of the cabinet, because thanks to the way paint ages, you'll see the difference clearly if you just paint in the one patch. If there's a ding in a stained cabinet, you probably can't fix it. Most stained cabinets are veneered, meaning there's a thin sheet of wood glued onto the face of the cabinet. This means you have only 1/32 inch to work with, and chances are if you have a ding in the veneer, that thickness has been broken into. Now you are into another material, which will become very apparent when you try to sand and restain. On the outside chance that you have a very old or very fancy cabinet, you may have solid wood on the doors. In that case, you can sand the ding out. Do not fill the ding with putty because it will be visible. Finally, restain the entire door. If you have double doors, you may have to restain the door next to it.

281 Adding a clothes hanger rod to a closet

This is a relatively simple operation that can turn any empty closet into a useful storage space.

PREPARATION
Before you decide to make this upgrade, measure the depth of your closet. It will need to be at least 22 inches deep. That is the

minimum clearance for a coat. Then measure the width of your closet. The rod you will buy has to be the closet width minus 2 inches to allow for the hardware you are going to install and for wiggle room in the closet itself. You'll need two blocks of plywood, measuring 4 by 4 inches and ¾ inch thick. You'll need a Lucite or metal rod that should be 1⅛ inches in diameter minimum and should be longer than your closet is wide so you can cut it down at home, using a hacksaw, or have it cut down at the hardware store. (This is the better idea.) You will also need flanges, which are the pieces, usually in metal, that hold the rod to the wall. There are two kinds of flanges: U-shaped ones that allow you to take the rod in and out, and the circular variety, which needs to be removed if you want to remove the rod. We recommend the U-shaped, because this style makes it easier to change the closet around quickly.

INSTALLATION

The most important thing is to hang the rod high enough so that you can see shoes and other items on the floor, but low enough so that you can have a shelf above the rod. The ideal distance from the floor to the pole is 66 inches. The space between the pole and any shelf above it should be 3 inches. Measure 66 inches from the floor and mark it with a 5-inch pencil line on the left or right wall. Then measure on the same wall from the back forward 11 inches minimum (12 if you have the space) and cross the first mark you made with another 5-inch pencil line.

Now you have two crossed marks on the wall. Repeat on the opposite side wall. Place some white glue on one of the plywood blocks and place

1. Hammer nails through the glued block to help fasten it to the wall.

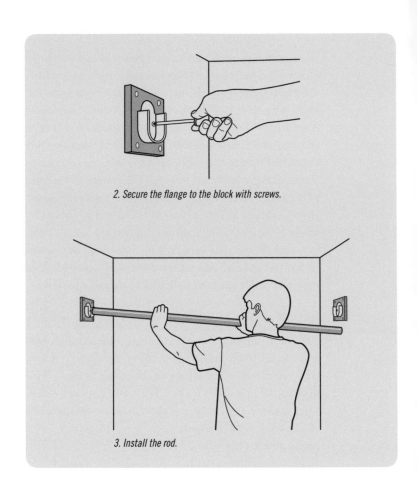

2. Secure the flange to the block with screws.

3. Install the rod.

that block directly over the crossed lines, centering the block over
the crosshairs. Knock two to four sixpenny finishing nails on a slight
angle on opposite sides of the block (fig. 1), securing the block to the
wall. Repeat on the other side. Assuming you have U-shaped flanges,
center the flange on the block and fasten it to the block with ¾-inch
pan-head screws, or with the screws that came with the flange (fig. 2).
Place the rod onto the flange and bring it to the other side. Use a
level to make sure you are doing a level installation. Mark in pencil
the right spot to place the flange, then install the second flange.
Install the rod, and you're done (fig. 3).

If you have fine antique furniture in your house, or think you might, do not repair it yourself. You will ruin its value. If, however, you have basic, modern wooden furniture, you can make simple repairs. What can go wrong with furniture? Basically, the wood will crack somewhere, or an arm or a leg will loosen or break off.

To repair cracks, you will need these supplies: clamps, rags to protect the wood, plenty of white glue, and a wet rag to clean the excess glue. Fill the crack with as much glue as you can force in there, wipe away the excess glue, and clamp the crack for twenty-four hours, placing rags between the clamp and the wood. When you remove the clamps, you may end up with bits of rag stuck to the area. If you dampen it with water, then the rag will come off. The damage may be so great that once you are done putting the piece back together, you will have to either stain it yourself and finish it, or take it to a professional finisher. There are hazards in trying to match the original stain and finish yourself.

In most cases furniture arms and legs are separate pieces of wood attached to the main body of the piece by dowels. A dowel is a cylindrical piece of wood that is inserted into a hole in the body of the furniture and a corresponding opening in the arm or leg; the entire thing is held together by glue.

The process here is the same for an arm or a leg, so let's just talk about a leg. Turn the piece of furniture upside down. If the leg is loose, you want to put it in the proper position and squeeze as much glue—regular white glue is fine—as you can in there. If that doesn't work, pry the leg off. Sand the glue off the dowel. This is important, because the dried glue has to come off so that the new glue can set. Add new glue to the dowel and install the leg. For a tighter fit, try inserting a few wooden toothpicks. If the leg is broken off and the dowel is broken in half, take a power drill and use a bit of the same diameter as the dowel, drill it out on both sides, and buy a new dowel. The dowel should go ½ inch minimum into both sides. Glue the dowel and insert it into the leg first. Let it set overnight. Insert the leg into the body of the furniture.

household carpentry

Doors and Locks

A piece of wood or metal hinged into an opening in a wall, the door is one of the most simple and basic of household objects. Yet the more we started thinking about doors, the more we realized how much we had to say about them, and eventually we ended up giving doors their own chapter. Why? Well, there are just so many small, nagging things that can go wrong with doors, and when you add locks into the picture, forget about it. With all the squeaking, sticking, warping, and whatnot, there is no end to the trouble doors can put you through.

283 What kind of door do I have?

Doors come in two standard heights: 6 feet 8 inches, which is 80 inches, and 7 feet, which is 84 inches. In fact, however, doors can come in any height. They can be ordered in other heights at the factory for a nominal fee. Standard door widths go up in 2-inch intervals, beginning at 16 inches and ending at 36 inches. For doorways that are wider than 36 inches, many builders will opt to put in double doors. The standard thicknesses for doors are 1⅜ and 1¾ inches. Doors can come in a variety of substances, from vinyl to metal, but most doors used in the home are made of some kind of wood or wood product. The most basic doors are flat—an apt description for a plain, flat door. An upgrade from this is the paneled door, which has one to fifteen decorative panels on it. In the United States you can find doors made of any kind of wood you can think of. Flat doors are usually created out of man-made materials. Paneled doors are made from solid blocks of wood, typically pine and oak. They also come in finer woods like hickory or cherry, which are much more expensive.

Flat door   *Paneled door*

284 What's inside a flat door?

Flat doors are typically made of particleboard. This is an engineered substance that is made by taking wood chips or sawdust and binding it together with some kind of resin and forming it into a door shape. The three main advantages of particleboard are that it's cheap, it's light, and it's made up of material that would otherwise be turned into waste. The particleboard is then covered in a thin veneer of natural wood. Usually the edges of the door, which will take the most wear and tear as the door opens and closes, will be constructed of a solid wood like pine. The section of the door where the lock goes will also be made of solid pine. Flat doors may be hollow-cored, meaning they are hollow inside. These are the cheapest type of doors on the market, and as a consequence you will find them in many houses. Flat doors may also be what is called solid core, which doesn't mean the door is solid, exactly. What it means is that the door has weighty wooden ribs inside to give it heft and add sound-blocking potential.

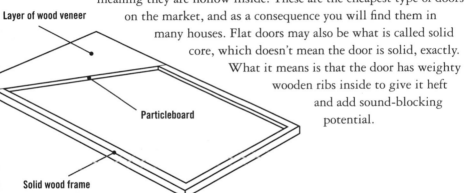

Layer of wood veneer

Particleboard

Solid wood frame

285 Why do some doors have fire ratings?

You may have noticed that you have the option of buying fire-rated doors, which means the door in question has been tested in the factory for its ability to hold off a fire for a certain amount of time, which could be as few as twenty minutes or as much as ninety minutes. These doors, which are usually made of metal and other nonwooden materials, are often found in public buildings. You can, however, install them in your home as a safety feature. But you should keep in mind that the doors need to be installed properly, and if the walls of your house are constructed from single-layer Sheetrock, which is likely to go up in flames in relatively short order and burn around the fire door, that fire-rated door isn't going to do you much good.

TRICK OF THE TRADE: *When buying a door, make sure that it hasn't warped in the store. That happens a lot.*

286 Doors are attached to walls by hinges

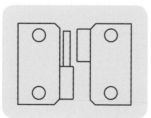

Consider for a second the unheralded door hinge. Not a part of your house you spend much time thinking about, but it is really the hinge that makes the door a useful item, and you use doors all day, every day. Hinges come in all shapes, sizes, and looks. You can select hinges on aesthetic grounds, as most hinges will work with most doors. The two most common sizes of hinge are 3½ by 3½ inches, which will work well with standard 1⅜-inch-thick doors, and 4 by 4 inches, which work best with 1¾-inch-thick doors. Make sure to choose a rustproof hinge for exterior use.

You'll also have to decide how many hinges to use. Standard 6-foot-8-inch-tall doors will be fine with two hinges. Anything taller or wider or very heavy, and you should consider using three hinges. The hinge consists of two metal pieces that look something like butterfly wings interlocking to form a central tube, into which a metal pin is inserted, and the hinge opens and closes on the pin. Most hinges come with a removable pin.

287   How to lubricate a squeaky hinge

In an ideal world, you should lubricate every hinge in your house once a year. That would keep the hinges healthy and ensure they'll be in good working order. We understand that you probably aren't going to do that, but when you think about it, try to. There's a quick way to lubricate a hinge and a more comprehensive way. The quick way isn't exactly the wrong way, but it may not really get the job done. Basically, you take some lubricant—for example, oil in a spray can—and spray it on the hinge, opening and shutting the door, trying to get the lubricant into all the nooks and crannies. This may work just fine, but it won't get the lubricant into the really important part of the hinge: the pin. Some of the cheaper hinges come with pins that cannot be removed, but most hinges have removable pins. If the pin does come out, take it out, place a nail in the hinge to keep the door from falling down, lay the pin out on some newspaper, and spray it with lubricant. That will do the trick.

288   Can I fix a rusted hinge?

Even a hinge in an indoor room can rust over time. There's the regular humidity in the atmosphere and condensation caused by changes in temperature brought on by central heating, and the moisture that you and your family are putting into the air with your breath. If a hinge becomes rusted you could replace it, but you may want to save the hinge, since it matches the other hinges in the house and you don't want to replace all of them, or because it is old and irreplaceable. In that case, there is a fix for a rusted hinge: fire.

For this fix you'll need a handheld propane torch. This is a dangerous item. (You knew that.) So wear safety gloves and glasses,

doors and locks

257

and for the love of Pete, make sure you are somewhere away from flammable objects. Take the hinge off the door. Go to a safe, nonflammable area, preferably outdoors. Put the hinge down on a nonflammable surface, like stone, concrete, or asphalt. Turn on the propane and light the torch. Aim the flame at the hinge, moving the flame around and around the hinge, until it begins to glow with heat. Shut off the torch and put it away. Let the hinge cool and then—*only* once it is cool—spray the hinge with a spray-on lubricant. Holding both sides of the hinge with two pairs of pliers, move the hinge back and forth. Watch the rust fall off the hinge. Give it another lubricant spray. Reattach it to the door.

289   When hinges falter

The single biggest problem with hinges is that the screws that hold them to the wall and door loosen over time. This is caused by the weight and the motion of the door. Hinges can also loosen because whoever installed the hinges overscrewed the hinges into the wall. When the hinges loosen, you may not actually see the door moving in a funny way. What you may notice is that the door is sticking or scraping against the doorframe. To fix a loose hinge, just take the appropriate screwdriver and tighten all the screws that attach the hinge to both the door and the door frame. If you have tightened all the hinges and the door is still scraping, you may have one of two problems. Either the screws are loose in the wood, or the door may have expanded or warped.

290 Tightening loose hinges

If you're not sure whether you have a loose hinge or another problem, try opening and closing the door while looking at the hinges. Do they shift or move at all? If you hold the door by the handle and jiggle it, do the hinges move? If they do, then they are loose. The screws attaching the hinge to the wall can loosen for a variety of reasons, but the most common would be from the motion of the door itself. If the hinges have been allowed to sit there loose for a while, their screws may have moved around so much in their holes that they will no longer sit tightly in those holes. To get a tight fit again, try using a larger screw. You can also take a small piece of wood, like a narrow dowel, and tap it into the hole with a hammer, then try screwing the old screw again. Either of these fixes ought to give you the nice, tight fit you had when the screw was first installed.

291 Fixing a door that has expanded

In places that have different seasons with wide temperature changes, wood doors tend to expand in the summertime, when the air is humid, and contract in the winter, when central heating dries them out. So, you'll usually find that doors stick during the warmer months. To determine where a door is sticking, look at the side of the door and find the scratch marks; or shine a light behind the door and look for the spots where there's no light coming through. The fix for a door that's sticking from expansion is to shave or sand down the door at the spot where the sticking is occurring. You may be able to sand down the spot by hand with some 80-grit sandpaper. If that doesn't work, you may need to use a tool.

doors and locks

You can use a hand planer, which is a tool that shaves a thin layer off wood. The hazard with using a planer is that it's really easy to gouge the wood. If you are going to use a hand planer, it's best to buy a piece of scrap wood and practice on it. The easier way to go is to buy or rent a radial-belt sander, which is a commercial-grade power tool that has sandpaper on a revolving belt. Use this machine sparingly. Sand a little away, and try the door. Repeat until you have done the job.

A SEASONAL WARNING

You've identified the squeaky door and you've figured out where the door is sticking. Now you are all ready to sand that portion of the door down and fix the problem. But wait a second. Ask yourself what time of year it is. If your door is sticking during hot and humid weather, do not under any circumstance sand it down. Simply take note of exactly where the door is sticking. Then wait a few months until the weather cools. During the summer, the door has expanded from the humidity, and if you sand at that time, you run the danger of overdoing it because the door is so much larger than normal. If you wait until the temperatures cool, you'll have a better sense of just how far you need to go. If you get to the winter and the door is no longer sticking, just sand down the trouble spot very slightly and wait for summertime again. If the problem returns, just try a little more sanding and see how that goes.

292 The warp factor

Just as wood doors expand and contract, they also can warp. Tall, wide, and heavy doors, especially those taller than 8 feet, are more susceptible to warping. Doors warp in two basic ways. They belly out from the center, or the tops and bottoms warp out, with the center caving inward.

For a door whose top and bottom have warped and whose center has caved in, you'll need to clamp it. This is a complex and time-consuming activity that should not be undertaken unless you are a really good carpenter. If you want to save the particular door, you may be able to take it to a local woodshop, and they'll do the clamping for you. If not, you may want to consider a new door, especially if the door in question isn't an expensive or one-of-a-kind item. In the end, it's much cheaper to buy a new one.

It's much easier to fix a door that's bellied out than one that has caved in. You can correct a bellied-out door by adding a third hinge at the center of the door.

293 How to find a hinge to add to an already installed door

You may need to add a hinge to keep a door from warping (see entry 292). Find a hinge that matches the existing hardware in size, finish, and type. That might sound like trying to find a needle in a haystack, but actually hinges come in pretty standard formats. Take a look at the hinge; if you can find its manufacturer and model number, you might be able to buy it off the Internet. Failing that, you can always take one of the existing hinges to the hardware store and get as close a match as you can. Remember, most door hinges sit quietly in their spot on the side of the door, unobtrusively minding their own business. They rarely get noticed. Chances are if you find a hinge that is a close-enough match, it will attract little or no attention.

In order to attach the new hinge, you will have to take the door down.

294 Project: Remove a Door and Add a Center Hinge

This is the basic door project, because there may be various times you'll want to remove doors and replace or add hinges.

1. Begin to mark the door for the new hinge. On the side of the door where you see the existing hinge pins sticking out, measure the distance between the two existing hinges and mark the dead center point. Center the new hinge over that mark, hold it there, and make marks on the door and the door frame where the top and bottom of the new hinge are.

2. Remove the door. Start at the lower hinge and remove it by disassembling it. At the bottom of the hinge, beneath the pin, is a small hole. Find a screwdriver, nail, or other object that fits into that hole. Place the object in the hole and hammer upward until the pin comes out. Do the same for the top hinge. Take the door down.

3. Continue marking the door for the new hinge by using a ruler or other straight edge to extend the marks you already made for the hinge around the face of the door and across its inner edge. But keep in mind that when installed, the hinge will not lie across the entirety of the door's thickness. So take a ruler and measure how much space there is between the existing hinges and the end of the door's edge. Mark that distance on the two lines you've made for your new hinge and connect those marks, drawing a line through them. You now have a complete outline of where the hinge will sit.

4. Sink the hinge in the door. Hinges are made to be flush, so you'll need to carve out spaces to lay the hinge into. The tool that does this is called a router or Dremel (see entry 295). Once you have mastered the router and marked the space for the hinge in the door, sinking the hinge should be easy. Find a friend to hold the

door for you, or place the door between your legs, and, using the router, cut out the space you've marked.

5. Attach the hinge. Remove the pin and detach the wings. Take one wing and place it on the door where you've carved the space for it. Take a pencil and mark the screw holes. Be careful to use the correct side of the hinge, because some hinges have a top and bottom and others don't.

6. Mark the door frame and install the door. You are going to now repeat on the door frame what you did with the door. Mark the midpoint between the two existing hinges in the door frame. Place the new hinge wing centered over the midpoint mark and delineate the upper and lower boundaries of the new hinge. Join those two lines to create an outline of where the new hinge will sit. Attach the door to the doorjamb with the old hinges. When you have it lined up properly, route the door frame and mark the holes for the hinge. Screw the appropriate wing of the new hinge into the door frame. Reattach the door, doing the top hinge, the bottom hinge, and then the middle hinge. You're done.

Center mark

Step 1

Step 3

295 How to use a router

To install a new hinge, you are going to have to use a router (often called a Dremel), a power tool that has various bits that can be attached to it. These bits carve out spaces in wood. The bit you'll need for this job is Z-shaped. It's a basic bit for removing wood from surfaces. There are two kinds of routers: fixed routers and plunge routers. A fixed router is best for this kind of job. Explain what you're doing down at the hardware store, and they'll know exactly what you need. Before you start, please realize that the router is one of the most dangerous of all power tools. Make sure you attach the bit to the router firmly and properly, following the instructions that come with the appliance. Otherwise, when you turn the router on, you'll launch a flesh-gouging missile somewhere, maybe at yourself. Now set the depth of the router. Your depth will be the thickness of the hinge, which is usually ⅛ inch. But basically you'll have to eyeball the job, and the best way to do this is to do a dry run on a piece of scrap wood. Carve out a space, and if the hinge sits in it flush, you have the right depth.

TWO TRICKS OF THE TRADE:

1. *Make sure you have your router plugged into an extension cord, so you have freedom of movement.*
2. *When you start working with the router, you are going to be spewing sawdust everywhere. So cover the room you're working in with a plastic drop cloth and your eyes with glasses.*

296 Installing a door from scratch

You already know how to install a hinge, so installing a door is really just a matter of repeating that process two or three times. Still, there are some things to think about. The door should be ⅜ inch narrower than the opening. The door should be about 3⁄16 inch below the top of the door opening. The bottom is a little trickier. You need to know what the door is swinging into. Is there a threshold? Is there a carpet? Is there a doormat? Take that measurement into account and add ½ inch clearance beyond that for an interior door. For an exterior door, add a bit less—maybe ¼ inch—to keep out the cold air.

297 How to weatherize a door

There are two steps you can take: installing a door sweep, and using weather stripping. Weather stripping is self-explanatory. It's a strip of material that is available at the hardware store, comes in a length that can be trimmed, and has an adhesive side that you simply attach to the doorjamb to form a tighter seal between the door and the door frame. Weather stripping is cheap and easy, and it comes off the door all the time. So you'll replace it at least once a year.

A door sweep is a metal strip that typically comes with a rubber gasket, which touches the floor to form a seal. Buy a sweep wider than the door and cut it down to fit the door's width. Measure the width of the door and mark it on the sweep. Find any flat surface above the floor that you aren't afraid to scratch. Place the sweep on the flat surface with the portion of the sweep you want cut sticking out. (Place the sweep on a rag to cut down on scratching.) Press the sweep down onto the flat surface with the palm of one hand, and with the other cut the sweep with the saw. Saw gently at first to develop a

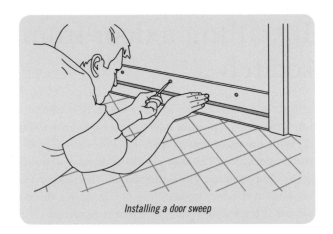

Installing a door sweep

Using weather stripping

groove and then saw with greater vigor. Once the sweep is cut to size, you can file down its edge. Lay the cut-down sweep against the door so that the gasket is bending on the floor about ⅛ inch when the door is closed. If you've had to cut into the premade screw hole at the end of the sweep, then you'll have to create a new one, using a drill, about 1 inch in from the end. Mark the openings for the screws on the door sweep, drill screw holes, and install the sweep.

TRICK OF THE TRADE: *Take note of any doormats or other obstructions that may be in front of the door and will affect the easy opening and shutting of the door when the door sweep is installed.*

298 What kind of door handles are there?

Most of the door handles in the world can be divided into two main categories: knobs and levers. The knob is the more old-fashioned of the two. Knobs can come in a wide variety of shapes and styles, but the classic is a ball of some sort. You turn a knob by gripping it with your fingers. Legend has it that the lever began in hospitals for use by people who were unable to, or had a hard time, using their hands. A lever typically has a longer handle that is positioned horizontally across the front of the door. You turn the lever by pressing it down. The difference between these two types of handles is a matter of style. The door handles are attached to something called a lockset, which is the door's inner workings, the mechanism that keeps the door closed when you shut it.

TRICK OF THE TRADE: *If you have problems with your hands, or are getting older and think small-muscle coordination might become a problem, consider lever handles.*

299 How the inside of a door handle works

You have a handle on either side of the door. The handles are attached to each other, and this attachment passes through something called a lockset. The lockset is perpendicular to the handles, sits inside the door, and emerges at the door's edge in the form of a metal tongue. The tongue is retractable, and when the door is closed, the tongue sits in a hole in the door frame, which keeps the door closed. When the handles turn, the lockset retracts the tongue, and the door opens.

doors and locks

Door handles are attached to each other in one of two ways. The old-fashioned design was to screw both handles into a rod, called a spindle, which passes through something called a mortise lockset. The mortise lockset is a rather large, rectangular box that sits inside the door itself. The newer method of connecting the two handles is to build them to interlock inside the door like a puzzle. With this system you have something called a cylinder lockset. It's almost certain that if you buy a new set of door handles, they'll come with a cylinder lockset, which is easy to deal with. By contrast, mortise locksets are very expensive, costing hundreds of dollars each. They're hard to install, and they are high maintenance. You may, however, have to use a mortise lockset if you are building or renovating a house in an older style, or if you are in an older house and all the doors have mortise locksets.

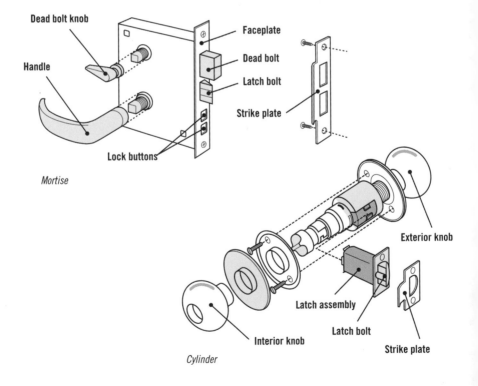

Mortise

Cylinder

300 Before you buy a lockset

Before you go to the hardware store, measure the thickness of
your door, because locksets are made to work with specific door
thicknesses. If your door is paneled, you'll want to measure the
distance from the edge of the door to the edge of the nearest panel.
Check whether the door's hinges are on the left or the right of the
door (do this while facing the side of the door where the hinge pins
are located). If the hinges are on the right side from this angle, you
have what's called a right swing door. If the hinges are on the left,
you have a left swing door. Finally, you will need to decide whether
you want a lockset that can lock, which is called a privacy set, or a
nonlocking model, which is called a passage set.

301 How to install a mortise lockset

Pick up the phone and call an experienced locksmith, because you
are *not* installing a mortise lockset. They are a kind of bulky, complex
lockset that was used back in the day. They're usually found in old
doors, where they are already installed, obviously. If you want to put
one in a new door, you're going to spend a lot of money to buy one.
Moreover, the installation is a serious bit of woodworking. The problem
is that mortise locksets are really big. That means you are going to
have to find a way to dig out a very large rectangular hole into the edge
of the door and then poke another hole through the rectangular hole
at the precise point where the handles need to go. That isn't easy to
do, and if you mess it up, you'll have effectively ruined your door. If
you really want an old-fashioned lockset installed in a new door, hire
someone to do it for you. Chances are this job will take a professional
carpenter about two hours, which shouldn't result in a massive charge.

302 How to install a cylinder lockset

Installing a cylinder lockset is a relatively quick job that you can do yourself, saving a locksmith's fees. However, if it's not done carefully, it could ruin the door. So read the following first to decide whether you're up to taking this task on yourself.

GETTING STARTED

What you will be doing is drilling two crossing, round holes into the door—one wider hole for the handles that goes from the inner face of the door to the outer face, and a narrower hole for the lockset, which goes into the edge of the door and through the hole for the handles. For this task you'll need a power drill with two bits, a screwdriver, a router or a hand chisel, and a hammer. Before you go to the hardware store to buy a new lockset, remember to measure the thickness of your door's edge and the distance from the edge to the nearest panel. (If you are installing the lockset into a flat door, you don't need to worry about this issue.)

When you are choosing locksets at the store, the most important information on the package is what the lockset's backset is. The backset (we know this is confusing) is the distance the center of the handle mechanism inside the door will sit from the door's edge. For a paneled door, try to find a backset equal to about half the distance from the door's edge to the edge of the first panel. For a flat door, take a backset of 2¼ inches. Once you've selected your lockset, you'll know what size of drill bits you are going to need. One bit should match exactly the diameter listed on the lockset package for the handles. The other bit should be ¹⁄₁₆ inch larger than the diameter of the cylinder lockset as listed.

MARKING AND DRILLING YOUR DOOR

The standard height for a lockset is around 38 inches. To mark where your handles will go, draw a 4-inch line from the door's edge, straight in, at the height you want them off the floor. Cross this line

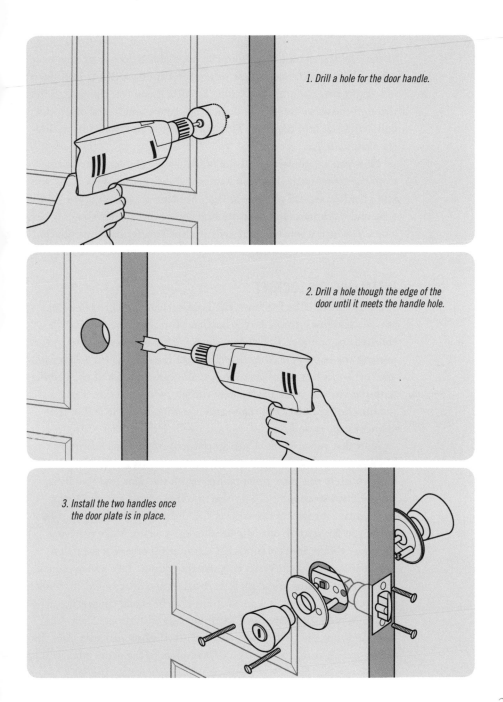

1. Drill a hole for the door handle.

2. Drill a hole though the edge of the door until it meets the handle hole.

3. Install the two handles once the door plate is in place.

at the backset, as measured from the edge of the door. You now have a T marked over the exact spot where the handles will sit. Drill your hole right there, going slowly (fig. 1). When you feel the drill going through the other side of the door, stop, go around to the other side, and drill back into the door. This will prevent you from splintering the door's surface.

Now you are going to drill the hole for the cylinder. Draw a line from the center of the hole you just made to the edge of the door, and take that line around the door's edge. Measure the width of the door's edge and mark its center over the line you've just made. You now have a new T, which is where you'll drill. Fit the smaller drill bit into the drill and drill a hole until you intersect the first hole you made (fig. 2).

INSTALLING THE LOCKSET

Place the cylinder lockset into the hole at the edge of the door and the two handles into the larger hole and interlock the two handles through the cylinder. Before you do anything else, make sure you are putting the handles on the correct side of the door. If the lockset is one that locks (not all of them do), make sure you install the handle with the keyhole underneath it on the *outside* of the door. Turn the installed handles, and make sure the tongue at the end of the cylinder goes in and out.

Now that you know it all works properly, there's one step left: installing the rectangular plate that surrounds the tongue. Unfortunately this plate must be flush with the door, and that means cutting out a space for it. To do that you'll need to route or chisel a rectangular indentation the same size and thickness as the plate. But before you get started, take the handles apart again. Make sure you have the cylinder in its hole so that the angled portion of the metal tongue is facing the direction that the door closes. Take a sharp pencil and trace the outline of the plate as it sits on the door's edge, marking the screw holes as well. Take your router or chisel and cut out the depth needed to make the plate flush with the edge of the door. Then drill your screw holes with drill bits that are just slightly narrower than the screws you are using. Screw the cylinder plate to the door's edge, install the two handles, and screw them into the door's surface (fig. 3).

303 Remember the strike plate

If you've just installed a lockset into a door, you are probably feeling pretty good about yourself right now. So, go ahead and close the door. Something isn't right? You don't hear that clicking sound a door makes when the lockset tongue clicks into a hole surrounded by a metal plate in the door frame. That metal plate is called a strike plate. The strike plate is there to protect the doorjamb from damage as the door opens and closes and to give the tongue something to catch onto. Close the door and estimate where the tongue is sitting on the door frame. Make a line at this point on the door casing, open the door, and draw that line around to the interior of the doorway (fig. 1). Now you have the height where the strike plate will sit. To get the width, measure the doorway and cross your line at the center. You now have a T at the point the strike plate will sit over. Take a drill bit larger than the diameter of the hole in the strike plate and drill in around an inch deep (fig. 2). Take your strike plate, center it over the hole you've drilled, draw a line around the perimeter of the strike plate, and mark the screw holes. Take your router or chisel and carve out the indentation you'll need to fit the strike plate flush with the door frame. Drill the screw holes and then screw the strike plate into the door frame (fig. 3).

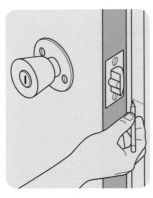

1. Mark the spot on the door frame for the strike plate.

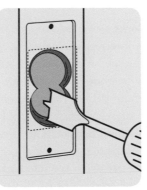

2. Drill the hole.

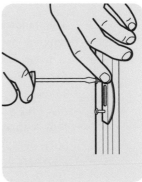

3. Screw in the plate.

304 Why doesn't the tongue click when I close the door?

Sometimes you've done everything pretty much correctly, but when you close the door, the tongue doesn't click into the strike plate hole. What's happened is that you've positioned the strike plate hole just a hair off. To figure out what's gone wrong and where, place a drop of white glue, the kind that wipes off easily with a wet rag, around the perimeter of the tongue and close the door. Open the door and see where the white glue has hit the strike plate. Where you see the glue on the strike plate, that's where you've gone wrong. As long as you are just a bit off, you can fix this by filing down the tongue or the opening to the strike plate. If you are off by a lot, read the preceding entries again—you are going to need to start over.

305 When do I need to install a dead bolt lock?

The standard locks we've been discussing in this chapter have metal tongues that will retract when force is applied to them, even if there is no key used in the lock. In other words, if someone really wants to break into a door with a regular lock on it, and that someone is a reasonably strong person, they are going to get in. If you want to make the door safer, you might think about installing a dead bolt lock. Sometimes dead bolt locks are used on their own, but more often they are added to doors that already have standard locks. A dead bolt lock differs from the standard lock because the dead bolt will move only when the lock itself is turned and the dead bolt extends more deeply into the door frame.

306 How to install a dead bolt lockset

The process here is similar to what you would do when installing a standard lockset. The usual practice is to install the dead bolt lock above the standard lock, at a height of around 50 inches. Most dead bolt locksets will come with a paper template that you can affix to the door with tape to show you where to cut into the door. Use a sharp object like an awl to mark where you are going to set the holes for the lock cylinder on the face of the door and for the bolt on the edge of the door. Drill the proper-size holes, making sure to drill almost all the way on one side, and then drilling from the other side to prevent splintering the wood. Use a drill to create a space for the bolt. Mark the space for the faceplate of the bolt on the inner edge of the door. Use a chisel or a router to carve out that space. Install the bolt, and then screw in the faceplate. Insert the lockset. Mark and drill the doorway with a space for the bolt to go into and for the strike plate.

TRICK OF THE TRADE: *Dead bolts come in single- and double-cylinder models. The single cylinders have a key on the outside of the door and a twist knob on the inside. Double-cylinder locks have keyed entry on both sides, making them even more secure.*

307　When door handles go bad

The problem common to all handles and locksets is that the tongue sometimes wears down at the sharp edge where the angled side of the tongue meets the flat side. For a tongue to work properly, this edge should be sharp. When it dulls, the tongue doesn't catch properly in the hole. This is an easy fix. Take a metal file and file the flat side and the angled side. After every five swipes of the file on each side of the tongue, try the door again. When it catches properly, you can stop.

If cylinder handles come loose now and then, just tighten the screws. If you hear any squeaks, use some spray lubricant. With mortise sets the knobs are always coming loose off the spindles. Typically when you put a knob back on the spindle, you actually have to screw it on, because most spindles are threaded. But don't screw the knob too far—if you do, the tongue won't come out of the mortise, staying inside the door. If that happens, unscrew the knob a half turn and see if the tongue comes out. Now you have to attach the knob to the spindle with a small screw. Remember, the spindles are actually square shaped and the screw is supposed to catch onto a flat side of the spindle. If the screw is sitting on an angle of the spindle, it won't catch properly, and when you try to turn the knob, the tongue won't operate at all. Loosen the screw, give the knob a turn, tighten the screw, and try again. Repeat this process until you get the tongue moving.

308 How to lubricate a lock

Now that you understand exactly how a lockset is installed, you can easily undertake this simple household fix for any sticking locks, which is a nagging issue that tortures many households. The first thing you should try is to spray some oil lubricant right into the keyhole. Once you've sprayed, let the door sit for two minutes and then put the key in and take it out of the lock a few times, just to spread the lubricant around. If that fails to solve the problem, consider taking the lockset apart. Unscrew the handles from the face of the door. Unscrew the plate with the tongue in it from the edge of the door. Remove the door handles and pull out the cylinder lockset with the tongue. Spray the entire mechanism with lubricant and then let it sit on newspaper until the excess lubricant drips off. Reinstall the lockset.

309 Removing a key that's broken off inside the lock

It will happen now and then that the business end of a key will get broken off inside the lock, meaning the handle end of the key will break off and the teeth of the key will end up in the lock. If you cannot see what remains of the key, meaning it is all the way in the interior of the lock, you are going to have to call a locksmith. But if you can see a bit of the key sticking out of the lock, save yourself a lot of time and money and pull the thing out. How? Simple. Take some spray lubricant and try to get it in around the key piece and into the lock. Take a pair of needle-nose pliers, get as firm a grip on the key piece as you can, and gently ease the key out of the lock. This ought to work every time and save you enough money to take yourself and a friend out to a nice restaurant.

310 How do sliding doors work?

There are many different kinds of sliding doors. They are often found in front of closets, decks, and patios. Sliding doors run on small rollers that fit into metal, wood, or vinyl tracks. Typically there are two doors—one door installed behind the other so that they don't get in each other's way. Heavier doors, such as those you find leading out to patios, tend to run on a bottom track, whereas lighter doors, such as those found on closets, are typically hung onto upper rails. There will also be a guide at the bottom, to prevent the door from swinging as it travels on the rollers. A variant on the sliding door is the bifold door, which has doors on hinges and pivots that allow the door panels to swing inward when they are opened.

311 Installing sliding track doors on a closet

GETTING STARTED

We are talking about installing two sliding closet doors for a closet that is 6 feet wide. If the closet is much wider than that, you'll need to install three or more doors. Normally you'd use flat, hollow-core doors, which are unobtrusive, cheaper, and lighter. Measure the width of your opening. If it is 6 feet wide, you'll want to order a 40-inch door for the front and a 42-inch door for the back, so that you won't be able to see in between the doors when they're closed. Then you measure the height of your opening and order doors that are ½ inch less than the height so that the door doesn't rub against carpet, the saddle, etc. At the hardware store, buy a double-track system that fits the width of the closet's opening and the thickness of the door. For wider closets, you may need a three-track, three-door system. Buy a width longer than you need and cut it down with a hacksaw. You'll buy two rollers per door—they're called wheel hangers in the biz. The rollers come with brackets that screw into the door. Finally, you'll need one guide per door for the bottom of the closet. It is a little piece that keeps the doors on track.

THE INSTALLATION

Screw the track into the header of the closet, meaning the top of the closet opening (fig. 1). Screw the wheel hangers onto whichever part of the door, the back face or the top edge, the instructions tell you to (fig. 2). Hang the back door on its track, then the front door on its

1. Install the track at the top of the closet.

2. Secure the wheels to the top of the closet door.

3. Hang the front door on the track.

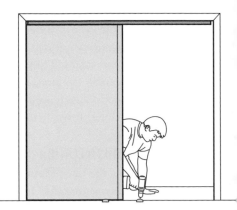

4. Screw the guides into the floor.

track (fig. 3). Eyeball the doors to make sure they are even. If they are not hanging straight, there's a nut on the plate that attaches the rollers to the door. You can adjust it to lift or lower the door. Taking the overlap point of the doors, measure about 10 percent into each door, and that is where you'll screw in your guides (fig. 4). They are screwed right into the floor.

312 Maintaining sliding doors

The truth about sliding doors is that they break. They don't last as long as they should, and there is no perfect model. The number one thing that breaks is the guide at the bottom. You'll find that you are kicking it all the time, and eventually the plastic will snap off. If you can, and it may not be easy, try to find a metal guide. The second most common problem is that the rollers and tracks will start to stick over time from dirt and use. So once a year just take a rag and a dab of water and clean the dust and lint out of the tracks. Then apply lubricating spray to them and the wheels. Third, the screws that attach the wheel-hanging system to the door are going to loosen. Every once in a while tighten them, without overturning. Do the same thing with the track header, which will loosen over time. If you don't tighten the screws, they'll start to fall into your closet, and you won't be able to find them. Then more screws will fall, and eventually you'll have a failed system. So be vigilant and maintain your sliding doors at least once a year.

313 How to install a door closer

A door closer is a hinged device that when properly calibrated will automatically close any door in a gentle fashion. This can be incredibly useful, particularly on front doors that see a lot of traffic from children or careless adults who regularly forget to keep the door in question closed. Door closers are also useful for restraining doors that are routinely slammed. Each manufacturer will have a slightly different installation, but essentially the main part of the mechanism is screwed into the upper part of the inner face of the door, then there is an arm with a small faceplate that is screwed into the upper part of the door frame. A small screw on the side of the mechanism allows you to adjust the door closer to allow for the weight of your

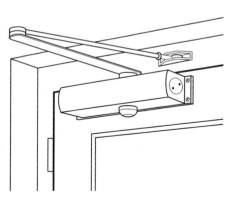

door. Typically you will turn the screw to the right to slow the door's motion, and to the left to speed it up. In cold-weather climates, a device like this can save you money on your heating bill and prevent wear and tear on your house.

Sheetrock, Painting, Wallpaper, Tile, and Stonework

Most of your house is walls. Today, most walls are made of a prefabricated material called Sheetrock. There are so many things you can do with it: paint, wallpaper, even tile and stone can go on it. It may be a bit flimsy, and the stone walls of yore were certainly more durable, but Sheetrock is a whole lot easier to work with, fix, and change.

SHEETROCK

314　What is Sheetrock?

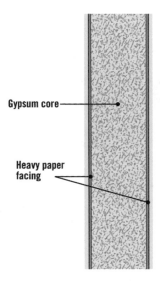

Gypsum core

Heavy paper facing

Cross section

It's called Sheetrock, drywall, gypsum board, and many other names, but whatever you call it, we call it Sheetrock, and it is the standard material used to create interior walls in all new construction. It is made of kiln-dried plaster wrapped in thick paper and comes in either 3-foot-by-5-foot boards or 4-foot-by-8-foot boards that range in thickness from ¼ inch to ⅝ inch. (The standard thicknesses for Sheetrock walls are ⅜ inch and ⅝ inch.) These boards are screwed onto wooden or metal framing, and then the builder fills up the wall with a patchwork of Sheetrock pieces. The seams between these pieces are covered with a special construction paste known as compound, and that is covered with a kind of tape and more compound to create a seamless wall. The indentations where the screws were placed are also filled with compound and then sanded flat. When a flat, seamless wall has been created, it can then be painted.

315　About wall framing

The framing behind Sheetrock is made of wood or metal. Wooden framing is usually made up of 2-by-4 pine planks. Metal framing is made up of horizontal tracks, which establish the perimeter of the wall, and vertical studs, which the Sheetrock is attached to. Both the studs and the tracks are made of steel and are shaped rather like squared-off Cs. Wood framing is more expensive; it can warp, is subject to termites and fire, and is heavy to carry around. Steel framing is light, durable, and cheap, but it is also a little more difficult to cut down to size.

Wood is still what most builders go with because it's more solid and stable. You can decide yourself which one would work best for you, but here's a good rule of thumb: if the wall you are building will have to bear any weight, wood is the better material; if you are pressed for time, metal framing goes up in a jiffy.

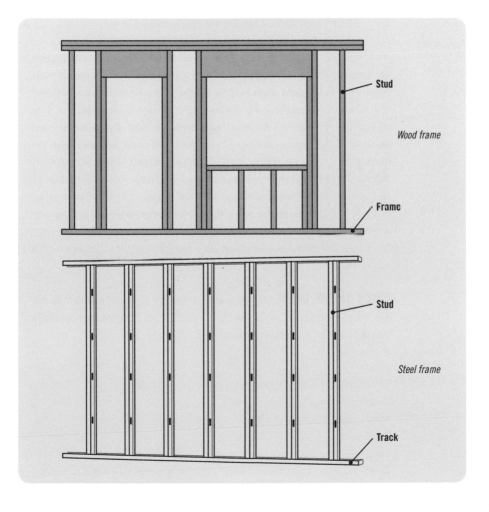

Stud

Wood frame

Frame

Stud

Steel frame

Track

316 How to frame out a wall in metal

Let's say you are adding a floor-to-ceiling partition to an existing room. Measure your new space carefully, remembering to factor in the thickness of your new wall, which will equal the thickness of the track plus the thickness of the Sheetrock on two sides. Try to run your new wall perpendicular to the joists or studs in the ceiling framing (for how to find studs, see entry 318). On the ceiling, measure and mark the four corners where the top track will sit, making sure the placement of the track is straight and true to the existing walls in the room (fig. 1). Cut the track to the length you need (fig. 2), using a metal clipper, which is a tool you can buy at the hardware store. Screw the tracking into the ceiling (fig. 3). Use a plumb line and an extension ruler to mark (fig. 4) and install the bottom track (fig. 5) directly underneath the top track (for how to use a plumb line, see entry 319). Then mark and install the two side tracks. Always use the right fasteners: Sheetrock screws for fastening to studs or joists; wood screws for wood floors; screws with toggle bolts for Sheetrock surfaces with no studs behind them; anchors and screws for plaster. Attach a vertical stud every 16 inches down the track (fig. 6). Metal studs screw into tracks using small screws called zip screws.

TRICK OF THE TRADE: *For extra solidity, you may also want to measure, cut, and install cross braces, which are short studs that are attached from stud to stud, perpendicular to the studs and parallel to the floor and the ceiling.*

1. Mark corners for the top track.

2. Cut the metal stud to the correct length.

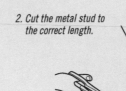

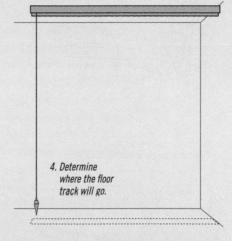

3. Screw the track into the ceiling.

4. Determine where the floor track will go.

6. Attach the vertical studs.

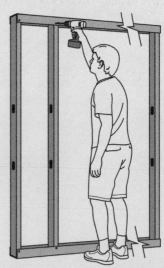

5. Install the bottom track.

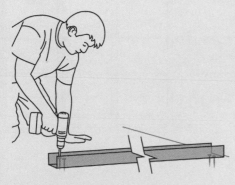

1. Clamp the base and the second top piece together.

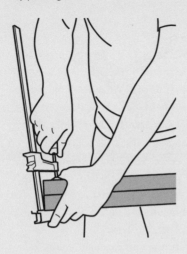

2. Mark for studs every 16 inches.

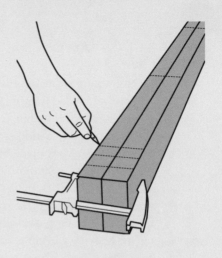

3. Nail vertical studs between the second top piece and the base.

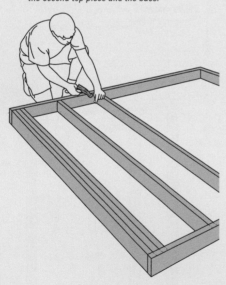

4. Stand the frame upright and screw it in place.

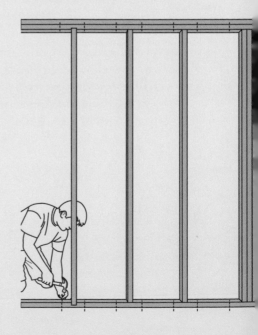

317 How to frame a wall in wood

Metal framing is cut and installed straight into the space where it is going to sit. Wood framing is slightly different. You install the top piece into the ceiling, but you measure the rest of the wall carefully and construct it as a kind of box, on its side, on the floor. Only then do you raise the box up and attach it to the ceiling piece and let the box become the wall's framing.

Measure and mark the space where the top plate will go, making sure it is straight and true to the rest of the room (see preceding spread, fig. 1). Then cut the piece and install it (preceding spread, fig. 3). Measure and cut a second top plate of the exact same dimensions as the first. Use your plumb line and extension ruler to mark and cut the base plate for the floor. Clamp the base plate and the second top plate together, side by side (fig. 1, opposite), and mark the spaces for the studs on both pieces, every 16 inches, using a pencil to mark the thickness of the wood boards you are using for studs (fig. 2). (This will typically be 1½ inches.) At the end of the wall, mark out a space for three studs together for strength. Measure and cut your studs, remembering to factor in the thickness of three boards: bottom plate and two top plates. Nail the studs into the top and bottom plates using sixteenpenny nails (fig. 3). Stand the new wall up and screw it into the top plate and the floor (fig. 4). You may also decide to install cross braces.

318 How to find your studs

Studs, the vertical wooden or metal framing that Sheetrock sits on, can be found behind walls and behind ceilings. Studs are usually placed at 16-inch intervals behind the Sheetrock. If you don't mind making a mess on your wall, you can find the studs by taking a sixpenny nail and hammering it into the Sheetrock. Once you've found a stud, you have a pretty good idea that the ones next to it are about 16 inches away.

There is also a high-tech solution to locating studs. It's called the electric stud finder, and you can buy a decent one for less than twenty dollars. How do these little machines work? Well, the explanation is an involved one, but essentially they sense the difference in density behind the wall, which tells them where the studs are. We strongly recommend you use one, but be aware that most stud finders do a poor job of differentiating between studs and other objects you might find behind walls like ducts, electrical equipment, and concrete foundations. So the best thing you can do is double-check your stud finder with a hammer and nail before you take any further action.

319 How to use a plumb line

This ancient and simple instrument, which is also known as a plumb bob, is used to show you the straight, vertical line from a ceiling to a floor. It is nothing more than a weight attached to a string. The weight is carefully balanced, has a pointed tip, and is made of steel, brass, or even plastic. Using the plumb line is easy. Hold the string over a spot and let the weight fall gently down to the ground, allowing it to swing. When it stops, the pointed end of the weight will be pointing at the exact spot below the point to which you have held the string. The plumb line can tell you, for example, the precise point on the floor that corresponds to the end of the track you have installed on the ceiling.

320 Cutting Sheetrock

As we said before, Sheetrock comes in large boards of either 3 by 5 feet or 4 by 8 feet. In a perfect world all walls would also come in these dimensions, but of course that isn't the case. So you'll need to cut Sheetrock. The best tool for this is a good old everyday utility knife. (There is also a tool called a Sheetrock saw, which has a serrated blade, but this is really best adapted to cutting holes out of already installed Sheetrock.) Mark the piece of Sheetrock you want to cut lightly in pencil. Take your utility knife and cut the outer layer of paper on the Sheetrock along the pencil line, scoring the plaster beneath. Don't worry about cutting too far into the plaster. Just score it with the knife. Holding the Sheetrock board, give it a solid bang with your hand or fist on the opposite side from where you made the cut. The board should fold right along where you made your cut. Straighten the board out again and cut along the crease of the fold, and the board should come apart right where you cut it. When doing this, please be aware of how you are holding the Sheetrock and do not slice through your hand.

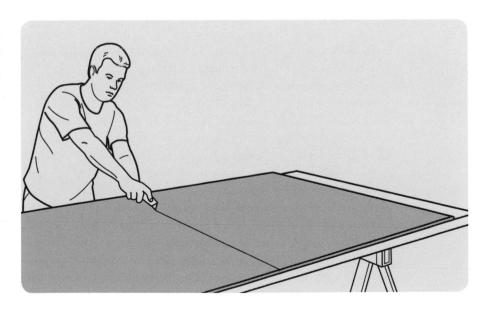

321 Drilling screws into Sheetrock

The usual fastener for attaching Sheetrock to studs is something called a Sheetrock screw, which is a sharp metal screw. You want a screw of the length that will penetrate the Sheetrock itself and a solid ½ inch into the stud beneath it. So if you have a ¾-inch-thick piece of Sheetrock, you need a 1½-inch-long screw. When you go to buy your screws, also take time to purchase something called a drill countersink. This is a kind of metal sheath you put on the end of your electric drill to stop it from drilling too deeply into the Sheetrock. The tricky thing about installing screws in Sheetrock is that you want them screwed in just deep enough so that they form a small indentation in the Sheetrock, but not so deep that they break the Sheetrock's paper covering. If the paper is broken, that screw will not hold in the wall and should be removed. Before you start installing a Sheetrock wall, take a piece of the Sheetrock, your drill, and your countersink and practice with them, trying to get the feel of exactly how far you need to go. After a while it will become second nature.

322 Installing Sheetrock on a framed wall

Before putting Sheetrock up, always make a pencil mark on the floor at the exact, measured center of each stud. That way you'll know where the studs are, even when the wall is up. The goal here is to fill the entire wall space with Sheetrock, and inevitably you are going to have to use a patchwork of Sheetrock pieces to do this. If you can, start at one end and install an entire Sheetrock board. Assuming you can, place this piece up against the framing and on the floor, and screw it into a central stud and studs as near to the four corners of the piece as you can. Once the board is secured, install screws along every stud the board is sitting on, including interior studs, placing one screw every 8 to 12 inches. Fit the next complete piece of Sheetrock onto the wall, next to the first one you have installed. But don't line the sheets up to create a single, long seam. Install the big pieces in a way such that you create a staggered seam—for example, one piece on the floor, the other piece on the ceiling. Once you fit in all the big pieces, you can cut boards down to fill in the smaller spaces.

323 How to tape and spackle a Sheetrock wall

Once the Sheetrock wall has been installed, you need to fill in the seams. You will be using something called joint compound, which you can buy premixed at the hardware store. For a large wall, consider using a five-gallon can. This stuff isn't expensive. The compound is applied with a Spackle knife. We recommend a 4- to 6-inch model. Joint tape comes in paper or vinyl mesh. The mesh is more expensive, but it is worth it, because it's easier to work with. Lay a wide but thin layer of compound along the open seam between two Sheetrock boards, at least to the width of the tape (fig. 1). Start from the top and press the tape into the compound with the Spackle knife (fig. 2). At the end, rip the tape off, holding it down with the knife. You now will put a slightly thicker layer of compound over the tape, completely covering the tape (fig. 3). After you've taped the seams, you will fill in the screw holes with dollops of compound but no tape (fig. 4). The following day sand down the compound on the seams and the screws (fig. 5). Sand by hand. You need a light touch, because you aren't sanding the compound off; you are just sanding to

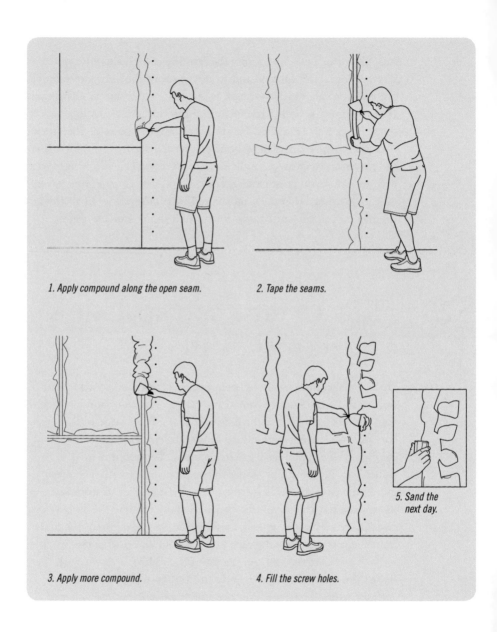

1. Apply compound along the open seam.

2. Tape the seams.

3. Apply more compound.

4. Fill the screw holes.

5. Sand the next day.

make it even with the wall. You will apply a thin layer of compound over each sealed seam, wait a day, and sand again. You need to use the tape just on the first application, not the second.

324 How are edges created in Sheetrock walls?

You don't just create an edge to a wall with compound, because it would look terrible and wouldn't last too long, with people bumping into the corner and running their hands over it and all the other things people will do. Instead, every corner and every finished edge on a Sheetrock wall is made with something called a corner bead. It is a thin piece of metal that is shaped at a right angle and tapered a little. Remember, every edge of every wall has a stud at it. So the corner bead can be screwed right into the stud. Then compound is applied along the entire surface of the corner bead on both sides of the right angle. It is left to dry. When it is sanded, you end up with a perfect, sharp corner. Rounded beads, for gentler corners, are another option.

325 Can I repair a hole in Sheetrock?

Sure. If you have a small hole, say ¾ inch wide, you can take some compound, mix it with some dried plaster on a sheet of cardboard, fill the hole with the compound, let it dry, sand it, and paint it. If you need to do a speedy job, a blow dryer will supercharge the drying. For a bigger hole, you may be able to cut a Sheetrock piece to fit that hole and screw it into a stud. Chances are, however, that wherever you get a hole, there will be no stud there. In that case, take the hole you have and use a Sheetrock saw, which is a tool designed to cut Sheetrock, and enlarge the existing hole so that it is in a general rectangle shape with straight lines. Buy some 3-inch-wide, ¾-inch-thick plywood in lengths that will fit approximately into each side of the hole. Buy Sheetrock of the exact same thickness as the Sheetrock on the wall. Place a piece of wood in the hole and hold it along one side of the hole so that half the wood is showing and half is behind the existing Sheetrock wall. Using 1¼-inch-long Sheetrock screws, screw the pieces of wood into the mouth of the hole so that there is wood lipping out over the edge of the Sheetrock all the way around. Cut a new piece of Sheetrock the shape of the hole and ⅛ inch smaller all the way around. Insert the Sheetrock piece into the hole and screw it into the wood you have installed around the hole. Use compound and tape on the seams, following the method described in entry 323.

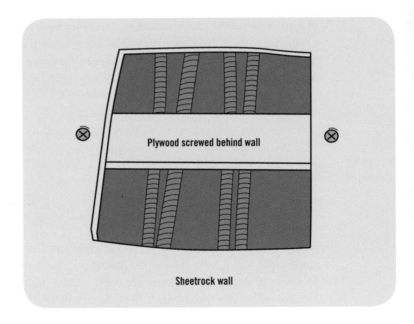

Plywood screwed behind wall

Sheetrock wall

326 Why do screws in drywall pop out?

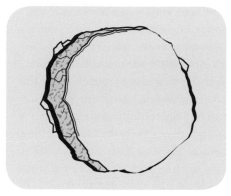

You've seen them all over the place, those little eruptions on walls. They look sort of as if someone took a dime, glued it to the wall, and painted over it. Sometimes the paint is broken around the eruption, and sometimes it isn't. What's going on here is that a screw in the drywall is popping out. This happens for a number of reasons. Sometimes the screw missed the stud and is therefore loose in the Sheetrock. Sometimes in wood-framed drywall, the wood has expanded and contracted with humidity, which pops the screw out. With new construction, houses will actually settle on their foundations, and this will cause shifting in the walls, which sets the screws popping.

There's only one real fix for this. Take a Spackle knife and cut out the paint and compound over the popped screw. Then clean the compound out of the indentation of the screw head. Try turning the screw to the right, tightening it. If it continues to turn without tightening, it isn't in the stud and you can pop it right out with the edge of the Spackle knife. If the screw is in a stud, tighten it. Then you will want to fill in the hole, whether it has a screw in it or not. After you let the compound dry, sand it flush and paint.

327   Installing a cabinet on a Sheetrock wall

Place your cabinet up against the wall, and using a level inside the cabinet, mark exactly where you want the cabinet to be. You don't need to draw a line all the way around the cabinet, just around the four right angles at the corners. Now you'll want to look for studs. If your house is post–World War II, you'll have Sheetrock walls; if it is pre–World War II, you'll have plaster walls. Assuming you have Sheetrock, ideally you'll want to find the vertical wooden or metal framing (called studs in the business) to nail your cabinet into. Ideally you should screw the cabinet into at least two studs as close to the ends of the cabinet as possible. Do the math to mark on the cabinet where your screws are going to go so that they hit the studs. Ideally, you want three screws up and down along the studs as close to the ends of the cabinet as possible. If you have a largish cabinet, you'll want four screws at each perimeter and every 16 inches where the studs are in between. Mark the spots for the screws and predrill the holes, from inside the cabinet going out, to avoid splintering the interior finish. Use a pan-head screw, or a flat-head screw with a washer. Make sure your screw can go through the ½ inch of backing, through the ½ inch of drywall, and into the stud. So figure on using a screw that is a minimum of 1½ inches long.

WHEN YOU CAN'T FIND THE STUDS

If you are dealing with Sheetrock, but can't find the studs, you will use a butterfly, also called a toggle bolt (see entry 24). We described these in chapter 1, but the idea is that once the screw goes into the Sheetrock, the toggle bolt opens up behind the Sheetrock to secure the screw. You'll predrill holes in the cabinet and the drywall, wherever you want the screws to be, which should be at the four corners and, in the case of a larger cabinet or one holding heavy objects like dishes, at the center of each perimeter, or even every 16 inches. The holes in the cabinet backing should be just wide enough to accommodate the screw. The holes in the drywall will be big enough to accommodate the screw plus the toggle bolt. Push the screws through the holes in the cabinet and screw the toggle bolts onto the screws and right up to the cabinet backing. Have a friend help you place the cabinet against the wall and match the screws to the holes in the wall. Make sure all the screws—every single one— match up before you do anything. Then tap the screws into the wall with a hammer until the toggle bolt snaps open behind the wall. You will now, holding the screw with your finger, pull it back toward you while at the same time screwing the screw into the wall.

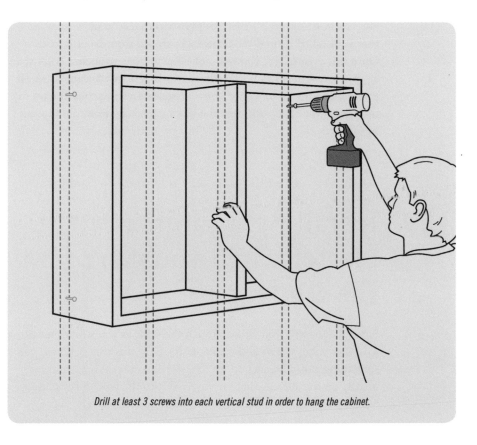

Drill at least 3 screws into each vertical stud in order to hang the cabinet.

328 One more idea for installing heavy cabinets onto a wall

When someone is hanging something heavy onto a Sheetrock wall—it could be a cabinet, a flat-screen television, or something that has pressure exerted on it, like a grab bar in a bathroom—the most secure and professional way to do it is to install blocking behind the Sheetrock. Blocking is a piece of plywood that is ½ or ¾ inch thick that is installed behind the Sheetrock, affixed from stud to stud. Once this is installed, you will not need to use any anchor other than a wood screw, and you'll never have to worry about finding studs. If you want to install blocking onto an existing wall, you will have to take down the Sheetrock, add the blocking to the studs, and install new Sheetrock.

329 Installing a cabinet on plaster when you can't find the studs

For a plaster wall, you will do much the same as you would installing a cabinet using screws and toggle bolts, only this time you will use something called an anchor. As described in entry 24, anchors are usually plastic sheaths that are inserted into the hole in the plaster wall to help the screw bite into the wall more effectively. Locate and mark where you want the cabinet to go following the directions in entry 327. Mark the points on the cabinet where the screws are going and predrill holes in those spots. Place the cabinet onto the wall, and mark where the screws are going into the wall. Predrill the wall with holes that are a hair smaller than the diameter of the anchor. Place the anchors in the holes, and hopefully you'll need to tap them in with a hammer. You want a snug, not a tight, fit. The whole anchor should go into the wall, but if you have a lip left, take a utility knife and cut the excess off. Now you can place the cabinet against the wall and screw the two top corner screws halfway into the anchor holes. Double-check that you are level before tightening. If you are level, tighten again, but not 100 percent. Add the screws at the bottom and tighten them some of the way. Check if you are level. Then tighten around the entire cabinet.

330 How a plaster wall is installed

If your home was built before 1940, your walls are likely made of plaster. Plaster is a cementlike substance that includes lime, and it was the primary wall material until World War II. A plaster wall

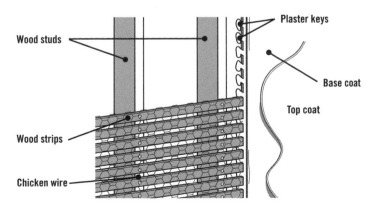

Wood studs

Plaster keys

Base coat

Top coat

Wood strips

Chicken wire

Cross section showing plaster supported by wooden slats

begins with the same kind of framing as a Sheetrock wall would, except it is always wood framed. Horizontal wood strips were put across the vertical wood framing, and chicken wire was nailed onto that. The plaster was mixed wet and applied directly onto the chicken wire to form a finished wall. That surface was then fine-tuned, primed, and painted. Plaster might sound a bit fragile, but it is actually quite durable—more durable, in fact, than Sheetrock walls. Plaster is also a better sound buffer than Sheetrock. But plaster isn't so much better than Sheetrock that it's worth the effort to install plaster walls in most cases.

331 When should I fix a crack in plaster?

A cracked wall is a kind of alarming thing. It looks as if your house is falling apart. But the truth is, except for in rare circumstances, there's nothing dangerous, or even particularly significant, about hairline cracks in a wall. If you can see through the crack behind the wall, you need an engineer—however, cracks that large are rare. Usually you're faced with narrow cracks. The best thing you can do with those is leave them alone until you are ready to paint the entire room where the crack is situated. The reason for this is that the color of the paint on the wall changes over time. If you fix a crack and paint only the area where the crack was, you are going to see the difference on your wall, even if you use the same paint. So wait until you are ready to paint the entire room and then fix the wall.

332   Plaster: THE DARK SIDE

Among the components in most plaster is limestone, and the limestone in plaster walls will expand when it comes in contact with water. Yet you will find plaster walls in bathrooms. If you have a tiled wall in your bathroom and the water penetrates the plaster wall, then the wall will expand and those tiles will pop off.

But by far the biggest problem with plaster walls is that they crack. There are a few reasons that plaster will crack. It may have been mixed poorly. There may not be enough moisture in the home, and the dried plaster becomes brittle. Vibrations from doors being slammed, movements of people in the house, and passing cars and trucks can all be culprits. But the main reason plaster cracks is that houses—all houses, old and new—move and settle, and over time those movements may cause the plaster to move.

333   How to fix a hairline crack in plaster

With the pointed corner of a Spackle knife, pry gently into the crack, and keep prying until the crack stops expanding (fig. 1). You will have opened a larger crack, but you will have exposed the true extent of the damage. Go to the hardware store and buy a special bonding agent, which comes in a can, premixed, and is designed to fill in plaster cracks. The bonding agent comes in liquid form. You take a paintbrush and liberally brush it into the crack you have just opened and let it dry for a few hours (fig. 2). When you come back and look at it, don't be alarmed. The crack is going to look exactly the same, except it may have changed color. But inside, the walls of the crack have been sealed up and the bonding agent has hardened. Now you are ready to fill the crack with compound. Compound, also known as joint compound or mud, is a kind of premixed plaster. Apply it liberally to the crack with the Spackle knife, filling the crack to overflowing (fig. 3). The following morning, sand the crack flush (fig. 4). If the repaired area doesn't look quite right after sanding, do another application. This repair usually requires two coats of paint.

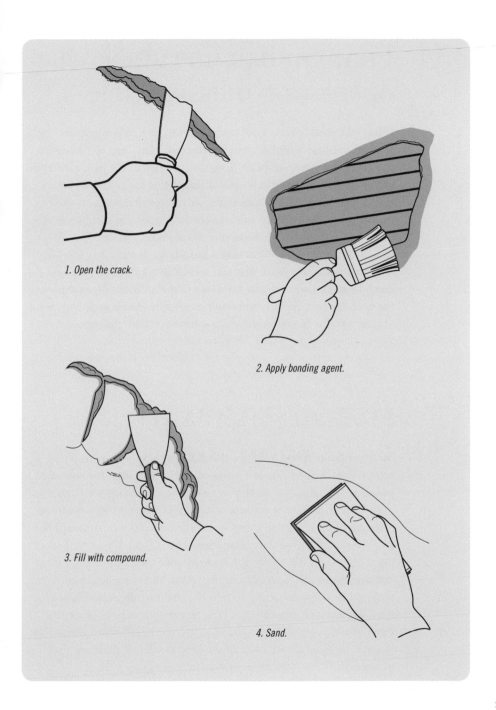

1. Open the crack.

2. Apply bonding agent.

3. Fill with compound.

4. Sand.

334 Fixing a hairline crack that opens to a massive hole

If you take your Spackle knife and open the crack, and when you are finished you have a big old crater in the wall, don't panic. You can fix it. For this fix, however, you will now have to go to the hardware store, buy some real plaster, mix it, and fill the hole with it. The reason we are telling you not to use the premixed joint compound is that it shrinks. If you apply it to a wider surface, you need something stronger, and that is plaster. You will need to mix the plaster (see entry 335). Once you have your plaster mixed, take a Spackle knife and fill in the hole with the plaster. Be aware that you are not going to be able to sand this down later. You will actually be filling in the hole just shy of flush with the wall. Let that dry overnight and then apply joint compound on top of that, which you can sand until you have a smooth, flat wall.

335 How to mix plaster

Mixing plaster is not difficult, but you may need to use trial and error to get it right. There's no special plaster to buy. Just tell the people at the hardware store you are filling a hole in a wall and need plaster for that. You never mix plaster in large amounts because it dries too quickly, so don't empty out the bag. Take a cardboard box and open it up on the floor. Put a small hill, about a quart, of the dried plaster on the cardboard, and use your finger to create a large indentation in the center of the pile. Pour lukewarm water into the plaster. Use a Spackle knife to fold the water in. Repeat this process until you have no more plaster dust and the plaster has become a paste. If the paste is soupy, you've added too much water, a situation you can fix by adding a little more dried plaster. If there are dry patches, then you need more water.

336 The final step to finishing a plaster wall: skim coating

Because of the way plaster works, plaster walls are put together bit by bit, and that makes it inevitable that the resulting wall will be slightly uneven. So to look right, a plaster wall must be evened out, and that is done by skimming the entire wall in joint compound. Using an eight-inch Spackle knife, smooth a ⅛-inch layer of joint compound onto the wall. There's no real science to this. You eyeball it and spread the compound like icing on a cake. Many people choose to merely skim noticeably indented areas. Once the wall has been skim coated, it is left to dry for a few hours and then sanded under very strong lighting that will show all the imperfections. Then you skim the wall again and sand it down. People do not usually skim Sheetrock walls. They will pay attention only to the seams and screw holes, because Sheetrock is by its very nature flat.

TRICK OF THE TRADE: *If you want to do something that real old-school builders do when they are skim coating walls, add a handful of dried plaster into the premixed compound, to make it a bit stronger.*

sheetrock, painting, wallpaper, tile, and stonework

PAINTING AND PRIMING

337 Oil versus latex

All common household paints and primers are oil based or latex based, but these days more and more people are turning to latex. Years ago people used oil-based paints inside and out of the house. Then more and more people began to conclude that oil-based paints should never be used on interiors, because oil paints smell terrible on application, make some people sick, and are thought by many people to be bad for the environment. These days there are many people who say oil-based paints should never be used at all, and indeed there are some states where it is illegal to use oil-based paints on interiors. Nonetheless, others—including some professional painters—think oil paints are more durable and give a smoother texture, and they will use oil paints on interior wooden surfaces and even walls when they can get away with it. Latex paints do not have the terrible smell, dry quickly, and are just fine for painting any surface apart from metal. For metal, you must use oil paint. As long as you are acting within the law, however, the choice is yours.

338 Choosing the right variety of paint

The brand and color of paint you choose is a matter of personal preference. But you should be aware that there are different kinds of paint for different surfaces. When you go to buy your paint, make sure you tell the employees at the store exactly what kind of surface you are dealing with. There are different paints for indoors and outdoors, cold-weather and warm-weather climates, and different surfaces, like metal and cement. There is even fire-resistant paint for areas around barbecues and fireplaces. So be aware of what the job is and ask someone at the paint store to help you.

Paint comes in seven sheens: flat, matte, satin, eggshell, semigloss, gloss, and high-gloss. Each of these will give a slightly different look to the surface, with each surface being shinier and shinier as you go up the scale. Another way to put it: you are going from a wall that looks dry to a wall that looks freshly painted. The higher-gloss paints are more durable, but they also show imperfections. That is why you rarely see high-gloss paints on walls, because a high-gloss wall will show every bump and blemish. Most walls and ceilings are painted in matte or flat finish, and most wood trim is painted in satin—not only because it is easier to clean, but also because many people think having the moldings glossier is a nice look and that you never want to see walls and moldings in the same finish.

339 How do I buy the right amount of paint?

Buying the right amount of paint and primer is not that hard. Calculate the height of each surface you are painting times the width, add the results, and that is how much you are painting per coat. Paint cans will tell you how much surface the paint inside can cover. Remember, you'll need to account for the number of coats you are laying down. In general, lighter-colored paint over primer will need two coats. Darker colors will need more. The darker the color, the more coats. A dark green, red, blue, or black wall will require four coats of paint. You will also need more coats of paint if you are painting over a darker shade of paint, but you should always prime a wall like that. Most can be primed with one coat of paint.

340 Protecting yourself and your home while you paint

Start with yourself. Wear something you don't mind getting paint on, and that includes your shoes. Next consider removing or covering all furniture in the room. Items you are covering should have plastic sheeting draped on them. If there's a wood floor, lay either plastic sheets and drop cloths or resin paper, which you can tape down with painter's tape (see entry 349). If you have a carpeted floor, place plastic sheeting over the carpet, and tape it down into the crease between the carpet and the wall. There is also a new product for carpeted floors, which is plastic sheeting with a light adhesive on it that will stick to your carpeted floor. As you paint and sand, you will create a great deal of fine dust. Much of it can be swept up, but not all of it. Don't use your home vacuum cleaner—the dust will ruin it. Instead, go out and rent or purchase an industrial vacuum, which is reasonably priced.

341 How to buy the right paintbrushes

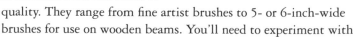

The general rule of thumb is that you use paintbrushes for wood, the corners of walls and ceilings, and hard-to-reach places. For the main surface of walls and ceilings, you use rollers. Brushes come in different sizes and levels of quality. They range from fine artist brushes to 5- or 6-inch-wide brushes for use on wooden beams. You'll need to experiment with what brush makes you feel comfortable, but for finishing a wall, we recommend a 2- to 3-inch brush. For latex paint you use brushes with nylon bristles, and for oil paints you use brushes made with natural bristles, which is horsehair. In general, the more expensive brushes will be of higher quality, and what you are mostly paying for is durability, meaning the brush won't shed bristles onto the surface you are painting. It's fine to use a cheap brush, but if you choose to do so, take a moment to see if any stray bristles are present on the surface you are painting.

342 How to buy the right rollers

Rollers come in different widths and degrees of texture. A standard roller will leave the painted wall with a kind of orange-peel pattern on it. You've seen that, and it is fine. If you don't want that pattern, make sure you purchase a roller designed to leave a smooth surface on the wall—your hardware store can help you pick the right one.

Rollers are measured by their widths. The average width is 7 to 9 inches. And they are measured by something called pad thickness, which is not the diameter of the roller but the actual thickness of the padding that is rolled up to make the roller. There are three standard thicknesses: ¼, ⅜, and ½ inch. The term for this thickness is the nap. In general, the thicker the nap, the more pronounced the orange-peel pattern you will see on the wall. When you are about to use your roller, take some masking tape and roll it all around the roller so that it is covered in tape. This will take off the lint that has accumulated on the roller in the factory. Make sure to buy a roller with a long handle that can help you paint up the side of a wall without using a ladder.

343 A primer on priming

Primer is a paintlike substance that is used not for its color but because it is a sealant. There are different kinds of primers for different jobs, but you should buy an all-purpose primer. There are oil-based and latex-based primers, just as there are paints, and just as with paints, oil is being replaced by latex in all instances except for painting on metals.

You need to use primer before almost any paint job: before painting any surface that is unpainted wood or unpainted Sheetrock; before painting a surface that has been newly skim coated or patched with compound; or if you are painting a wall that has already been painted and are changing the finish or changing the color. The only circumstance where you don't prime is when you are covering an already painted surface with a paint of the same finish and in a similar color.

The reason you need primer for most surfaces is that it helps the paint adhere properly and smoothly. The primer does two things: it seals porous surfaces and provides a flat surface for the paint to adhere to. Primer also cuts your painting time in half by reducing the coats of paint you need to use. You apply primer to a wall just as you would any paint (see entry 347).

344 How to paint a room: The overview

Painting a room isn't just applying paint to the walls. It's a process that has many steps within it, each one important to ending up with the desired finished result. You need to begin with smooth, clear walls. In most cases you would then prime the walls, and finally you would paint the walls.

The processes for priming a room and for painting a room are much the same. In each case, there's a particular order of how you will apply the paint or primer to the walls. In addition, using painter's tape is essential to make the transitions between painted surfaces and any trim crisp, clear, and defined. You will also want to protect the room by laying down or taping down plastic and cloth coverings over the floor, ducts, and furniture.

The entries that follow describe the whole process, but to recap: the order of business is create smooth, clean walls; prime; and paint.

345 Start with a clean wall

There are two factors involved here. The first is what kind of wall you are starting with. The second is how intense you want to be about the finished paint job.

Just to keep you on your toes, let's begin by discussing that latter factor first. A good professional painter will always prepare a wall, no matter what kind of wall it is, by skim coating it in the manner we described in entry 336. You can do that and the result will be beautiful, but it must also be said that most amateur painters will likely not bother with skim coating.

If you're starting with a new Sheetrock wall, you should make sure to finish all the joints between the pieces of Sheetrock and all the screw holes as we described in entry 323.

If you are starting with a painted wall, you should cover the floor with a cloth, and using a tool called a paint scraper, scrape the wall to remove any areas where the paint has come loose or chipped. Then wash the wall with a new sponge or sponge mop dipped in warm water and household detergent. Dry the wall. Then go over any rough areas with a thin layer of joint compound. Sand the wall down lightly and you are ready to prime.

346 How to mix and strain primer or paint

Before using primer or paint, you should always mix and strain it. The reason is that you don't know how long the primer or the paint has sat on the shelf at the store. If it has been there for a while, it may have formed dried areas at the top; when you open the lid, these dried bits will fall into the can and may end up as unsightly formations on your wall. Straining the primer or paint gets rid of those dried bits.

At the paint store, buy a two-gallon bucket and some paint strainer, which will come in the form of a sheet designed to be placed over the two-gallon bucket. (Larger sizes of bucket and strainer are available, but we recommend the two-gallon variety.) Open the can of primer or paint, stir it with a stick, and then pour it slowly through the strainer into the large bucket. Then you can pour the primer or paint back into its original can.

347 How to prime or paint a room

Again, there are two issues here: the order you will paint the parts of the room, and the order you will paint the sections of each wall.

In any room, you start with the ceiling. Then you do the walls. The trim comes last.

When priming or painting an individual wall, begin by painting the perimeter of the wall carefully with a brush and then fill in the large central area with paint rollers. Only after you've finished the flat wall surfaces do you paint the trim. Before you start the trim, you'll want to tape down the wall to make sure none of the paint from the trim gets on the wall (see entry 349).

There's also a logical order to painting the trim. Start with any window casings, proceed to any crown and baseboard moldings, and finish with the door casings. You do the door casings last, by the way, because they are easy to bump into, so you want to do them on your way out.

348 Applying primer or paint to an individual wall

First you do the perimeter. Take a brush and, using careful up-and-down strokes for vertical applications and left-to-right strokes for horizontal applications, paint the perimeter of the wall and any nooks and crannies that are hard to get to.

At this point you will not be focusing on any wood trim around the wall. If this is a new construction project, you don't need to worry about getting some primer on the wood trim. If you're repainting a room, tape down the trim to protect it.

Now you'll tackle the center of the wall. Take your roller. Place the primer or paint in a roller pan and use a roller to fill in the center of the wall with up-and-down strokes, moving from left to right or right to left. The key is to be consistent and move in one direction.

Here are some general techniques for painting:

• Never dip the brush all the way into the paint. It should go no more than ½ inch into the paint, and you will use the tip of the brush on the wall.
• Always paint in one direction and be consistent.
• Be aware that different finishes require slightly different techniques. If you are using eggshell, which is a special finish, you will actually need to paint the perimeter and the center of the wall simultaneously; therefore, if you choose this finish, you'll need someone to help you paint. On the other hand, if you are using any finish glossier than satin, in order to finish the wall you will have to use a brush over any sections that have been painted with a roller.
• When painting a ceiling, make sure you paint the first coat in one direction, let's say horizontally, and the next coat in the perpendicular direction—let's say vertically. This will ensure that you won't see lines in the sunlight when you look up.

349 How to tape down a paint job

Most paint jobs are going to involve painting contiguous walls, or walls and trims, that are being done in different colors, or in different glosses. Imagine, for example, a white ceiling with a red wall. To have crisp boundaries between these two walls, you are going to need to tape. The tape used is called painter's tape, which is a kind of tape that has less adhesive on it. Imagine you have painted the ceiling white. Let the paint dry overnight. Then take your tape and place it along the entire perimeter of the ceiling, getting the tape right up to the wall. Now you can paint the wall carefully without getting any paint on the ceiling. Once you have the wall painted, wait about thirty minutes and take the tape off the ceiling. Never leave it on overnight or the paint will seal it to the wall. When you remove the tape, you should see two surfaces, each totally painted, and a crisp transition between the two. If you find there are places where you have let a little paint get over the border onto the other wall, you can fix it by waiting for the paint to dry and touching up with a small brush, or tape down the dried wall again and repaint that section of perimeter.

350 Priming and painting wood trim

A lot of the moldings and trim around walls have uneven surfaces, and to make sure you are getting a nice coat of paint onto an uneven surface, use a narrower brush, like one with a 2-inch width. Again, the same techniques apply. Mix and strain your paint. Use just the tip of the brush. Brush up and down or side to side in a consistent manner; don't mix the two up. Assuming you have painted the walls and have primed the trim and let everything dry, you will now tape the walls and paint your trim.

351 How many coats of paint do you need?

The general rule of thumb is that if you have light-colored paint, you need one coat of primer and two coats of paint. If you have a dark color, you need one coat of primer and at least three coats of paint. An excellent professional painter's technique when using dark paint is to "thin the primer." This means to tint the primer with the same color as the paint. The store where you buy the primer and the paint can actually do this for you, and you should let them.

WHAT TO DO BETWEEN EACH COAT?

Here's an old-school painter's way of doing things that is a good idea: sand between each coat of primer and paint. Most homeowners who undertake a paint job will not sand between each coat. But if you want a supersmooth, professional look, you need to sand. You sand by hand and gently. A different kind of sandpaper is used between each coat. Before the primer you use 150-grit paper; after the primer you use 180-grit paper; between the first and second coats of paint you use a 220-grit paper.

Oil-based primers and paints need to dry overnight. Latex primer should also be left overnight, even though it may be close to fully dry in a few hours. Latex paint can be painted over after three or four hours in most cases.

352 How do I repair damage to a painted wall?

Let's say you have a blotch on your wall or the wall has been scratched or marred in some way. You are going to want to paint over it, but the sad truth is you probably aren't going to be able to do that. There is really only one case where you can get away with patching a blotch on a wall, and that is if you have a flat or matte finish on a wall that has been recently painted and you have the same can of paint you used to paint the wall. In any other circumstance, you are going to have to repaint the entire wall to fix that one blotch. There are two basic reasons you can't attempt a patch in any other circumstance than the one we described above.

1. If the wall is in any kind of finish glossier than matte, you will see where you have patched, because each coat of the glossier paints will dry a little differently.

2. If the paint job you want to patch is older than six months, you'll see the difference between the old paint and the new, because the paint on the wall will have changed color subtly with exposure to the sun and oxygen. If you have to go and buy a new can of paint, you'll still see the difference, because each can of paint is slightly different.

353 The skinny on lead paint

If your house was painted before 1978, chances are some of that paint was lead based. Up until then, paint had lead in it, because the lead made the colors more vibrant and the paint more durable. The only problem is that the lead in paint is toxic and can cause neurological damage, especially to children. If you are worried that you have lead in your house, you can hire someone to do a lead check on it, or you can buy do-it-yourself lead test kits, which are cheap and easy to use. Families can be exposed to lead from dust from walls that are cracking, or from paint chips that get swallowed accidentally—or in the case of small children, on purpose. This becomes a particular issue when you are sanding down a wall to repaint it. Be aware of lead and the risks associated with it.

LEAD PAINT SAFETY

If you are considering doing work on an older house that has lead in it, you should really hire a professional and make sure that the crew uses proper practices.

But if you insist on doing the work yourself, follow these five steps:

1. Seal off the area you are working in with plastic sheets and covers, or, better still, remove all furniture from the room.

2. Since lead travels in dust, mist your wall with a spray bottle before you sand to reduce dust.

3. Wear a mask, goggles, and gloves when you are sanding.

4. When you finish, vacuum and mop the entire room with great care.

5. When you are finished for the day, remove all your clothes, put them in a plastic bag, and leave them by the washing machine. Don't hug your kids with paint dust on your clothes. Remember, lead dust is not visible.

WALLPAPER

354   What's the deal with wallpaper?

Wallpaper isn't always paper anymore. It would be more accurate to call it wall covering. There are wall coverings that are made of paper, but there are also wall coverings made from fabric, plastic, vinyl, grass, cork, and even wood veneer. What puts them in the same category is that almost all of them are glued to the wall in rolls. We can't go through every option out there. What we are going to do is walk you through the application of the three most common types of wall covering, which are paper, vinyl, and fabric. What we are talking about is a basic installation, but always be sure to read the instructions that come with any kind of wallpaper, because there may be special steps you need to take to make the application come out right.

355 Project: Install a Sheet of Wallpaper

Wallpaper comes in rolls, and each kind of wallpaper comes in different widths and lengths. This information is on the packaging of the wallpaper. Traditionally wallpaper is installed vertically, and in fact it's designed to be done that way. We are going to describe that kind of installation.

1. Figure out how much wallpaper you need. Assuming you are installing the wallpaper in vertical strips, start by measuring the height of the wall. You need strips that are the height of the wall or taller. Then measure the width of the wall and purchase enough strips to cover the width. This is actually a rather complicated calculation, and the best thing to do is take your measurements to the store and ask the professionals to determine exactly how much wallpaper you need, given the kind of paper you have chosen and the size of your wall.

2. Acquire the right equipment. You'll need a ladder and a level; a table that you are not afraid to beat up; a tool called a wallpaper smoother; a wallpaper brush; a utility knife or a one-sided razor; a miter, which is a tool that looks like a Spackle knife but is less sharp; a pair of scissors; a plumb bob; a seam roller, which is like a small paint roller; a regular paint roller; wallpaper primer, which is a special kind of primer that helps the wallpaper adhere to the wall; a damp sponge; dry towels; and wallpaper glue. You should use a different kind of glue for each different kind of wallpaper: for paper wallpaper, use a clear vinyl glue or wheat paste; for vinyl, clay-based glue; and for fabric, a kind of ultraclear glue. In essence, installing vinyl and fabric wallpaper is the same as installing paper wallpaper.

3. Begin with a wall that is spackled or primed or painted. If the wall has wallpaper on it, you should remove the wallpaper first

(see entry 359). The first step is to prime the wall with your special wallpaper primer, using the same painting technique you would use to prime a wall for paint. The only difference is that you need to let the wallpaper primer dry for just one hour.

4. Inspect every roll of wallpaper before you install it to make sure they all have the same dye and lot numbers. Remember, the paper is printed, and there are subtle differences between different lots of papers, so use ones from the same lots. On that note, always buy 10 or 15 percent more paper than you need so you have extra from the same dye and lot number to make repairs. Take note of the width of the wallpaper.

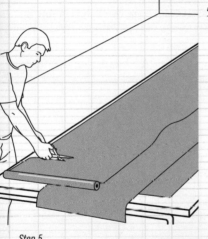

Step 5

5. Measure your wall carefully. Starting from one end of the wall, measure out the width of the paper on the wall, and draw a plumb line up and down the wall at that point (see entry 319). Open the roll of wallpaper on the table, and if you are dealing with a large wall, you'll cut the first three panels of paper with your scissors. Make sure to cut the paper 4 to 6 inches longer than you will need to fill the height of the wall. You don't have to worry too much about cutting a straight line because you are going to cut the top and bottom edges of the paper off on the wall.

6. Turn the first sheet of paper you are installing onto its printed side, the side that will be facing out into the room, and use the regular paint roller to apply glue to the back of the paper. (Some wallpaper comes preglued, but you still need to wet it in a special tray.) Be sure to use a thin and even coat of glue or the wallpaper will look uneven when you install it. Crease the glued paper in half and fold the glued sides onto each other (we know this sounds strange, but that is how you do it). Go up the ladder, open the paper, and starting at the top, lay the paper onto the wall using your hands. Take care to fit it flush against the line you have

marked for its boundary on the left or the right. If you don't fit the paper exactly against this line, you will have messed up the installation. Install the paper 2 to 3 inches up onto the ceiling and 2 or 3 inches onto the baseboard. Use the plastic smoother to smooth the paper down onto the wall, taking out any air bubbles you see and pressing the wallpaper into the crease between the wall and the ceiling and the crease between the wall and the baseboard. You now need to cut the excess paper off the top and the bottom of the wall. Use your miter blade up against the ceiling or the baseboard to give you a straight edge to cut along, and cut gently with the tip of the blade of your utility knife or one-sided razor. Once you have cut away the top and the bottom of the paper, you will see excess glue. Wipe this off gently with the damp sponge, and then wipe the moisture from the sponge off the wall with the dry towel.

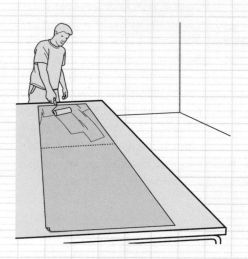

Step 6 (applying glue to the paper)

Step 6 (applying the paper to the wall)

356 How to install the second sheet of wallpaper

You install the second sheet next to the first, with the sides of the two sheets of paper touching each other but not overlapping and the pattern of the wallpaper matching. Use the same method as you did with the first sheet of wallpaper. Measure out the space you are fitting it into, apply glue to the paper, fold it, take it up the ladder, install it from the top, fit the paper in snugly at the side, and overlap the ceiling and baseboard by a few inches. However, with the second piece of paper you also have to make sure you are matching the pattern of the first piece. There's no exact set of instructions for how to do this, because each wallpaper pattern is different. But after you cut the first sheet of wallpaper, open the roll of wallpaper next to it. Match the pattern of the first sheet of wallpaper to the wallpaper still on the roll, and cut the new sheet of paper of the exact same length and matching the pattern of the first. To do this, you may have to cut off a small strip of paper at the bottom. When you are installing paper on the wall, please make sure you are matching the pattern very carefully. Once the paper is installed, smooth it down onto the wall and cut off the excess at the top and the bottom, as you did with the first sheet. Once you have the second sheet installed, use your seam roller and roll it a few times over the seam between the two sheets of paper on the wall until the seam between them is tight.

sheetrock, painting, wallpaper, tile, and stonework

357 Wallpaper: THE DARK SIDE

The first thing you might see on a freshly installed wallpaper wall is air bubbles. They might appear even if you have been very careful in your installation. To fix an air bubble, take a sewing needle or the tip of a razor blade and poke a small hole. The bubble should collapse. If it doesn't, you may need to take a wallpaper syringe and inject a small amount of glue behind the bubble. Then use a smoother to squeeze it out.

Right after installation or over time, you might see the edges of the paper coming up. The fix for this is easy. Take a small brush with some glue and paint the back of the paper, smooth it out, and wipe off the excess glue with a damp sponge.

After some installations, the wallpaper may shrink on the wall. If this happens, you need to take the wallpaper down and start over. The reason that most wallpaper shrinks is the temperature. Never install wallpaper with the air conditioner on. Central heating is fine, but do not hang wallpaper in conditions colder than 70° Fahrenheit.

If the wallpaper becomes nicked or scratched, it can be filled in with a colored artist pencil of the same color.

358 How do I deal with fabric wallpaper?

Fabric wallpaper has a paper backing and some kind of fabric or padded fabric over it. Handling this kind of wallpaper is trickier than handling plain paper wallpaper. You cannot get any glue on the fabric. When you are smoothing the paper down, make sure to smooth away from the paper, and use a damp sponge to wipe away the glue as you are working. Use the same process after you cut the paper as well. But you should not wet the fabric paper. So as you get glue on the smoother, wipe the smoother with the sponge, but do not wipe the wallpaper. You must be aware of the humidity in the air when you are installing fabric wallpaper because it may shrink. If you do get glue on the fabric, let it dry before cleaning it. Here's where the wallpaper brush comes in handy. You will use the brush to try to get the glue to flake off. If it doesn't, then you can try using a scrap piece of the wallpaper itself to rub the glue off. If that doesn't work, dampen the wallpaper ever so lightly with seltzer water and dry it immediately with a blow dryer.

359 How to take wallpaper off a wall

There are three ways to take wallpaper off a wall.

1. You can put some dishwashing soap in hot water in a bucket and use a roller to roll the soapy foam onto the wallpaper. Let it sit for ten minutes. Do it again. Then you will see that the paper is buckling. Take a Spackle knife and start peeling the paper away.

2. Rent a wallpaper steam machine. This comes with instructions, but essentially you put it against the wall, and it steams the wallpaper off.

3. Buy a wallpaper remover in the hardware store. It comes in gel or liquid. Follow the instructions but apply the remover with a brush or roller, and then use a Spackle knife to lift up the wallpaper.

Please be aware of your flooring or carpeting. Always lay down a plastic covering and a drop cloth when you are removing wallpaper. But there can be another issue: leftover glue. To get that off, take plain lukewarm water and sponge off the glue. Do not use any kind of soap, because it may interfere with any primer you will apply thereafter.

TRICK OF THE TRADE: *You may encounter a wallpapered wall that has been painted over. If you see painted wallpaper, do not try to get it off the wall. It won't work. Just prime it and paint, spackling and sanding at the seams. If there are loose portions, cut them away, spackle the area, prime, and paint.*

TILE AND STONEWORK

360 How tiles work

Tiles are pieces of durable material that are used for covering floors, roofs, showers, walls, and even tables. They come in a wide variety of styles, shapes, and colors. Tiles are typically made from either ceramic, stone, glass, or metal.

- Ceramic tiles are the classic. They've been around for centuries and are typically the least expensive.
- Stone tiles can be made of natural or man-made material. Stone can be expensive, and some kinds of stone are porous and prone to staining.
- Glass is an increasingly popular material because of its look, but it is expensive, it cracks easily, and it's hard to install fixtures onto glass tiles.
- Metal tiles are quite expensive and show scratches.

The basic issue with all tiles is choosing between machine-made and man-made. Machine-made tiles are identical in size and shape and therefore easier to install. Man-made tiles can be slightly irregular, but that is a look some people like.

361 Using the right kind of tile

In theory you can install any kind of tile anywhere, but in reality there are some applications that make more sense than others. The best tiles for floors are ceramic and stone, because they are the most resistant to scratching and cracking. For this reason, ceramic and stone are also the main players in any outdoor situation. Glass and metal are used mostly for interior walls. For kitchens and bathrooms, you can use almost any kind of tile you want, but be aware that some stones, most notably limestone, are porous, and even with proper sealing methods, you'll see water marks with repeated use.

362 Selecting the right grout

When you are having a tiled surface installed by a builder, you will be called upon to select the kind of grout that will be used. There are many different manufacturers that make grout, and each company will have its own specific colors. One company's white may be quite different from another company's white. So if you are asked to choose a grout for a project, go down to the store and pick up the color charts of a few different grout manufacturers. Some people like to see the grout contrast with the color of the tile. Others like the grout to blend in. Once you have chosen a grout, write down the manufacturer, color, and number for future reference. You'll need that information when you have to make repairs. In general, if you choose a grout of a lighter color, be aware that it will show more stains and wear and tear over time. By contrast, a darker grout will wear better. Once you've chosen the color you are going to use, you need to choose between sand-based and non-sand-based grout. You use a sand-based grout for situations where the tiles are spaced ¼ inch or farther apart. Non-sand-based grout is better for tighter applications.

363 The basics of tile

We're not necessarily recommending you install tile yourself, but we want you to understand how tiling works so that you can fix tiled surfaces and get the best work out of a contractor. When ordering tiles, always get at least 10 percent more than you will need, so that you can replace cracked tiles in the future. You need to begin with a flat, durable, clean surface that has no cracks in it—any faults in the surface will show up eventually once it is tiled, so it needs to be sound. The tiles are then glued down onto the surface. The tiles are spaced evenly with small plastic bits called (not so surprisingly) "spacers." Some tiles come evenly spaced in premade sheets. In general, you can space machine-made tiles tighter than man-made, because the machine-made are uniform in shape. Once the tiles are laid down, the spaces between them are filled in with grout, which is a kind of paste made from water, sand, cement, and sometimes gravel. If the tiles are made of a porous material, then they may need to be sealed with two coats of a premixed solution that will prevent staining.

364 Maintaining a tiled surface

The beautiful thing about tiles is that there is very little maintenance. All you need to do is clean them off with soap and water as much as you want. Avoid abrasive detergents and sponges. Otherwise, go for it. The truth is that the Achilles' heel of a tiled surface isn't the tiles themselves: it's the grout. Over time the best grout job is going to crack and start to fall out. This will typically happen at the seams where the tile meets another surface—for example, the corner between the wall and the floor, or the seam between a tub and the wall. The best thing you can do to maintain the grout is to spot the places where it is wearing away and fill them up. For this reason, it is important to keep the brand and color of the grout you used on file.

365 Can I mix my own grout?

It takes a little practice, but you can indeed mix your own grout. If you are making a repair, chances are you're going to need a tiny amount of the stuff. You can literally mix it in a small, disposable cup. Grout comes in a powder, and the key to mixing it is getting the right amount of water. Put some of the powder in your small cup and add just a little bit of water. Mix it in. Keep adding water until you see no more powder, and you have a paste. The paste should be wet in consistency but not move around, and it should stick to the sides of the cup. You do not want a soupy paste, and you do not want to see any dry patches. If your paste is soupy, add grout. If your paste is dry, add water.

TRICK OF THE TRADE: *In bathrooms, where the tub meets the tile, you'll see a lot of grout cracking. Don't fix this with grout; use a flexible caulking that matches the grout color. The caulking will last longer and be easier to apply.*

366 How to regrout a problem area

You can use your fingers, a Spackle knife, or a dedicated grout applicator, which you can buy for a tiny sum of money at the hardware store. You will also need a wet sponge. Examine the problem area. If the grout there is cracked, stick your nail in there or use a Spackle knife or some instrument to test how solid the grout is. If it's cracked, but the crack is stable, just apply the new grout on top of the crack and the good grout around it, pushing it into the crack and spreading it around. If the old grout is moving around, try to pry it out. Then fill the hole with your new grout. In either case, once you have applied the grout, wait five to ten minutes for it to

Applying grout

dry and then gently wipe the excess grout with a damp sponge. If you are dealing with a large surface, you may want to have a bucket of water with you.

367 How to fix a cracked tile

Another common problem with a tiled surface, especially floors, is that one tile will crack. Believe it or not, you can fix this problem yourself—provided you have extra tiles to work with. (That's the reason we told you to buy more than you needed in the first place.) Assuming you have an extra tile to work with, the first thing you need to do is remove the cracked tile. Use a blunt screwdriver and a hammer. Start in the center of the tile. Bang the screwdriver into the tile, crack it into pieces, and lift up each piece with the screwdriver. Stay away from the margins so that you don't damage the neighboring tiles. You need to get all of the tile and the glue residue off the subsurface.

Now you'll need to glue down the new tile. There are two kinds of adhesive you can use: a ready-made product that is easy to apply but not as durable, or a cement-based mix, which you blend yourself but which lasts better. Lay down a thin layer (around ⅛ inch thick) of adhesive with a trowel. Then set your tile into it. Make sure the tile is flush with the surface and that the spacing is uniform all around. Leave it to dry overnight and apply grout all around it. Please note that for glass tiles, you need to use cement mix in the color white or the tile will not look right.

368 Selecting the right material for a countertop

Countertops are generally 1¼ inches to 1½ inches thick. They are made of natural stones like marble and granite, man-made stone materials, wood, stainless steel, poured concrete, tile, and laminate. The laminate and tiled countertops are the least expensive and also the least durable. Stainless steel and wood countertops are a little more expensive and show wear, but they are meant to show their wear. The most durable and the most expensive are the natural stones. Man-made stones are slightly less expensive than natural. They are typically made from small pieces of quartz that have been pressed together with resin, and they come in a range of solid colors. The man-made stones are more heat resistant and scratch resistant than natural stones. Poured concrete is equivalent to man-made stone in price, but it can have durability issues if it is mixed badly. With concrete you need to have a good craftsman making the countertop.

369 Maintaining a countertop

You can wash most countertops with soap and water. You don't need to go much further than that. You should, however, reseal your countertop every two or three years. There are special sealants for stone, which are solutions that are applied with a rag and left to dry. Basically, sealants fill in the microscopic holes in the counter and prevent staining. Having said that, all countertops, no matter what they are made of, will stain. Especially if you leave things that stain on the countertop, like oils, salts, fruits, wine, or, in the case of the bathroom, makeup. Once a counter is stained, it is very hard to get the stain off. There are pastes you can buy that will take a stain off a counter. If that doesn't work, you may need to bring in a professional to sand down the counter and refinish it. If your countertop looks generally grimy, you can have a professional come in and repolish the entire surface, which will make the countertop look brand new.

370 Fixing a countertop

There is very little that is going to happen to a countertop. You will see nicks, dings, chips, and on rare occasions, if a heavy object is dropped at exactly the right point on a natural stone, a crack. You can try to fix these things on your own, but for a really fine countertop you've made a big investment in, think about hiring someone. In general, all of these fixes are the same. You buy a special stone epoxy, a paste you mix with a dye to match the stone, which is designed to fill in a crack, or a chip that is at least ⅛ inch deep. If the chip is shallower than that, you should leave it alone. Make sure the surface of the stone is clean and that the chip or crack is free of loose material, even minute bits. Mix the epoxy, getting it to the consistency of peanut butter. Fill in the damaged area, using your finger. Wipe away the excess with a wet sponge, making sure the surface is even, and let it dry overnight.

Basement, Yard, and Garage (and Fireplaces Too)

Now for a tour of some of the peripheral areas of the house. We start with the basement, an often underutilized resource that can account for up to a third of many homes. Then we head into the yard, not to offer you gardening tips but just to lay out some of the basics that any homeowner ought to know. Finally, we talk a bit about the garage and offer you a handy project to organize that space, which so often is reduced to a jumbled storage area.

BASEMENT

371 How the foundation of a home works

There are two basic kinds of foundations for the home. The first type is nothing more complex than a slab of concrete, usually around a foot thick, which is poured directly onto the ground. Houses on this kind of foundation will not have a basement. You might find houses like this in a flood zone. This kind of foundation is also cheaper to make. The other common type of foundation begins with a hole in the ground. The hole is excavated, and the sides of the hole are shored up with plywood. Then a form is created, outlining the exterior perimeter of the house with plywood on both sides, and cement is poured into it over rebar, which is a framework of reinforced steel bars. After seventy-two hours of curing, a cement floor is poured, and you have a basement.

Slab on ground

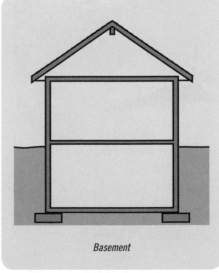

Basement

Foundations develop cracks. This is almost always going to occur. Cement is fickle stuff. It will crack from vibrations, from variations of temperature, or when tree roots grow into it. When this happens, water will get into the cracks and into your basement. Typically the cracks will be on the outside of the foundation and you won't even see them. What you will see is water. Often it is hard to find out where the cracks are, but you can make a good guess about which wall has been penetrated by the proximity of water to the wall. If you actually see some small cracks in the foundation, don't be too concerned, even if you have some water. That's normal. You should start to get worried if you see a large crack, one that you can put your hand into, or if you see a crack where one lip is sticking out over the other, or if your entire basement floods during a storm. If anything like that goes down, you will need to call a foundation professional. Similarly, if the doors and windows in your home are not opening and closing properly, the house itself may have shifted, collapsing the rectangular openings. That is a bad sign, and you will need to call a pro.

TRICK OF THE TRADE: *If you see a massive crack in your basement, don't immediately panic. The crack could be in a stucco finish to the foundation wall and not in the wall itself. If you open the crack and see smooth cement behind it, you don't have a major problem.*

373 Waterproofing the foundation

Back in the day, foundations were just laid down, and the house slapped on top of them. These days, however, most foundations are waterproofed. After the foundation is poured and allowed to harden, a layer of epoxy, a sealant, is painted onto the exterior side of the foundation to seal the concrete and make it waterproof. This is the same idea as applying sealant to wood after you have stained it. There are also houses that will get a sheet of waterproof rubber membrane, which will make the foundation even more impervious to water. This would be used in a place that gets a lot of rain, such as the Pacific Northwest.

374 Why is my basement wet?

The first thing you want to do is check to make sure it isn't a plumbing issue or something to do with your washer/dryer. Flush your toilets and run your sinks, run the washer, and see whether water comes into the basement right away; if it does, then begin to narrow down the source and call a plumber. If that isn't the source of the water, look at your walls. Chances are the water will begin at a wall and puddle on the floor near that wall, or you will see a wet mark that shows you where the water came from before it puddled. If you see the water leading from a specific wall, then that is the wall where the problem has occurred. Now, if this happens a few times a year, in one spot, just when there is a bad rainstorm, you really can live with the problem. Keep a few old towels around and jam them into the space during a big rainstorm, and let that be the end of it. But if the puddling happens every time it rains even lightly, or if the water is coming from all around the walls, then you have a real problem and are going to need a major fix.

TRICK OF THE TRADE: *If you have water in your basement, there are two possible culprits. Faulty rain gutters around your roof could be a cause—check the roof for dams or issues in the gutter. Also, basement windows could be leaking water into the foundation—if this is so, at one angle of the window, you'll often see a crack.*

375 What to do about a leaky basement

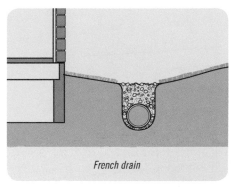

French drain

You aren't going to do anything yourself if you have a leaky basement. This is a job for a professional. There are two strategies. The first is a system called a French drain. The perimeter of the basement is dug up and a drain is installed all around that perimeter, which will carry the water away from the foundation to a pump that will send the water to the main waste pipe of your house. The second possible fix is to excavate the entire foundation and have a waterproof membrane installed around the house.

Both of these operations are expensive and time-consuming, but neither of them will bankrupt you, and if you are having a problem with water in the basement, you will have to do this. You can't live with the situation. Eventually it will create mold in your house, and that can be deadly. Every case is different, but as a general rule, we recommend the installation of a French drain, because it makes less of a mess in your landscaping and also protects the entire foundation from water. With a French drain you are covered.

376 When water comes up through the basement floor

Water may come up through cracks in the floor and even through your drains in the floor. If you are seeing water below your house forcing its way up through the floor of the basement, then you likely have a high water table in your area. If this is so, then the only thing you can do is hire a plumber to dig into your basement floor and install a pump to take the water away from the house and deposit it into the main waste pipes. You will also need an electrician, because in order to funtion, the pump needs an electrical connection.

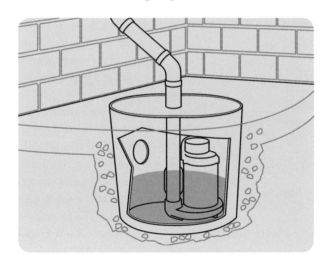

377 The whys and wherefores of mold

Mold is a fungus that can grow in your home. A fungus needs moisture to grow, so it will most likely begin in whatever part of the home is consistently damp, and that is often the basement. As the fungus grows it generates spores, and these can get into the air in your house, spreading the fungus everywhere. Fungus can make people sick. It can cause asthma and other serious medical conditions. Some molds are more dangerous than others, but it is best to treat all mold with caution. You'll see mold most usually on walls and floors in the form of black, green, or gray dots, circles, and patches. To determine whether the splotches you are seeing are mold, apply some hydrogen peroxide to them. If the mixture merely runs down the wall, no worries. If the blotches on the wall foam and bubble, then you have mold. If you have a small patch of mold, you can wipe the walls with a regular detergent or even vinegar, and that will work. If you have a big infestation, you need to hire a company to come in and do a mold remediation. To keep the mold from coming back, you have to solve the problem of moisture in the house.

378   A short note on finishing your basement

If you have a basement, and some money and some energy, we recommend that you think about finishing that space. It's a quick and easy way to add up to a third more space to your home. We suggest acoustic tile on the ceiling to give you easy access to pipes and wires. For the walls, use mold-retardant Sheetrock. For the flooring, you can leave it as is or, better still, put in a subfloor, plywood, and carpeting. Be aware that placing carpeting directly down on a basement floor is asking for wet carpeting, which is a short trip to mold. Basements make excellent playrooms for kids, home offices, man caves, exercise rooms, gyms, and, if there is some kind of window, guest rooms. The choice is yours.

379 How landscaping can affect your basement

In some cases landscaping can be the culprit in a basement flood. The dirt close to your house should be higher than the dirt farther away from the house. To put it more succinctly, the landscaping should be graded away from the house. Water travels through dirt, and if the dirt isn't sloped properly, the dirt could literally be carrying water to the foundation. A good rule of thumb is that the dirt 10 feet away from the house should be 6 inches lower than the dirt near the house, which is a 5 percent slope. You can try to fix this by adding some dirt around the house. If the problem persists, you should think about calling in a professional landscaper.

380 Some tips for landscaping

• At the end of the summer, prune your flowers, trim your hedges, get rid of all dead bushes, and call a tree company and have any trees that are near power lines or the house pruned back. (In general, it is better to leave trimming trees to the pros, because you can not only hurt yourself but also overprune a tree, which can kill the tree.)

- If you are planning to plant new bushes or trees, think about the size they will be at maturity, not what they look like in the garden center. Make sure that any tree you plant is at least 3 feet away from the house at maturity, which means you should plant it at least 5 feet away from the house. Think about the shade the tree will throw onto your house, the leaves you will be raking, and how deep the roots will grow.
- Buy a gardening encyclopedia that can tell you which plants thrive in your area.

381 The care and feeding of lawns

Lawns are a huge pain, but if you have a healthy one, it can be one of the nicest aspects of your home. We're not gardeners, this isn't a garden book, and lawn care is a complicated process about which many books have been written. But in general terms, there are two kinds of lawns: cool-climate lawns, which thrive in places that have cold winters, and warm-climate lawns, which thrive in places that are always warm. There are three main areas of lawn care. One is the application of fertilizer. In cool-climate places you fertilize in the early autumn and then in mid-November. In warm-climate places you fertilize in early spring and then late summer. The next area of lawn care is irrigation. It is best to water in the mornings, twenty or thirty minutes a day. Finally, you need to mow and maintain the lawn. A healthy lawn should be mown once a week, on a day when it is dry.

TRICK OF THE TRADE: *Those nice flowers that you have in planters during the summer can come into the house and survive a few months longer, making your house beautiful and, because they add oxygen, healthy.*

382 What you should have in a well-stocked suburban toolshed

We're calling it a toolshed, but you can also leave these tools in the garage. The tools you'll need are mostly the ones you will use around the outside areas of the house. Here's a list of the basic tools you'll want in your shed.

- Leaf blower
- Rake
- Lawn mower
- Shovels
- Hand shovel
- Pots and planters
- Fertilizer
- Sprinklers
- Small workbench
- Second set of hammers, screwdrivers, and other tools
- Gallon of gasoline for lawn mower
- Six- or 8-foot standing ladder
- Extra roof tiles
- Twenty-by-20-foot tarpaulin

TRICK OF THE TRADE: *If you have a snowblower, don't keep it in the shed. The last thing you want is to have to walk across your lawn in the snow, get the snowblower, and bring it back to the driveway. The blower belongs adjacent to the driveway, and the obvious place for it is your garage.*

383 How to buy and store a hose

There is nothing more convenient than a way to bring water to multiple places around the house. The way to do this is with a hose. You can use that water to clean decks, clear driveways, sluice out rain gutters, wash screens, and water plants. We recommend getting a hose that is at least 50 percent longer than your driveway. Spend some money and buy a quality garage hose, because the more expensive ones don't tangle. Buy a hose that has a roller with it, and always put it back properly after every use. Hoses break, crack, and get stepped on and crinkled when they are left snaggled up in a pile.

384 Do I need a sprinkler system?

If you have property of any decent size and you don't have all day every day to wander around your yard wielding a hose, and if you care about how your lawn looks, the answer is a resounding yes! If you buy a house with one already installed, you are lucky. If you need to put one in, it will cost you the price of a modest weeklong family vacation. These systems are all pretty much the same. A hose attached to the main water supply of the house runs underground around your property. The system is put on a timer and can be zoned, so that the landscape is watered one section at a time over the course of the day. If you want one of these, you need a professional to put it in for you. There are various different kinds of systems, and your best bet is to consult with a pro on the best system for your house and grounds.

basement, yard, garage, and fireplaces

385 How to light up your landscape

There are two types of outdoor lighting: line voltage, which works with regular bulbs and the central power system of your house, and low voltage, which is a lower-energy system that works with special bulbs. Most of the nicer lighting schemes use low voltage, which lasts longer and gives off a nice cool light. As you would with low-voltage lighting in your home, you will need a transformer box to make the transition between the low-voltage lighting and your regular-voltage power system. The biggest enemy of any lighting system is someone doing gardening or landscaping on your property. If the wires aren't buried deep enough—at least 18 inches—the landscaper may cut the wires or knock over the light with his lawn mower. If you hire a landscaper, show him where all the lights are and ask him to avoid them.

TRICK OF THE TRADE: *With a low-voltage system, you may see that the lights farther from the transformer box are dimmer than those closer to it. That's because the power is running from light to light away from the transformer. There's an easy solution for this: use a hub. A hub is a box that takes power from the transformer and delivers it to five to ten lights. If you make sure that every light in the system is attached to a hub, you will avoid the problem of dimming.*

386 What's on your patio?

A patio is a paved area on the exterior of your home that adds a nice outdoor space for cooking, entertaining, and hanging out. Patios are typically made from slab concrete, paving stones on concrete, or paving stones on sand with gravel around them. The paving stones themselves can be made of brick, man-made materials, slate, bluestone, or many other choices in all shades, shapes, and sizes. If you are going to put in a new patio, we recommend paving stones with sand and gravel. It's the cheapest to install, it lasts the longest when properly maintained, and we really like the way it looks. The problem with the other two kinds of patio is the concrete—basically, it is going to crack, break, and lift away with the weather.

TRICKS OF THE TRADE: *If you have a concrete patio, there's nothing to do but wait for it to break and then add mortar to the cracks. For paving stones with sand and gravel, you do a once-a-year maintenance in the spring. Cover the patio with ¼ inch of sand, then sweep the sand off the paving stones into the cracks between the stones, and then wet it down a bit, so the sand goes into the cracks.*

387 Dealing with a deck

A deck is an extension of your home, usually a raised platform made out of wood or some composite material. Decks are great. They give you a level surface, usually a little above the ground with a nice view, to enjoy the outdoors without being in the thick of it.

Decks made out of wood will be either stained or painted. They are beautiful, but the downside with wooden decks is that they are susceptible to rotting.

Decks made out of composite material don't have that classic wood look, and composite material is also about twice as expensive as wood. But it lasts. There really isn't that much maintenance with a composite deck—you just clean it when you think it's dirty.

388 Maintaining a wood deck

With a painted wood deck, you need to patch the paint every twelve to eighteen months. Power wash it with soap or detergent. Make sure to stand at least a few feet away to avoid damaging the wood. Let the deck dry for a day. Sand down any visible imperfections, like splinters, accretions of tree resin, and loose paint. Then repaint those areas. With a stained deck, you should apply a layer of sealer every two years. The process is similar to painting. Take a power washer with some detergent and wash the deck. Let it dry for one day. Sand down the entire deck, taking care to smooth out any splinters, stuck-on resin from trees, and other imperfections. Then apply a layer of sealer. The question with sealers is whether to use a clear sealer or a pigmented sealer. We recommend the pigmented version, because it protects the wood from UV rays.

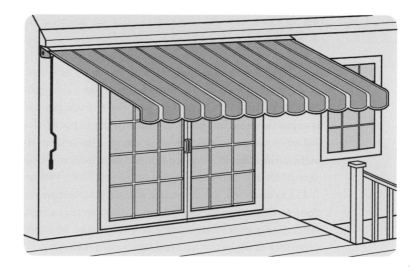

389 Think about putting in an awning

If you have a deck or a patio, you really ought to consider putting a retractable awning over it. The awning, which will be made of fabric or metal, allows you to use the area in question in sunlight and light rain, and it also provides a nice, calming effect. A quality retractable awning is a great asset. It will set you back anywhere from the cost of a good watch to the cost of a used car. Because most of the companies that sell awnings want you to buy them, they often install them for a reasonable fee. For a supercheap alternative you can think about using a pop-up canopy, which is a collapsible tent without the walls that you can put up and take down in a few minutes. A slightly more expensive alternative is a stationary awning, which is nonretractable and attached to the side of your house. Of course, you can also use just a table umbrella.

basement, yard, garage, and fireplaces

390   Fences make good neighbors

You understand all the reasons that fences are a good idea. The cheapest type is the chain-link variety, made out of aluminum (which rusts) and vinyl (which doesn't). The next on the expense scale is the standard wooden fence. These have to be painted every year or stained and sealed every few years. Then you have wrought-iron fences, which are expensive and need to be painted and scraped and painted where there is rusting. An even pricier option is electric fencing. Then there are stone and brick walls, which are the most expensive of all but don't need much maintenance.

When putting in a fence, be sure you are aware of the exact property lines and any height restrictions in your locality.

391   How to install a fence

In general terms, you can install any kind of store-bought fence. The key to installing a fence is that you have to dig holes that are deep enough to allow each post to sit upright. We recommend an 18- to 30-inch hole that is 10 inches wide. The distance between the posts shouldn't exceed 10 feet. Generally, you will be digging the holes with something called a posthole digger. It is a specialty tool that will dig a deep, narrow hole for the posts to go into. There is a power-tool version of this tool.

Beyond that, it is really a matter of following the instructions of whatever fence you are installing. Putting up a chain-link fence is kind of a tedious process, because you have to put the fence together, and it has a lot of different little pieces. Wooden fences are much easier to deal with. Our advice: if you have a lot of fencing to install, or if you are considering any kind of fencing other than wooden

1. Dig holes with a posthole digger.

2. After sinking the post into the hole, fill in around it with dirt.

3. Attach the fence to the post.

fencing, hire someone. Also, avoid doing your work in winter when the ground is frozen.

TRICK OF THE TRADE: *Make sure you know where your power lines, sewer lines, and other buried utilities are located before you start digging holes all over your property.*

392 How to maintain a pool

Pools range from the plain aboveground types to fancy in-ground models. They have various cleaning and filtration systems. But there is a basic philosophy to maintaining any pool. In winter, every few weeks, turn on the filter pumps, heaters, and spa systems for five minutes. That will dislodge any insects and debris that have collected there. If you live in a cold area, then you need to drain your pool. In the spring, check the entire system, including water levels. If your system requires it, add any chemicals that are needed. Wash out your filters at this time and check for any loose or worn hoses. Check the pilot light in the heating system if you have one. If you have any lighting in the pool, look for burned-out bulbs. Make sure any diving boards are tight and sound. During summer, run your systems at least two hours a day and test your water three times a week. Make a special note to test the water after a party, when you have lots of people in the pool (a buildup of suntan lotion can be bad for a pool). A call to your pool company might be warranted at that time. In autumn, make sure that leaves aren't clogging up the works.

393 What's on your driveway

There are four common types of driveways, and they correspond to the surfaces you'll find in patios. The most common type, and the most expensive, is concrete, poured 4 to 6 inches thick. Like all concrete, these driveways tend to crack from variable weather and tree roots and require professional attention. Slightly less expensive are surfaces in paving stones or brick. Over time the sand among the stones will wear away, but regular maintenance will keep this surface working well. Next in price is asphalt, which is the same black surface that you see on city streets. Asphalt cracks like concrete, and perhaps a little more often, and it also requires a pro to fix it. Finally, there's the gravel driveway. Over time you will lose gravel and you will have to replace it and rake it to make it look neat.

TRICK OF THE TRADE: *You will sometimes find small potholes in a gravel driveway. Fill them with dirt and cover them.*

394 Maintaining a driveway

The best way to keep your driveway in good shape is to patch it quickly when cracks appear. When you have cracks, water can get into them, and if that water freezes and expands, you'll have a bigger crack.

Crack-repair compounds are available at hardware stores. They're used with a caulk gun or a Spackle knife. Work on a day when it isn't going to rain. Clean the crack and fill it with the compound. The repair should last. If you have a crack that is bigger than ½ inch, you may want to put in a layer of compound as a base, then a layer of sand, and then a top layer of compound. Push the layers down with a Spackle knife to make sure the mixture is filling the crack well.

The other problem that plagues driveways is oil stains. They don't hurt the driveway, but they're pesky and unsightly. Use laundry detergent and a heavy scrub brush. Get down on your hands and knees and scrub. Many stains will wipe away with some warm water. Then go and have your car checked—it's leaking.

You can actually avoid staining by putting down a sealer on concrete or asphalt annually. Once a year, in early spring or early fall, wash your driveway with a hose to get rid of all the leaves and pebbles. Locate all your stains and clean them as we describe above. Hose down the driveway again. Let it dry. Then apply the sealer. Most people use a kind of applicator that looks like a large squeegee-type window cleaner. When you're done, you'll have a bright, shining driveway that everyone will admire.

GARAGE

395 How to maintain your garage

People don't realize how important the garage is. You are in and out of the garage every day and never even think about it. But the garage is part of your home, and it should be inspected and maintained. It is the most underappreciated and overused room in the house. Every year you should subject your garage to a spring cleaning and maintenance. Take everything in the garage and put it in the driveway and sell or give away as much as you can. Organize what you are keeping and put it back in an orderly way. Check your garage door (see entry 398). Hose down the garage floor and clean it. If you see cracks in the concrete flooring, patch them with a store-bought concrete patch. Check the walls for any cracking, mold, or damage. Refurbish the weather stripping on the door that goes from the garage to the main part of the house. Scan the room for rodent droppings. You are done.

396 A great way to execute perfect parking

Many of us have cars that are just a tad smaller than our garages, and we need to fit them in there snugly against the garage wall. At the same time, we don't want to ding our car every time we drive into the garage. There is a way, however, to park perfectly every time. Take a string and tie it to a screw and screw it to the garage ceiling right where you want the tip of your hood when you park perfectly.

Let the string touch the floor. Pull your car into the perfect location. Grab a tennis ball. Take another screw. Tie the string to the screw, and screw the screw into the tennis ball. Raise the string up so that the tennis ball touches your hood when you get to the point of a perfect parking job. Cut the string and reattach it to the ceiling. This gives you a guideline for perfect parking.

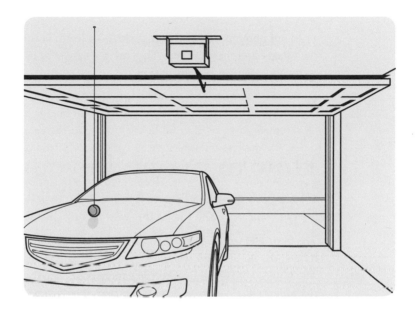

397 A rundown of the different types of garage doors

Garage doors can be made out of wood, vinyl, steel, or aluminum. Now they all come automated, but older ones can be retrofitted to be automated.

Canopy: one-piece door that swings up and in.

Retractable: one-piece door that resembles a canopy but is wider.

Sectional: a door in four to six sections, like a watchband that rolls up.

Roller: has narrower slats and can roll up more tightly.

Around the corner: an early model of garage door. It slides horizontally.

Side hinge: works like a door in your house, or a barn door.

In our opinion the ideal garage doors in terms of function are the canopy and the sectional. They are the easiest to use and offer reasonable security and insulation.

398 How to maintain your garage door

The basic elements you need to deal with in a garage door are the rollers, the hinges, and the track. The rollers lift the garage door. The hinges hold the rollers to the garage door. The track is where the rollers sit. If you have a metal system, then you want to lubricate the track every six months to keep the rollers running smoothly and protect them from moisture. If you have a plastic system, there is really no maintenance. The newer ones are even self-lubricating. If you have a leaf blower, you should blow the tracks, removing the gunk that has fallen in there. If you don't have a leaf blower, use a hose. There is a soft gasket around the perimeter of the door for insulation. Inspect it and make sure it hasn't suffered too much wear and tear; if it has, order a new one from the manufacturer. If you have electronic sensors, clean them. Change the battery on the remote control.

399 Project: Organize Your Garage

The art of garage organization is all about the walls. Along the side walls you'll use a system of Peg-Boards and hooks to store small and large items. Against the back wall, you'll place steel shelving. (The most important noncar items you might keep on the garage floor are a snowblower and/or a portable air compressor for filling tires.) Some items you might consider for the garage are the retractable ladder, brooms, tools, sporting equipment, off-season clothes, beach chairs, paint cans, and folding tables and chairs. Make a list of what you want to store, do a drawing of your garage, and make a reasonable plan of what you are going to hang and where you want it. Create a map, and bring it to the hardware store.

1. For storage of smaller items you'll buy one or more Peg-Boards. A Peg-Board is a board with rows of holes or slots. They work with hook systems that allow you to hang items off the board. The Peg-Board is attached to the wall with screws.

2. For larger items you will buy metal hooks that will go directly into the wall. For example, two hooks for a ladder.

3. For more storage of smaller items you'll buy a system of steel shelving. They come in different heights, widths, and depths for your garage needs.

4. To install the hooks and Peg-Boards, be sure to identify what kind of wall you are dealing with. When you go to the hardware store, you will need to buy your fasteners for the correct type of wall.

5. You are now ready to install your storage system and get your junk out of the way.

FIREPLACES

400 Anatomy of a fireplace

The hearth is the stone base in front of the fireplace. Then you have the firebox, which is the opening in the wall where the lumber sits and where you start your fire. When the fire is lit, the smoke goes up the flue, which is a hollow opening that allows the smoke to duct up and out of the house. The flue is inside the chimney. In the old days, most chimneys were made out of brick, and the flue was the inside of the brick chimney. These days flues can be metal lined or ceramic lined. Right at the start of the flue is a metal door with a handle on it called the damper. It allows you to close up the chimney when you aren't using the fireplace and want to seal up your house.

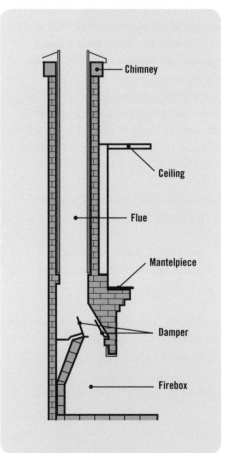

Chimney

Ceiling

Flue

Mantelpiece

Damper

Firebox

401 How to maintain your fireplace

The most important element to maintain is the brick inside the firebox. If some of the mortar has loosened in the firebox and you have a crackling fire that sends flaming cinders, those cinders might get into the spaces among the bricks and set off a fire inside your wall. Make sure your damper is always fully open when you are lighting fires. If it doesn't open the entire way, you need someone to come in and fix it. You can try a little petroleum jelly to lubricate it and see whether that works. You also need to keep your flue clear, and if you use the fireplace a good deal, you'll need to have the flue cleaned once a year. A great time to do this is after the leaves have fallen in autumn. If not, once every couple of years will work. Remember, a good, healthy fire means the flue is drawing. If the fire isn't that strong, you may have a blocked flue. You can also, if you think you can handle being up on the roof, go up and check the chimney, and if there is loose mortar between the bricks, replace it.

Safety and Security

This is the most subjective chapter in the book. We all know what it means to fix a toilet so that it flushes properly, but you and I could argue all day about what makes a house safe and secure. Or to put it simply: one person's safe is another person's paranoid. In the end, the choice is yours. We wrote a good deal of this chapter in the form of advice for making the house safe for children, because we noticed that there are few written guides for childproofing out there and thought it would be useful.

SAFETY

402   Smoke detectors and carbon monoxide alarms

We all have them and we've all seen them. They are those disc-shaped (sometimes rectangular) plastic things on the walls and ceilings of all our houses. Most municipalities have regulations about how many of them you need. But as a rule, to be safe, you should have a smoke alarm on every floor and outside every part of the house where people sleep. When you think about it, a person who is awake shouldn't need an alarm to tell her the house is burning. Smoke alarms are there to wake you, so placing them near bedrooms is important.

We also recommend you put a smoke alarm in finished basements and in the attic—basically, there should be at least one on every floor. Smoke alarms are always installed on ceilings, because smoke rises. Carbon monoxide alarms, which alert you to leaks of this highly toxic colorless and odorless gas, can be installed on walls or ceilings. You need one on every floor. In the basement, put one as near the boiler room as possible. These alarms come hardwired to your main electrical system or are battery operated. Carbon monoxide alarms can also be plugged into an outlet.

TRICK OF THE TRADE: *Even though the kitchen is a place where fires occur, don't put a smoke alarm in your kitchen. It is going to go off every time you make a burger. Outside the kitchen door is much better.*

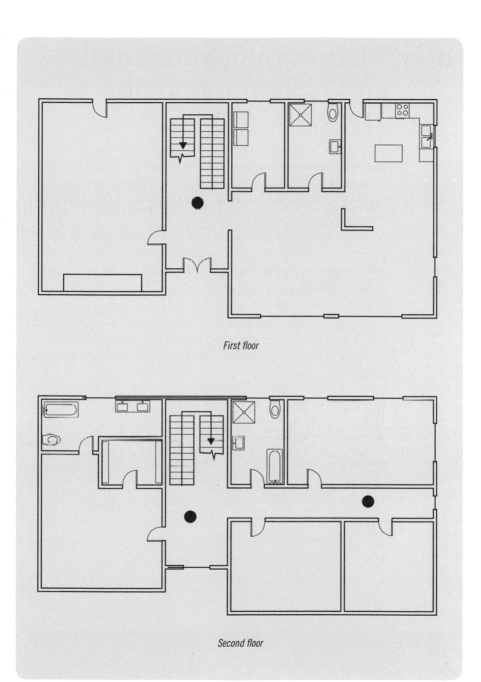

First floor

Second floor

403 Maintaining your smoke and carbon monoxide alarms

Every kind of alarm is different, but most have a battery in them (even hardwired alarms contain batteries as a backup system). Our advice is to change the batteries in each alarm every three or four months.

Most alarms come with a test button. When you change the battery, run the test. The test usually consists of pressing the button and listening to the alarm go off. If that happens, then the alarm is working. This is a much better idea than spewing carbon monoxide or smoke into the air and seeing if you get an alarm.

Every five years, regardless of the type of alarm you have, replace it. It is just better to be safe than sorry. A ten-year-old machine may not work. They aren't expensive. So change them. This is your family we are talking about.

TRICK OF THE TRADE: *Carbon monoxide alarms may give you a false alarm. No matter what, if it goes off, get out of your house! Then call the fire department. Don't be concerned that it might be a false alarm. If it is a false alarm, no one will give you a hard time. If you have two false alarms, change the machine.*

404   How to create a fire plan

A family fire plan is an established guide for what you will do if the house goes up in flames. It's the home version of all those tedious fire drills you had to deal with at school and now at work. Okay, it isn't fun, but there is a reason to plan for these things. When something goes wrong, people are less likely to panic and more likely to do the right thing if they've set up a plan in advance.

First, make sure everyone knows where the fire extinguishers are in the house. Show everyone what the smoke detector sounds like. (This is especially important for small children and for caregivers who may come from countries where they don't have fire alarms.) Show them where the escape routes and ladders are. Make sure people understand about feeling doors for heat before opening them. Then have a safe assembly place, like a spot across the street, where you can get an accurate head count. Remember to tell everyone that going back into the house is forbidden. Once or twice a year, run a drill. Make sure there are keys available to any doors or windows with locks on them.

405   How to buy, store, and maintain fire extinguishers

Fire extinguishers are a necessity. You have to have them. But they are used for small fires. If you are seeing massive floor-to-ceiling flames, get out of your house and then call the fire department. That said, a well-placed extinguisher can prevent a small fire from becoming a large one.

Extinguishers come in various sizes, and most of them will shoot either a chemical flame-retardant foam, a dry powder, or water. Remember that not all types of extinguishers will work on all fires, and some kinds of extinguishers will make some kinds of fires worse. Water, for example, may actually increase a grease fire. The dry powder is the best variety of extinguisher because it will work on almost every single type of flame, even electrical. We recommend you keep a small extinguisher in the kitchen and a large three-gallon one hanging on a wall near the stairs in the basement. If you don't hang the thing on the wall, it will get moved around.

TRICK OF THE TRADE: *Refill and check your extinguishers at least every two years, ideally twice a year. You can also hire a company to service your extinguishers twice a year.*

406 Deciding what safety measures you need

They call it childproofing—a misnomer, since you aren't making your home safe *from* children, but *for* children—but many child-safety tips make good general sense for you, as well as for older relatives and friends. Take a walk through your house with a notebook and a pen and create a checklist of dangerous areas. Do all your windows, including those on the ground floor, have gates on them? Are stoves, knives, refrigerators, and other potentially harmful cooking devices safe and secure? Are poisonous cleaning materials and medicines secured? How hot does the hot water in the house get? Is heavy furniture secured? Are there gaps in banisters large enough for a small head to get between? Are electrical outlets blocked off or covered? Are there tangles of electrical cords at hand? Are there coffee tables and other low-slung pieces of furniture with sharp edges?

407 How to choose the right kind of window guard

A window guard is a basic metal grid that sits inside the window frame itself or in front of the window and prevents children from falling out. The experts will tell you that children can die from falls out of ground-floor windows, and they also caution that window screens, like the kind designed to keep out bugs, do not prevent child falls. So you'll want to install proper window guards on just about every window in a private home. For windows on lower floors, however, you will also want to make sure that whatever window guard you choose can easily be opened by an adult, in case of fire or other emergency. Typically this kind of removable window guard can be telescoped in by an adult within a few seconds. Double-hung windows will usually take guards that fill most of the space occupied by the lower sash. Guards for casement windows must protect the entire window. There are scores of different kinds of window guards out there, and you should buy yours in consultation with a good retailer.

TRICK OF THE TRADE: *Look for guards that conform to the ASTM Standards code. This is an independent form of certification that the window guard is effective and safe.*

408 How to install a window guard

Every manufacturer will have its own specific installation, but we'll just go through the process in general. The typical guard for a double-hung window will be secured by two vertical metal rods that are screwed directly inside the window frame. Put the entire window guard together and fit it into the frame. If you have a wooden frame, you can take the screws that come with the guard and just screw them into the wood, using a power tool. If you have a metal-frame window, you are going to have to mark where the holes need to go, remove the guard, and predrill holes. Then put the guard back into the window and screw it in. This is essentially what you will also do for a guard in a casement window, except the guard will fill the entire window frame, not just the bottom half. With some windows you may have to mount the window guard outside the frame. If so, make sure to buy a kind of window guard designed for that application.

409 How to install a window stop

If you have double-hung windows and want even more protection than window guards can afford, you might consider adding window stops. At its most basic, a window stop is a piece of wood or metal drilled into the window frame that prevents the lower sash of a double-hung window from rising above a certain point. This is an effective tool against break-ins, and it also keeps children from falling out. There are many window-stop products you can buy, some of which are excellent and allow you to do things like adjust the height of the stop. But you can also easily make a window stop at home. Open the lower sash of your window to the maximum height you wish it to go, perhaps 6 inches. Mark the place where you want the top of the sash to go on the window frame. Find a piece of wood or metal that comes close to matching the color of the frame and cut it down to fit the frame. Place it against the side of the frame and use a wood or metal screw to fasten the piece of wood or metal onto the frame. You now have a window stop. You have also ruined the window as a way out of your house in case of an emergency. So have an alternate route in your mind if the window you have blocked was a potential escape route for your family.

410   How to make window treatments safe

Window blinds are popular with homeowners, but the cords from blinds are also a strangulation hazard for children and pets. When you are designing or decorating a child's room, please be conscious of the fact that you should never under any circumstance place the bed of a small child within reach of the cord of a blind. (Or near any window, for that matter.) In general, you should go through your house and make sure there are no blinds with cords accessible to the ground. If you can, you should replace all blinds with cords with other types of window treatments. If you can't or won't do this, you should cut the cords or tie them so that they are well off the ground. If you have the kind of shades that are operated by a cord or chain in a continuous loop, there are devices you can install that will keep the chain or cord under tension and therefore less likely to get caught around a child's hand or neck. If you have the kind of blinds that have cords that lock into place, always keep the cords locked.

411   How to choose the right child safety gate

A safety gate is installed in the doorway of a room, at the top or bottom of a set of stairs, or across a room to keep a child away from a hazardous situation. You can find these gates in all shapes and sizes. Gates come in wood, metal, or plastic and can be screwed into a wall or other surface, strapped onto an object like a baluster, or wedged into a doorway using a pressure system. They also come with a wide variety of locking systems. Choosing a safety gate is mostly a matter of common sense, but where you can, choose gates that screw directly into the wall rather than pressure-mounted gates; choose metal and wood over plastic; and make sure you are selecting a gate of a width that can properly cover the space you are intending to block off. In general, childproof gates are for use with children three years and younger, or at least children small enough so that the gate is above the child's shoulders. As much as some of you might want to keep your older children under lock and key, these gates will not help you.

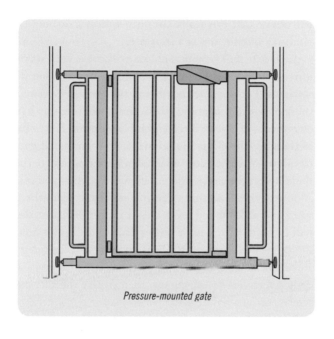

Pressure-mounted gate

412 How to install screw-mounted safety gates

This kind of safety gate is screwed directly into a door frame, a wooden baluster, the studs behind drywall, a plaster wall, or any other solid part of your house. A screw-mounted gate is by far the best option for blocking off an area, and many childproofing experts will advise that it is really the only option you should consider for a vital area like the top of a staircase.

Each gate will be different and will come with its own installation instructions, but the concept behind the installation will be much the same. Put the gate together as per the instructions, situate it in the spot where it is going to go, and make sure you have a surface on either side that will accommodate a screw. Place the gate firmly in the spot where it is going. Most screw-mounted gates will have faceplates on either side with holes to accommodate the screws. Line these holes up exactly where they will be when you install the gate and mark them. At this stage you can try to place the gate in its space and sink the screws in with a power drill, but the installation will be better if you use a power drill to drill pilot holes. A pilot hole should be of a diameter slightly smaller than the screw you are using and about half the depth you want the screw to go in. Once you've drilled the pilot holes, you can then situate the gate and sink the screws, using a power drill.

413 How to install a safety gate without screws

The standard safety gate is meant to be installed in a wooden door frame with screws. But the reality of life is that there are many situations where you might want a safety gate and using screws isn't an option. Or you don't want to. You may live in an antique home with a fine old staircase that shouldn't be drilled into. You may live in a new-construction home where the walls are all Sheetrock, which screws will not adequately fasten to. You may have a staircase with iron balusters, or a wood staircase with a handrail that curves in such a way that there's no surface thick enough for a screw.

In these cases and others, you will need to buy a special all-purpose safety-gate installation kit. Some will come with plastic straps that will go around balusters to secure the gate. Others will have special faceplates with toggle-bolted screws designed to remain secure on Sheetrock walls. There are systems with two posts that go on either side of a banister with a nut-and-bolt attachment that sandwiches the sides together. A quick call to a retailer should get you what you need.

414 What about pressure-mounted safety gates?

Pressure-mounted safety gates are held in a space by a spring inside the gate that presses out in both directions, wedging the gate between two solid surfaces. This is an attractive idea to most parents, because the gates cause no damage to the house and there is no real installation involved. You just set the thing up, place it in the doorway, for example, and your room is blocked off. Not only that, but pressure-mounted gates are portable and you can move them from room to room with your child.

So why not use these gates everywhere in the house? Because they slip. To stay in place, the pressure-mounted gate must maintain a delicate equilibrium between the levels of pressure on each side of the gate. If that equilibrium is lost, for whatever reason, the gate will actually push away from the surface it is adhering to. That is why most experts insist that these gates are not appropriate for the tops of stairs. They are better for short-lived situations, like being with your baby in a single room and keeping the child in that room for an hour or two.

415 How to use a door for child safety

If the idea of having safety gates all over your house seems unsightly and ungainly to you, and you have doors in front of all your rooms, you might be able to get away with simply securing the doors in your house. This is the simplest solution to keeping a child out of any room with hazards in it. There are three childproofing solutions for a door.

1. You can install a child-safety latch or lock on the door, much as you would on a cabinet or a closet.

2. If you have a door with a traditional doorknob, there are plastic knob covers you can purchase that you just slip over the knob. When an adult uses the knob, he or she can exert enough strength to turn the cover and the knob together. But when a child tries to turn the knob, the cover will spin, and the knob will stay in place.

3. Lever-style door handles are traditionally secured with a doughnut-shaped attachment that fits around the handle and is secured by adhesive. When the attachment is locked, the handle cannot move. Press a button, and the doughnut rotates with the handle, allowing the door to open.

416 Kitchen safety for children

The first question you need to ask yourself is: can you block the kitchen off altogether? The kitchen is just bristling with things that can harm a child, and the easiest answer is to keep small children out of there, period. Of course that may not be possible in a world where people increasingly favor open floor plans with kitchens that are accessible to the entire house. If you are going to have children in and out of the kitchen, here are some general guidelines you can follow.

- Keep all knives, sharp utensils, plastic bags, and hazardous materials, like cleaning fluids, in locked drawers.
- Strap down and secure appliances large and small that are sitting out in full view.
- Apply locks to refrigerator and freezer doors.

The next five entries detail specific improvements you can make for increased kitchen safety.

TRICK OF THE TRADE: *When cooking on stovetops, use the back burners, and turn the handles of pots and pans toward the wall, away from where little hands can get at them. Never use a stove while holding a child.*

417 How to make an oven safe

The typical oven has three main danger zones: the oven knobs, the oven door, and the cooktop. The solution for the oven knobs is simple. There are plastic knob covers that are installed by removing the oven knobs, placing the covers on the stove, and reinstalling the knobs. When you're done, you have a plastic lid over the knob that can be opened by an adult but not by a child. Oven doors can be secured with locks. Oven-door locks come front mounted or side mounted. You attach them by using a heat-resistant adhesive strip, and there is a childproof latch that keeps the oven door secured. For cooktops there are plastic screens that sit at the front of the cooktop and angle up and out to block small hands from reaching up to the stove. Most of these can also be attached to the face of the oven by using heat-resistant adhesive. The issue with door locks and stove screens is the adhesive. If you look up these products on the Internet, for example, you'll find a strong difference of opinion among consumers. Some say the adhesive works well, and some report that it fails rather quickly. Our advice is to just try some products. They don't cost very much, so it is worth a go.

TRICK OF THE TRADE: *Be sure to clean the surface carefully before you apply the product—nothing is worse for an adhesive than grease—and let the adhesive cure overnight to bond fully.*

418 How to make refrigerators and other appliances safe

After the oven, the refrigerator is the biggest safety hazard for children. Not only can children get stuck inside refrigerators, but there are also many potentially dangerous items inside the fridge, from alcoholic beverages and raw meat to glass containers that can be broken. There are a variety of different products available that act as child-safety locks on fridge doors. They work much the same way that oven-door locks do. One piece attaches to the refrigerator door and the other piece to the body of the appliance, and the two pieces click together with a latch of some sort. Countertop appliances such as toasters and coffeemakers should be unplugged when not in use and should be left as far away from the edge of the counter as possible. There are appliance straps with adhesive ends that you can buy, which will allow you to secure appliances to the countertop so that they cannot be moved. Just attach one end of the strap to the appliance and the other end to the countertop. You should think about doing the same thing for stereo systems, televisions, computers, and computer monitors.

419 How many drawers and cabinets should be secured?

We aren't going to lie to you: if you really want to secure all the cabinets and drawers in your home that might need securing, you are in for many hours of tedious labor. There are just so many cabinets in the house that could conceivably need protecting. In theory, you could apply latches to every single cabinet in the kitchen, all the bathroom cabinets, every cabinet in the living and play areas that contains electronic equipment, heavy books, and breakable glass items, and so on. You'll have to decide how far you want to go. Many people whose children are not climbers—and there are those kinds of children out there—will content themselves with securing the lower cabinets in the kitchen and bathroom. There's a wide variety of cabinet locks out there, but the most common ones fall into two basic categories: slide locks and latches. Slide locks will work on some forms of cabinets; latches work for most every other kind. Latches require some installation, but they are quite convenient to use when you get the hang of them.

420 How to install slide locks for drawers and cabinets

Slide locks are appropriate for cabinets with double doors with knobs or handles on them. They're great because they require no installation. The slide lock is a U-shaped plastic strap with teeth on it. You fit the U through the handles on both cabinet doors. Then there's a plastic piece that slides down over both tips of the U, locking the U and the two cabinet doors together. To release the slide lock, you press buttons on either side of the plastic piece. Sounds easy on paper, but in reality it can be quite difficult to get these things on and off.

421 How to install a cabinet or drawer latch

Latches tend to be made of plastic and are installed with screws or adhesives. What we are calling a latch is really both a latch (a plastic prong with a small hook on the end) and a catch (a plastic piece that catches the latch-hook and holds it in place). The trick when installing a latch is to line the latch and the catch properly. Typically you install the latch on the cabinet first. The latch goes on the inside of the cabinet door. Position it in the upper corner of the inside of the door on the side away from where the hinges are. The catch goes on the cabinet itself, on the upper part of the door opening, exactly across from where the latch is. To match up the two sides correctly, eyeball it. Many catches come with temporary adhesive strips so you can test out your latch and catch before you drill or apply permanent adhesive. After a proper installation, the latch should hook onto the catch automatically when you close the door. To open the latch, open the door as far as you can, stick your finger into the crack between the door and the cabinet, and push the latch prong down. Honorable mention should also go to the spring latch, which is a one-piece unit that hooks onto cabinets that have a lip in the drawer opening.

Please note that this installation can also work for any door in your house that isn't too heavy.

422 How to make a bathroom safe

In an ideal world you'd keep the child out of the bathroom except when he or she is using it and is supervised by an adult. The simplest and easiest way to accomplish this is to install a safety latch on the bathroom door, high up, away from small hands. If that doesn't work for you, or you'd like to have more protection, there are a few simple things to think about. Install safety latches on all bathroom cabinets, even ones up above sinks. Remember, some kids climb. Keep all sharp items, like nail clippers and razors, safely stowed away in the cabinets. Ditto for all medicines and vitamins. Any electric appliances you might use, especially blow dryers, should remain secured in latched cabinets at all times and should never be left anywhere near a water source. You should install nonslip tape in the bathtub or lay down a nonslip bathmat. If you have a senior citizen in the house, install a handrail in the tub.

Beyond that, there are two more complicated measures you should consider: securing your toilet seat (see entry 423) and turning down the temperature on your water heater (see entry 425).

423 How to make a toilet safe for children

Who would want to go mucking around in a toilet, you ask? Well, a toddler is the answer. Water is endlessly interesting to children, and from the toddler perspective one body of water is just as interesting as another. Beyond the obvious sanitary concerns for your child, there's also the fact that the little one who is interested in toilet water will likely want to drop things into the water. Some of these items will stop up the toilet and others will be ruined by contact with the toilet water.

There are various different models of toilet locks, so you'll have to experiment with what works for you. Please be aware that there are locks that will not work with every kind of toilet seat, so take note of the shape of your toilet before you go out and buy a lock. Beyond that, there are models that clamp onto the rim of the toilet

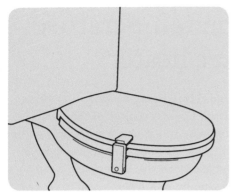

and then onto the seat. There are models that function like door latches with two pieces, both attached by adhesive strips. There are systems that have rigid pieces that close over the toilet lid, keeping it shut. Some latches require you to disassemble the toilet seat in order to install them. Some fit right over your existing toilet. In general, we favor the models that clamp directly onto the toilet without the use of adhesives.

424 How to make a bathtub safe

There are just so many ways a child, an older person, or even a healthy adult can come to harm in the tub: slipping and falling, banging a head into the faucet, being scalded by hot water, and the old standby—drowning. Be sure to install nonskid safety strips in the tub to prevent slips and falls. In most bathrooms a handrail can be simply drilled into the wall beside the tub. There are rubber covers you can buy that will go over faucets and handles to make them soft and to prevent children from burning their hands on hot metal. There are devices you can purchase that will shut down the water flow from a faucet when the water gets too hot. You may also want to look into controlling the hot water temperature in your house as a whole (see entry 425). As for drowning, never leave a child unsupervised in a bathtub, whether it is filled with water or has a small amount of water in it or no water at all. That is the best and only preventative measure against drowning.

425 Lowering the temperature on your water heater

It doesn't take much to be scalded by burning hot water in a house where the water temperature isn't properly controlled. The simplest way to avoid this problem is to make sure your water heater is set to no more than 120° Fahrenheit, which is more than hot enough for you to enjoy a nice shower and not so hot that your children can do themselves serious damage. Assuming your house has an electric or gas hot water heater separate from the boiler, or a new on-demand tankless system, this is a straightforward operation. There is a thermostat on the unit, and you simply set it to 120°. If your water is heated directly off the furnace, however, you may not be able to set the temperature yourself. Please also be aware that some plumbers consider 120° a touch low for maintaining the health of your heating system, because bacteria can grow at that temperature. They recommend keeping your hot water at a temperature of 130°. Of course, childproofing experts will say 130° is too high for your child's safety. The decision will have to be yours.

426 How to secure heavy pieces of furniture to the wall

Even if you don't have children, falling bits of furniture can pose a risk. But if you have children and they are climbers, watch out. You have a chest of drawers that is sitting in a friendly way against a wall, but what happens if one of those climbing children decides to crawl up the front of the chest of drawers while rocking it and wrenching back and forth until it hits the tipping point and comes crashing down on top of the child? The solution for this is a simple one:

straps. The straps have plates at both ends. One plate is screwed into the wall, at a point where there are studs behind the Sheetrock. (For a definition of studs and how to locate them behind a wall, please see chapter 9.) The other plate is screwed directly into the piece of furniture. As long as you have used at least two straps, one on each side, for larger pieces of furniture, you will prevent the furniture from tipping over. When installing the straps, please be sure to secure them on the upper half of the piece of furniture and to sink the drills into a solid wood portion of the furniture, not into flimsy plywood backing, for example. Please also think twice before drilling into any kind of valuable antique.

TRICK OF THE TRADE: *For antiques, fine furniture, and more expensive pieces, removing them for a few years might be preferable to making holes in them.*

427 How to make electrical outlets safe

There are two kinds of outlet faceplates: standard outlets with one screw, and decorator plates that have two screws. Make sure you determine which style you have before buying any childproofing products. There are three different solutions for childproofing an outlet, and they depend on how the outlet is used. For an outlet that always has something plugged into it, use an outlet cover. This is a plastic piece that goes over the outlet and the plugs, keeping it all away from small hands. Outlets that you plug appliances in and out of should have their faceplates replaced with so-called safe plates. The safe plates have sliding doors over the outlets, which allow adults to plug appliances in, but make it impossible for children to stick their fingers into them. For outlets that are rarely used, buy simple plugs. The early versions of these plugs were easy for children to remove, creating a choking hazard as well as leaving the plug unprotected, but now there are models that come with buttons that must be pressed in for the plug to release. You can also purchase covers for power strips.

Outlet cover

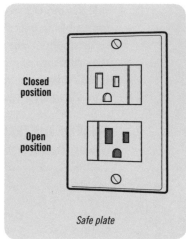

Closed position

Open position

Safe plate

428 How to make a garage door safe

Your garage door is a lethal weapon. It is big, it moves fast, and it is in a place where children, pets, and even a mindless adult or two may be walking around. What you want to avoid is having the thing come crashing down on someone. The best prevention for this is to install a motion detector that will stop the door and reverse it when someone or something is in its path. Many localities have laws mandating this kind of thing. Some automatic garage door openers aren't capable of reversing. If you have one of those, replace it or retrofit it so that it does.

TRICK OF THE TRADE: *Do not leave the garage door remote on your dashboard or in your glove compartment. Always keep it with you. There is no easier way for a burglar to get into your home than with a stolen remote.*

429 More home safety tips

Here are a few other things to think about.

- Install a fireplace grille.
- Place bumpers on all sharp corners and edges of furniture and remove all glass tables.
- Put nonslip pads on rugs.
- Never use a crib that has slats that are more than 2⅜ inches apart.
- Make sure the mattress of the crib is firm and fits into the crib snugly.
- Do not use pillows, comforters, or large blankets in an infant's crib.
- Do not place stuffed animals or other toys in an infant's crib.
- Place stickers on sliding glass doors to prevent children from walking into them.
- Install a fence with a locking gate around your swimming pool.
- Inspect outdoor play areas for sharp edges, loose screws, splinters, choking hazards, and areas that will heat excessively in the sun.
- Make sure all jungle gyms, playhouses, and other toys are stable and secure.
- Use trash cans that have lids that lock.

SECURITY

430 How to choose the right alarm system

Alarm systems are designed to alert you to the presence of an intruder. They do this by detecting whether windows and doors have been opened, or by detecting motion in places that should be empty. (You can also have your fire and carbon monoxide monitors hooked into your alarm system.) These systems come in all levels of complexity and cost. The two most important issues are whether an alarm is hardwired or wireless, and monitored or unmonitored.

The hardwired systems are more expensive and more labor intensive to install, but they are more reliable. Even the best wireless system can be affected by electrical interference.

An unmonitored system is nothing more than an elaborate alarm. A monitored system, by contrast, sends a message to a company that will call you and alert the police if you don't answer or if you tell them there's a problem. In our opinion, a monitored system is a must. Let's face it, there are so many alarms going off all the time these days that most of your neighbors will ignore it if yours goes off. The monitoring company won't ignore it. Also, if you make a plan with the security company, they may wire your home for free.

431 Smile, you're on security cam

As we've said, first and foremost, security cameras are a deterrent. Their mere presence may be enough to frighten off someone. But if you have a system of cameras that works and you choose the right system, the added benefit is that you have a record of what happened. This might come in handy for things that have nothing to do with crime. Imagine catching that kid who put a baseball through your window. You can go back to the videotape and nab him on tape. You can have as many cameras as you want, but we recommend one on the front door, one on the driveway, one in the backyard, and maybe one on the side of the house. That makes four. You need to ask yourself how well lit is the space you are filming. You may want a camera that can see all the way to the street so that you can get a shot of a license plate moving away.

TRICK OF THE TRADE: *Depending on how well lit the area around your house is, you may want night-vision cameras and film, or you may want to install lights on motion detectors. Those lights on motion detectors are a great deterrent in and of themselves.*

432 Interior cameras (the good, the bad, the nanny cam)

At first people started putting cameras inside their houses to check up on nannies. But you know how these things go: it didn't take long before these interior cameras were being used to keep tabs on a whole host of people in the home, from housekeepers to handymen and even contractors. There are those who will find something quite creepy about having all of these cameras in the house. That is why some people hide them. Other people just won't have them. To each his or her own. As with any other system, these can be hardwired or wireless. If they are hardwired, they can go right to your DVR or your computer. One way or the other, the most important thing this kind of system does, as opposed to outdoor cameras, which may be considered deterrents, is to record what is going on in the house.

433 Some cheapo deterrents

Most of the security measures we are talking about in this chapter are deterrents. That means they aren't going to be able to stop anyone from breaking into your house, but their mere presence may cause the bad guy to give your house a pass. But some of the cheapest deterrents you can put in place are signs: for example, BEWARE OF DOG or THIS HOUSE PROTECTED BY XYZ SECURITY SYSTEM. It would be great to have a massive Doberman or an upscale security system, but sometimes the sign is enough. You can install fake security cameras around the house. They aren't even wired, but so what? Is a burglar going to climb a ladder to check? Another cheap fix is to trim the bushes around your house so there is nowhere for a burglar to hide.

TRICKS OF THE TRADE Don't leave your valuable items within sight of windows. Put your lamps on timers to turn on and off while you are away from home.

434 Security systems and your computer

In today's world it is not that difficult to have the security systems, and also your lights, HVAC, and other things, connected to your computer. The only issue here is money. It is quite expensive. You will need to bring in a specialist company to do this. They will come in and connect all of the machinery in your house to a main computer. When this is done correctly, you can control the entire system remotely through another computer, from your mobile phone, or from a handheld remote control console inside the house. The plusses of these systems are obvious. You can keep track of your house from anywhere. The minus is that many homeowners may find a system of this type very hard to operate. You may be computer savvy, but what about your mother-in-law, who always comes over? The system is only as good as the least tech-savvy person who uses it.

435 Window and door security

When you think about it, the humble door was perhaps the first security item used, once people moved into houses. But doors can be more or less safe, depending on how you deal with them. The hinges of exterior doors should all be on the inside. You want good quality doorknobs, and you want good dead bolts, ones that go at least 1 inch into the door frame. You also want to make sure you use nice long screws in the installation of any door hardware. Remember, people kick doors in, and if you have short screws, this is going to be much easier. Think also about the quality of the door itself. Don't use hollow-core doors on the exterior of the house. A strong man could put his fist through a hollow door. Window security is simple:

make sure your windows have locks. If you have casement windows, leave the cranks off them when you are not opening them.

TRICK OF THE TRADE: *Believe it or not, a lot of people forget to lock their doors and windows. So, use your door lock. Lock your windows. Turn the security system on. None of this stuff can help you if you don't use it.*

436 Take our advice: get a safe

If you are the kind of person who has a nice house that needs maintenance, chances are you could benefit from having a safe in that house. Safes don't just protect valuables from robbery; they are also useful against fire, flood, or building collapse. You can spend a lot of money on a safe, but for the price of a dinner for two at a fancy restaurant you can get a safe that will do what you need. When shopping for safes, look for one that has an Underwriter Laboratories rating. The rating will tell you how long your valuables will be protected in a fire. Class A will keep your stuff safe for four hours at 2,000° Fahrenheit. Class B works for two hours at 1,800°. Class C will work for one hour at 1,700°. Most people will buy a Class B or C safe. The best kind of safe is one that is bolted into the floor, or even better, cemented into the basement floor.

437 How to keep your home pest free

There's nothing intrinsically wrong with rodents, bugs, and other little creatures. They play their role in the universe. Problems only occur when they decide to leave the outdoors, where they belong, and try to share your house with you. That's when they become pests. So why do they come in? It isn't for the premium cable channels on the television. Animals enter your home in search of three things: food, water, and shelter. There are all sorts of specific steps you can take to prevent pests from entering your home and for getting rid of them once they're inside, but your best overall strategy for keeping your house pest free is to eliminate access to food, water, and shelter. The bad news is that even if you do your best at this, you may still be infested from time to time. The good news is that most of the steps we will advise you to take are simple, everyday procedures that can easily be incorporated into your routine, and if you take these steps you'll save yourself money and anguish down the line.

438 How to handle ants

By all accounts, ants are the number one pest in the United States. There are around seven hundred species of ants wandering around in our part of the world. Most species live forty-five to sixty days. They can appear at any time of the year but are most active in the warmer months.

Ants come into the home looking for food, and if they find food, they will leave chemical messages behind them that will attract other ants. If you want to discourage ants, keep your food in sealed containers. Dispose of garbage early and often. Keep your kitchen counters wiped and get that message to any children in the house.

Train your dogs and cats to eat their food in a short amount of time and in one sitting. Do not leave pet food sitting around in bowls all day. That is an ant buffet.

If you have ants, you can try to contain them with over-the-counter sprays, but if the problem persists, you should hire an exterminator.

Please be aware that some species of ants, known as carpenter ants, can not only overrun your house in the usual way but also can chew up the wood in your home, potentially causing a great deal of damage.

439   Keeping termites at bay

These are the real bad boys of the pest world, because they aren't just yucky, they are also highly destructive. It is estimated that termites do around five billion dollars' worth of property damage each year, and most of it isn't covered by home insurance policies. There are around two thousand termite species in the United States. They can be found in any region but are most prevalent in the Southern. Termites eat the cellulose in wood; once they get into your house they will begin destroying any wood they can find and that means the structural beams of the home, staircases and antique furniture, to name a few key items.

One of the big problems with termites is that they often remain undetected until they have done horrible damage. You may have termites if you see unexplained damage to wood in the house and piles of sawdust inside or outside the home. Termites are white and see-through. In the spring they have wings, which fall off, allowing the termites to fit into small holes and gain access to the house. If you have termites, you must call a professional. Better still, get a termite contract, which will ensure that you have an inspection at least once a year. A few of the things you can do to prevent termite infestations include keeping wood mulch 15 inches from the home's foundation, storing firewood at least 20 feet from the home and bringing in wood only when you are about to burn it, and keeping your basement and crawl spaces dry.

440 Dealing with cockroaches

Most pests carry disease, but cockroaches excel at it. There are thousands of species of roach, and around thirty of them are known to hang out around humans. They carry at least thirty-three different kinds of bacteria, including E. coli, six forms of parasitic worms, and other human pathogens. Cockroach droppings are known to cause asthma attacks, especially in children. You know how people are always saying roaches are indestructible? Well, check this out: a cockroach can live for up to a week without its head, and the only reason it will die is the lack of a mouth to take in water. They are also superfast, being able to reach speeds of up to three miles an hour.

Here are a couple of easy ways to discourage roaches: make sure the garbage is taken out regularly; don't leave your pet's water bowl out all day; and make sure cracks and holes around the outer façade of the home are sealed up.

A big motivation for roaches is access to water. So make sure your pipes aren't leaking, especially underneath sinks and in kitchens and baths. Keep basements and crawl spaces moisture free. Believe it or not, a damp wall may provide enough water for a roach to get by on.

One final thing: clean your countertops regularly. It won't prevent roaches from coming in, but it will limit your exposure to the bacteria they carry. You can try over-the-counter remedies for roaches. Bait traps are especially effective.

441 Living rodent-free

We're not talking Peter Rabbit here. This is about mice and rats, which invade an estimated twenty-one million homes in the United States, especially in the winter. They are very good at getting into homes through tiny holes and cracks. Mice can squeeze through a space as small as a nickel, and rats can enter through a hole the size of a quarter. Once they get into your home, they start multiplying. Females can make a dozen babies every three weeks. So if you see one rodent in your home, you are probably infested or will be in short order. Rodents carry various diseases and spread them, especially through their feces, which can cause allergies. An average mouse drops around twenty-five thousand fecal pellets a year; that's around seventy times a day. Now, this is very important: you cannot eradicate rodents from your house by using poison or traps. You must block the holes they are coming through. To do this you need to hire an expert to come and find the entrance holes and then plug them, usually with steel wool, which rodents cannot abide. Once the home has been sealed, the rodents stuck inside will have to be eliminated with traps and rodenticides.

442 Stopping bedbugs

The bedbug, a small insect, is about the size of a lentil or an apple seed when fully mature. It lives off of human blood. Over the past few years there has been a growing bedbug crisis. Today, around 95 percent of pest control professionals report treating homes for bedbugs; a decade ago that number was fewer than 25 percent. There are various theories about why this problem has grown so much, but the theory most accepted by scientists and professionals is that it is the result of an increase in travel, which is spreading the problem, and bedbugs' growing resistance to insecticides.

To make matters more confusing, there are different strains of bedbugs around the United States, and different strains are resistant to different kinds of pesticides. Bedbugs can live up to a year without feeding. You will often find them around beds, especially where the mattress and box spring meet, and on the underside of dust ruffles. But bedbugs have nothing to do with beds biologically and will seek refuge between walls, in electrical sockets, underneath the couch, or wherever they can be warm and safe. They come out at night when people sleep, attracted by humans' release of carbon dioxide when they breathe out. They climb onto a body, inject an anesthetic so that the victim can't feel the bite, and bite away, sucking as much blood as they can.

HOW TO TELL IF YOU HAVE BEDBUGS

Bedbugs do not care how rich you are or whether you stay in first-class accommodations or cheap ones, and they are not at all affected by cleanliness or its lack. They simply get into clothing, luggage, and electronic equipment, jumping from person to person. In apartment buildings they will climb straight up pipes and go from flat to flat. Some of the most common places where people get bedbugs these days is on airplanes, trains, and other forms of public transportation; in movie theaters; and just from touching other people. The first evidence you may have of bedbugs is from the itching, weltlike bumps on your arms, face, and back. Often these bites appear in threes, along a line, the so-called breakfast, lunch, and dinner pattern. But not everyone will show signs that they have been bitten. You can also look for bedbugs, as we said above, on box springs, on dust ruffles, or even in sheets. The best time to check is at night, in the dark, with a flashlight. But if you suspect you have bedbugs, you need to call in a professional to tell you if you do, and if you do, where you do.

HOW TO PREVENT AN INFESTATION AND ERADICATE IT

Take extra special care when traveling, particularly if you are staying in a hotel. Always check an airplane seat, train seat, or hotel room for evidence of bugs. When you come home from a journey, wash your clothes in a hot cycle. Do not buy secondhand clothes or bring secondhand furniture into the house. If you discover you do have bedbugs, then you are in for a protracted and potentially expensive battle. Bring in a professional and develop a treatment plan. No two infestations are alike, so there is no standard treatment, but some of the methods include steaming, freezing, and insecticides. Often a combination of these treatments is needed. Most infestations will require more than one visit from a professional to eradicate them.

APPENDIX A

How to Hire and Manage a Contractor

Take care when you are hiring a contractor. This is going to be a long-term relationship. The contractor is often the person who helps maintain your home over time. The following are some quick tips on how to hire and manage your contractor.

HAVE A CLEAR IDEA OF WHAT YOU WANT TO DO
You aren't ready to call a contractor until you have a project written down, at least in your own words. If you are doing some kind of real construction, you need an architect's drawings. If you are doing a cosmetic renovation, you can make a list yourself and call a contractor directly.

FIND AT LEAST THREE CONTRACTORS
Ask your friends and family for referrals. If that isn't helpful, go to a local high-end paint or hardware store and ask around.

CALL FOR APPOINTMENTS AND JUDGE THE RESPONSES
If it takes a contractor more than seventy-two hours to respond, put him at the bottom of the list. He's either too busy to work with you or too lazy.

CONDUCT JOB INTERVIEWS
Have a sheet detailing the scope of work on it for the contractor and for yourself. Have him read it over and ask for his initial reaction. Then watch him. If he's in a hurry, if he doesn't take interest or ask questions, those are bad signs. You want someone who is creative, a problem solver, and has suggestions about good ways to do the job.

ASK FOR A BID

The bid is the contractor's proposal for doing the work and what it is going to cost. If you are getting multiple bids—and you should—make sure each one is for the same scope of work. That means each bid should include materials, overhead, insurance, filing fees, and the same miscellaneous costs. If they don't, then you are comparing apples to oranges. Once you're sure all the bids are for the same level of service, line them up and compare.

What to ask about bids

Once you get the bids, it is fine to call up the contractor and ask some tough questions.

- Is he open to working with people who have been working on your house for years, like your handyman or painter?
- Are he and all his subcontractors insured and licensed under the laws of your state? Usually, this means liability, disability, and workmen's compensation insurance for his employees.
- Is he going to take care of the permits and filings, or are you?
- Who is dealing with the garbage during demolition and construction, and where is the garbage going?
- Is there a project manager for you to deal with?
- Will the site be cleaned every day?
- Are the exact materials he is using specified, or is there an allowance for materials? If you are talking about an allowance for materials, how large is it, and will it cover the quality of materials you want?
- Is there a penalty for completing the job late?
- What is the size of the workforce that will be coming to the site?
- Does he have a real office, or does he work out of his basement?
- Will he give you an overnight number in case of an emergency?
- Will he service your project after he is finished?

HOW IS THE BID PRICED?

There are two ways bids are priced. The first is a single number for the project from start to finish with materials. The good thing about this is that you know the

al cost, however long it takes to do the job. The other way is called time and
material. That is when you are told the daily cost of labor and will be charged by
how long the work takes. Unless you really trust your contractor, you don't want
this, because it builds in a disincentive for the contractor to finish the job. The
longer he works, the more he makes.

HOW TO CHOOSE BETWEEN BIDS

You want a nice, complete, detailed, clear bid that spells out everything. The same
job can be described in one page or twenty. The twenty-page bid is the better
one, because it gives you more information. Also, don't judge the bid entirely by
what it costs. The more expensive bid could be worth it, depending on the level of
service. But a cheaper bid might really offer the same service for less. Just be sure
you are comparing equivalent bids.

SIGN A LEGAL DOCUMENT

Don't sign his bid and say it is a contract. In an ideal world you'd have a smart
lawyer draft up an agreement for you to sign, but that is expensive, and most
people don't do that. As an alternative, the American Institute of Architects, or
AIA, has a boilerplate contract that you can download for a small fee and use.

ARRANGE A WEEKLY MEETING

You want a meeting each week—same time, same day—so that you are guaranteed
face time with your contractor. No excuses.

DEMAND A DAY-BY-DAY SCHEDULE

You want to see exactly what is happening and what is going to happen daily, so
you can keep track of how the job is going.

DIVIDE YOUR PAYMENTS INTO FOUR

You want to pay in four installments. Begin with a 30 percent payment so that
the contractor can buy materials. After that use an AIA payment requisition form,
which you can get online. That will allow the contractor to tell you what percent
he has completed on various facets of the job. That tells you in detail what fraction
of the overall job is done, and you can pay accordingly. Withhold 15 percent until
thirty days after the job is done.

STOP BY THE JOB AS MUCH AS YOU CAN

The more present you are, the better the job will be.

ESTABLISH A PUNCH LIST AT THE END

A punch list is a list of your fine-tuning complaints after the job is done. When the work is completed, put a memo pad in the kitchen and write down little problems you see. That will establish the punch list to give to the contractor.

KNOW YOUR RIGHTS

When you have a licensed contractor, by law he has to fix for free anything he damaged because of his workmanship, not your carelessness. So be sure to inform the contractor about all problems within twelve months of completion of the job.

REALIZE THAT CHANGES COST MONEY

If you aren't clear about what you want before the work starts, or if you change your mind while work is under way, or add things or subtract things from the job, you are going to cost yourself time and money. The way most renovation projects get superexpensive is from people changing their minds during the job. Don't do it. Create a solid plan in advance and stick to it.

APPENDIX B

A Seasonal Checklist

We all have different kinds of homes in different parts of the country with different climates. But this is an example of a baseline, minimum list of vital tasks that should be performed, in order by season, on a typical house. For argument's sake, we had in mind a suburban home with a swimming pool located in the northeastern United States. The tasks aren't ranked by importance within the season. This is just to give you an idea of what a conscientious homeowner should do throughout the year.

AUTUMN
○ Fertilize your lawn in early September.
○ Check your roof for loose shingles.
○ Clean your gardening tools and put them away until spring.
○ After the leaves have fallen, clean out your gutters and clean your chimney.
○ Power wash algae, moss, and dirt off the house's façade.
○ Check the façade for damage and have it repaired.
○ Caulk all the outside windows and weatherize doors.
○ Take the screens down if you take them off.
○ Turn off your outside water, such as sprinkler systems, and drain the pipes.
○ Check the batteries on your smoke and carbon monoxide alarms.
○ Bring in potted plants.
○ Cover your grill.
○ Run swimming pool filtration once a week for five minutes.
○ Fertilize your lawn again in mid-November.

WINTER

- ○ Run pool filtration every two weeks for five minutes.
- ○ Buy salt and an ice scraper for snow and ice conditions.
- ○ Have your HVAC system serviced.
- ○ Check the grout lines in your bathroom and replace losses.
- ○ Go through the house and tighten all the hinges and knobs.
- ○ Check the batteries on your smoke and carbon monoxide alarms.

SPRING

- ○ Snake all the drains and traps.
- ○ Check your house's façade for damage.
- ○ Clean your gutters.
- ○ Repair any broken windowsills.
- ○ Check and repair your window screens.
- ○ If you have taken screens down, put them back up.
- ○ Turn on the outside water.
- ○ Check the batteries on smoke and carbon monoxide alarms.
- ○ Check spa jets.
- ○ Repair and seal the driveway.
- ○ Do garage spring cleaning.
- ○ Check and lube garage doors.
- ○ Run pool filtration every two weeks for five minutes.

SUMMER

- ○ Run pool filtration every day for twenty minutes minimum.
- ○ Late in the season have your boiler serviced.
- ○ Check the batteries on your smoke and carbon monoxide alarms.

Acknowledgments

We wrote this book together over the course of a year, sitting in Stephen's office, or sometimes over the telephone, talking the ideas out and getting them down on the computer. The information and advice in this book come directly from those conversations. We did occasionally clarify or fact-check a point in various reference works and catalogs, and on Web sites. But when there was an area of expertise we didn't possess ourselves, we picked up the phone and called an expert in the field.

So our gratitude goes to a group of top-notch professionals in and around New York City, who work with Stephen and who generously gave their time to us and helped us better understand what they do. They are John Schenone, president of Maspeth Roofing in Maspeth; Larry Nolan, president of Original Window in Flushing; Joseph Siniscalchi, president of Practical Plumbing and Heating in New York City; Greg Widelski, president of G&S Electric in Staten Island; Kenny Childs, president of My Guy Appliance and Electronics in Ridgewood; Howard Lang, president of Howard Mechanical in Woodside; Carl Conti, president of Air-Excel Service in Woodside; and Boris Abramovich, founder of Couture Interiors in Merrick. We also appreciate the assistance of Missy Henriksen at the National Pest Management Association in Fairfax, Virginia. Nevertheless, any errors are our fault.

Furthermore, we'd like to thank the entire staff of Fanuka, Inc., with a special mention to Sandra Sevilla and Frank Fanuka. Thanks to Artisan for encouraging us to dive into this fantastic project; to our patient editors, Trent Duffy and Ingrid Abramovitch; Artisan's publisher, Ann Bramson; Artisan's president, Peter Workman; and their brilliant colleagues, including but in no way limited to Susan Baldaserini, Kevin Brainard, Jarrod Dyer, Bridget Heiking, Sibylle Kazeroid, Laurin Lucaire, Allison McGeehon, Nancy Murray, and Barbara Peragine. Ralph Voltz did a fantastic job realizing the illustrations.

Stephen would like to thank his wife, Lisa, and children, Spencer and Avery, who tolerated his being missing for the year it took to write this book, as well as his publicist, Christina Juarez, who always believed he could turn the lights on if she could take him to the party.

Edward would like to thank Megan, Noah, and Charlotte, with hugs and kisses beyond counting, and everyone in his extended family from Massachusetts to San Diego. Many thanks to his agent, David Black. This is for his mother, Carol F. Lewine.

Index

About the Authors

STEPHEN FANUKA is the star of the DIY Network series *Million Dollar Contractor*. He is a frequent guest on *The Nate Berkus Show*, *George to the Rescue*, and Sirius/XM Martha Stewart Living Radio. A second-generation contractor, he runs Fanuka, Inc., which specializes in high-quality general contracting and luxury interior renovations. The business is based in New York City, and he and his family live in suburban Long Island. For more about Stephen and his business, visit www.fanuka.com.

EDWARD LEWINE writes the "Domains" and "Ask the Contractor" columns for *The New York Times Magazine*. His work has also appeared in the New York *Daily News*, *Wired*, *New York*, *Smart Money*, and *Fast Company*. Edward's superb reporting skills are much in evidence in his book *Death and the Sun: A Matador's Season in the Heart of Spain*, published in 2005 after he spent a year doing research among bullfighters. He lives in a brownstone in Brooklyn, New York, that continually needs repairs.

What's a doer to do?

Look for the quirky and comprehensive **What's a . . . to Do?**
series in bookstores everywhere or visit www.artisanbooks.com

ARTISAN